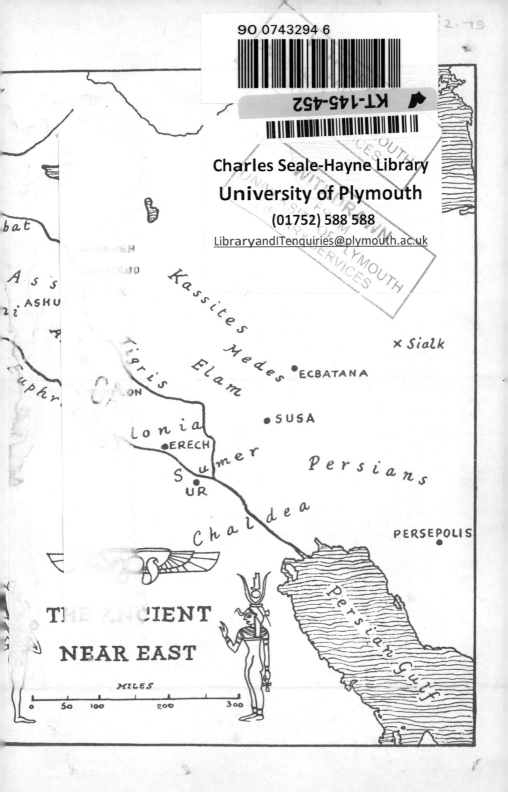

bat

NINEVEH
NIMRUD

A s s
ASHU

Tigris

Euphr

Kassites

Medes

Elam

Ionia

ERECH

Sumer

UR

Chaldea

× Sialk

●ECBATANA

● SUSA

Persians

PERSEPOLIS
●

Persian Gulf

THE ANCIENT

NEAR EAST

MILES

0   50   100   200   300

ANCIENT EGYPT

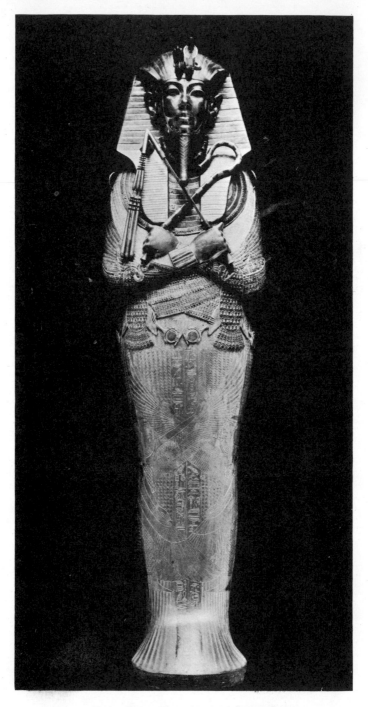

1. THE PHARAOH TUTANKHAMON
The inner coffin. From his tomb in the Valley of the Kings

ANCIENT EGYPT
Its Culture and History

by

J. E. Manchip White

LONDON
GEORGE ALLEN & UNWIN LTD
RUSKIN HOUSE   MUSEUM STREET

FIRST PUBLISHED IN GREAT BRITAIN IN 1952

SECOND EDITION 1970

This edition © J. E. Manchip White, 1970

ISBN 0 04 932002 5

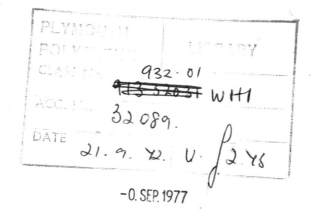
PRINTED IN GREAT BRITAIN
BY COMPTON PRINTING LTD,
LONDON AND AYLESBURY

Contents

Illustrations

Acknowledgements

Frontispiece, Plates 5, 6, 10 (top), 12, 23, 25, 29, 30, 32, 33:
courtesy of the Griffith Institute, Ashmolean Museum, Oxford.
Plates 2, 3, 4, 8, 11, 13, 14, 15, 18, 19, 24, 27, 28, 31, 34,
35, 36, 37, 40, 41, 44, 45, 46, 47: courtesy of Messrs.
Lehnert & Landrock, Cairo. Plates 7, 9, 10 (below), 20, 21,
22, 37, 38, 39, 42, 43: courtesy of the Metropolitan Museum
of Art, New York. Plates 16, 17, 24: courtesy of the Museum
of Fine Arts, Boston. Plate 48: courtesy of the Department of
Egyptian Antiquities, Turin Museum.

TO MY WIFE

Preface to the Second Edition (1970)

During the past half-century, field-studies in Egypt have been impeded by a number of factors beyond the control of Egyptologists. After legal disputes following the discovery of the tomb of Tutankhamon in 1922, the Egyptian authorities decreed that significant finds from future excavations must remain in Egypt. This ruling, though justified in principle, had the unfortunate effect of discouraging the directors of wealthy foreign museums who up to that time had financed expeditions with the aim of enlarging their collections; and World War Two brought to an abrupt halt any excavations that still happened to continue.

It is sad to report that the situation, as it exists within the boundaries of Egypt itself, has not greatly improved during the eighteen years since this book was first published. During the 1950s and 1960s, Egyptologists applied themselves with their usual diligence to their discipline: but their attempts to pursue their researches in the field have continued to be frustrated by the unsettled nature of Middle Eastern and Egyptian politics.

When I was engaged in writing this, my first book, in the spring and summer of 1951, Egypt was a monarchy; when it was published twelve months later, Egypt was a republic. An era had come to an end. The last two years of the reign of King Farouk had already been marked by serious riots in the Canal Zone, and his downfall signalled the beginning of two more decades of almost continuous crisis.

The first two years of the republic, from 1952 to 1954, were distinguished by revolutionary ardour and by a struggle for power between General Naguib and Colonel Nasser. In 1954 Colonel Nasser, then Prime Minister, ousted General Naguib, the President. In 1956, Colonel Nasser, now President in his turn, compelled the British to withdraw from their bases in Egypt. As a result, the British cancelled the financial contribution they had promised towards the construction of the High Dam at Aswan, a step in which they were followed by the Americans. In October of that year the Israelis invaded Egypt and the Anglo-French intervention occurred. In 1958 the formation of the United Arab Republic of Egypt, Iraq and Syria took place, only to collapse five years later; and in 1962 the Egyptians sent an army to the Yemen to support the rebels against the royalists, an ugly episode which dragged on for a further five-year period. Finally, in June 1967, came the briefest, bloodiest and most bitter bout to date in the series of Arab-Israeli wars.

Under the circumstances, it is scarcely surprising that archaeological investigation has been severely restricted. The British and French centres in Cairo, which for a hundred years had managed the majority of major excavations, were closed down after the Suez War, and other Western nations were hardly less popular. Funds and the leisure to excavate were in short supply. Furthermore, the young republic was passing through a xenophobic phase and wished to reserve to itself the glory of uncovering its own past. Fortunately the Antiquities Department of the Egyptian Government, in spite of the shortage of funds which is a condition of life in Egypt, has performed with great ability and devotion. Excavators of the quality of Mr Zakariah Goneim have undertaken important digs; museums have been reorganized; the business of conservation and preservation has gone steadily forward; and great strides have been made in opening up the main sites in an intelligent and tasteful way to tourists, as anyone who has visited the Valley of the Kings in recent years can testify.

Mr Goneim in particular has laid Egyptology in his debt. In 1949 he assisted Mr Abdel Azarik to excavate the magnificent royal avenue of sphinxes at Luxor, buried beneath 60 feet of rubble; and in 1953, as Chief Inspector of Antiquities at Sakkara, he discovered the foundations of a Third Dynasty step pyramid near the Step Pyramid of Zoser. After unearthing a cache of gold ornaments, his hopes ran high, and in May 1954 he reached a burial chamber that contained a splendid sarcophagus that appeared to be intact. He had visions of repeating the wonderful moment which Howard Carter had experienced when he opened the sarcophagus of Tutankhamon thirty years before. As he wrote later, in *The Lost Pyramid*: 'One by one my workmen clambered through the hole in the blockage and scrambled down into the chamber. They were mad with excitement and, catching their enthusiasm, I gave way completely to my pent-up feelings, kept in check for so long. We danced around the sarcophagus and wept. We embraced each other. It was a very strange moment in that dark chamber, 130 feet beneath the surface of the desert. Many of these workmen had been employed by great archaeologists such as Reisner and Junker and Petrie, and they told me that never in their whole lives had they seen such a thing.' However, when the sarcophagus was opened, on June 26, 1954, it proved, alas, to be empty. The pyramid was a dummy or cenotaph. Nevertheless, the cruel blow did not detract from Mr Goneim's great achievement.

During this difficult period the Western nations, by exercising much tact, still contrived to do useful work. Professor Walter Emery, for example, who had been working in Lower Egypt before the Suez incident, forthwith removed himself from that sensitive area to the far-distant reaches of Sudanese Nubia. There, in eight arduous seasons between 1956 and 1963, he excavated the huge fortress of Buhen. This was the largest and most impressive of a complex of forts built by the practical and tough-minded Pharaohs of the Middle Kingdom (see Chapter VIII following). They were specialists in constructing defence lines. In the Delta they built 'The Wall of the Princes' to guard the Suez isthmus, a system that endured for centuries. For their conquest and pacification of Nubia they erected a constellation of fortresses that comprised Buhen, Semna, Qaṣr Ibrim, 'Anîba, Ikkur, Kuban and Mirgissa.

By excavating Buhan, Professor Emery was therefore throwing light on the key to a whole military concept. He discovered that the site had been occupied during the Old Kingdom, when it was an entrepôt between Egypt and Nubia. There were workshops and foundries for smelting copper, and the remains of a town wall dating from the Fourth Dynasty. Then, in the Middle Kingdom, arose a tremendous fortress that bore an uncanny resemblance to the Crusaders' castles of the Middle Ages. This was destroyed by fire, no doubt as the result of a successful invasion by the Nubians, but was reconstructed during the great imperial epoch of the New Kingdom. Here the mighty Viceroys of Kush (see pages 51 and 189) had their headquarters, and erected boastful monuments to commemorate their martial triumphs. The Pharaohs of the New Kingdom consolidated the gains of the Pharaohs Sesostris I and Sesostris II of the Middle Kingdom, the frontier was advanced to the Fourth Cataract, and the land behind it became settled. Nevertheless, Buhen remained in active operation for almost another thousand years, until the reign of the Pharaoh Taharka of the Twenty-fifth Dynasty.

As Professor Emery was completing his work at Buhen, Professor J. Martin Plumley, under whom I had the honour of studying for a time at Cambridge, began work downstream at the associated fortress of Qaṣr Ibrîm, where Professor Emery had done some preliminary investigation. This was another structure of Crusader-castle type. In addition to the Ancient Egyptian finds, the site yielded a wealth of Christian material which greatly extended our knowledge of Christian Nubia. The past two decades have therefore seen a welcome increase of information about the interesting segment of Egyptian history that is contained in far-off Nubia. One of the fascinating queries raised by the British seasons there was the discovery at Buhen, lying on the pavement of a Middle Kingdom rampart, of the skeleton of a horse. Hitherto it had always been assumed that the horse had been introduced into Egypt by the Hyksôs kings during the Second Intermediate Period (see page 162). It now looks as if the introduction must be dated at least one or two centuries earlier.

In addition to the extensive and revealing discoveries at Buhen and Qaṣr Ibrîm, other important excavations were also undertaken within Sudanese Nubia. At Mirgissa, not far upstream from Buhen, Professor Jean Vercoutter and the French Archaeological Mission excavated the Middle Kingdom fortress on a hill above the Second Cataract. The fortress, which flourished about 2000 B.C., was situated in the centre of a town, many of whose houses had remained virtually intact. Expeditions from the Oriental Institute of Chicago, the University of Colorado, the University of New Mexico, and the Scandinavian Joint Expedition have also made substantial contributions to our knowledge of the region, while at Faras a Polish expedition under Professor C. Michalowski complemented the discoveries of the Christian era of Professor Plumley at Qaṣr Ibrîm. The Polish expedition discovered the largest Christian church found in Nubia, a veritable cathedral. The vast structure contained 169 superb frescoes and the intact tomb of the bishop who was its probable founder.

The emphasis on Egyptian and Sudanese Nubia and on Upper Egypt in the 1950s and 1960s was not due to political circumstances alone. In spite of the rebuff administered by the British and Americans, President Nasser, with extraordinary tenacity, pursued his dream of building the Aswan High Dam. In January 1960, backed now by the Russians, he began work on the dam, designed to supersede the old granite dam at the First Cataract completed by the British in 1906. As early as 1955, international teams of scholars had begun to record scenes and inscriptions of antiquities in the area which would be inundated. By good fortune most of the antiquities were of minor importance: but special arrangements had to be made to save many of the outstanding temples, in particular the famous temples at Abu Simbel (pages 81 and 177), the large temple dedicated to Ramses II and the smaller temple to his queen, Nefertari. Fifty-one nations initially subscribed $17 million to this cause, which ultimately cost twice that sum, the United States shouldering the main burden of the cost. Numerous architectural and engineering solutions were proposed. Some were bold in the extreme. A French engineer envisioned leaving the temple *in situ* behind an enormous coffer-dam. An Italian consultant suggested lifting the temple above water-level by means of gigantic hydraulic jacks. The Swedish technique which was eventually adopted and carried out by an international consortium was to cut up the temples into 1,042 blocks weighing between 20 and 30 tons, and hoist them by crane on to a cliff soaring far above the height of the old river-bed. The work took 2,000 men nearly five years to complete and was finished in 1968, the year when the High Dam was brought into operation. The dam is 3 miles long and 350 feet high, and by 1980 the lake which it has brought into being will be 300 miles long and 6 miles wide. The lake will irrigate two million miles of virgin or poorly irrigated desert and increase the Egyptian national income by an estimated $650-$700 million a year. If the Egyptian authorities can curb their country's alarming birth-rate, which is one of the most prolific in the world, then the Aswan High Dam could be a turning-point in Egyptian fortunes. Certainly its creation is a towering event in Egyptian history, a fitting culmination to Egypt's age-old obsession with water. No Egyptologist will grudge Egypt, a land where at the time of writing the average *per capita* income is below $250 a year, such a great boon in exchange for a few small sites. What effect the deliberate and awesome prevention of the natural flooding of the Nile and the permanent inundation of entire new regions will have on Egyptology, and on Egypt itself, is another question. It has been suggested that all the sites in the Delta will be lost for ever. This would indeed be a terrible blow. Because of the difficulties of excavating in waterlogged conditions, the Delta has hitherto been inadequately explored. Now it might never be.

In addition to the grandiose activity at Abu Simbel, no less than twenty-three other temples, some large and some small, situated between Abu Simbel and Aswan, have already been bodily removed or else scheduled for removal in the near future to higher, safer ground at other sites. Thus the Beit-al-Wali temple, containing fine polychrome reliefs of Ramses II's Asian and Nubian campaigns, was transferred to a new site at Aswan by the Oriental Institute of Chicago in conjunction with the Swiss Institute of Cairo. The splendid Graeco-Roman temple of Kalabsha, the 'Luxor of Nubia', was dismantled in 1962 with the aid of money and expertise provided by the Federal Republic of Germany. Almost the size of Notre Dame de Paris, it was cut into 1,600 blocks, many of which weighed 20 tons, which were placed on barges and floated downstream to Aswan, where they were re-erected. A very impressive achievement. Another Graeco-Roman temple, at Dakka, was similarly dismantled and removed to Wadi-es-Sebua by the Leningrad Academy of Sciences. Beneath it were discovered the remains of a temple built by Tuthmosis III, while at Wadi-es-Sebua itself the United States and the United Arab Republic combined in 1964 to dismantle and remove the temple there, and also uncovered an enormous temple of Amenhotep III. As a pendant to these remarkable feats of engineering, which have yielded an immense archaeological and epigraphical bonus, we might mention that plans are now afoot to resurrect the beautiful little temple of Philae, which Herodotus called 'The Pearl of Egypt'. Originally situated on a fragrant and flowery little island in midstream, and sacred to Isis and Osiris, since the construction of the first dam half a century ago it has been submerged for nine months in every year. Somehow the charming little edifice has survived its annual immersion, and the Dutch and Egyptian Governments are now to collaborate on building a system of dams and dykes that will shield it permanently from the movements of the water.

After the preliminaries of the High Dam were under way, and the hostility towards foreigners had somewhat abated, it was possible to resume operations in Lower Egypt. Once more Professor Emery put us in his debt. In 1956 he had been compelled to close down his work on the tomb of Queen Herneith at Sakkara. Now, in October 1964, he returned to Sakkara and set about excavating a site that had long interested him near the enclosure of the Step Pyramid (pages 65-68). He was eager to find the tomb of Imhotep (pages 50, 65-66 and 138), together with the Asklepieion or shrine and place of pilgrimage which was known to have been dedicated to that celebrated man-god. He had made a shrewd deduction. Two months after beginning work he broke through into a vast underground labyrinth with a network of passages and a frieze of rock-cut statues; it was filled with a bewildering mass of material dating from the Old Kingdom to Ptolemaic times. He also found a large tomb of the Third Dynasty into which in Ptolemaic and Roman times ceremonial burials of sacred bulls had been carefully inserted. Below them was a remarkable ibis catacomb—hundreds of ibis mummies, each bird enclosed in its own lidded pot. It was clear that Professor Emery had indeed hit on the location at Sakkara sacred to the cult of Imhotep. In 1966 my wife and I spent a day wandering around this interesting area, and I remember vividly the brittle feel of the sad little bird-mummies in their elaborate tindery wrappings as I turned them over in my fingers. Professor Emery is still working at Sakkara, although he is considerably hampered by the congested nature of that beautiful but over-crowded plateau. He is now faced with the problem of removing his own dumps in order to clear more space for excavation. As he has put it in one of his own interim reports: 'It would appear almost certain that the whole of the great valley area is covered by streets and streets of funerary monu-ments of the Archaic and Old Kingdom Periods.' A mouth-watering prospect, and one which would compensate to some extent for the possibility of having to write off the Delta.

It is worth mentioning that a British team went to the Delta in 1965 to excavate the 175-acre site of Tell el-Farâ'în. Possibly this is the venerable capital of Lower Egypt, the holy city of Buto. The team was in the middle of its third season when the June War of 1967 broke out and operations had to be hurriedly curtailed. Such, as indicated earlier, are the exigencies of excavating in Egypt in the middle of the twentieth century.

However, if work on the ground has been hampered, the business of speculation and study has continued unabated. There is no space here to discuss the scholarly *minutiae* of the past twenty years —the patient labours that continually enlarge the coral-reef. It must be sufficient to say that since the original publication of the present book a number of volumes of outstanding character have appeared. I have included the more important new titles in the revised bibliography (pages 207-209). I have also taken the liberty of inserting there the name of *Everyday Life in Ancient Egypt*, a second small contribution which I made in 1963 to the majestic field of Egyptology.

If, in conclusion, I may be permitted a short personal observation, I might state that, with every year that passes, my respect and admiration for the ancient people of the Nile Valley increases. In our brutal and distracted times it is a relief to be able to turn occasionally to the contemplation of a civilization characterized by dignity, tolerance, good humour and solid political, religious and cultural achievement. It refreshes the spirit to be reminded that a high culture once existed that was harmonious and disciplined, radiant, reverent and ceremonious. It makes one conjecture, in the middle of our battered and frantic century, as to whether the Ancient Egyptians may not have been right when they located the world's Golden Age not in the future, but in the past, and whether they are not themselves the retrospective inhabitants of that epoch.

It is a sobering thought that it needs only a bomb or two on such targets as the High Dam, the Cairo Museum, Luxor and Sakkara to cause the obliteration of the principal relics of Ancient Egypt. Modern high-explosive and atomic weapons can bring about in a few appalling seconds the destruction that the Copts, the Arabs and the Turks failed to achieve in two millennia. One can only trust that the spirit that conceived the High Dam will prevail over the impulse that would break it to pieces, and which would pour radio-active chemicals into the waters of a river that cherished mankind in its earliest years and was rightly worshipped as a god.

J.E.M.W.

Introduction

'Pyramids, arches, obelisks,' wrote Sir Thomas Browne with unwonted severity, 'were but the irregularities of vain-glory and wild enormities of ancient magnanimity.'

It is the intention of this book to give an account in general terms of the enigmatic civilization of the ancient Egyptians and to try to offer some explanation of the principles which animated it.

The book is meant to serve as a clear and comprehensive introduction to Egyptology. Each chapter is devoted to a different aspect of Egyptian life and the chapters are arranged according to the descending hierarchy of Nilotic society. In this way it is hoped to present a broad picture of life in the Nile valley in ancient times. The titles of the chapters are generalized and describe the activities of a class rather than an individual. Wherever possible needless repetition of information is avoided. What is missing or curtailed in one chapter is inserted or amplified in another.

To avoid distracting the reader, detailed references to sources are not given in the text. A short bibliography is included at the end. Scholars will readily recognize the origins of the quotations from ancient writings. They will also realize the debt which the author owes to the many Egyptologists whose publications he has consulted.

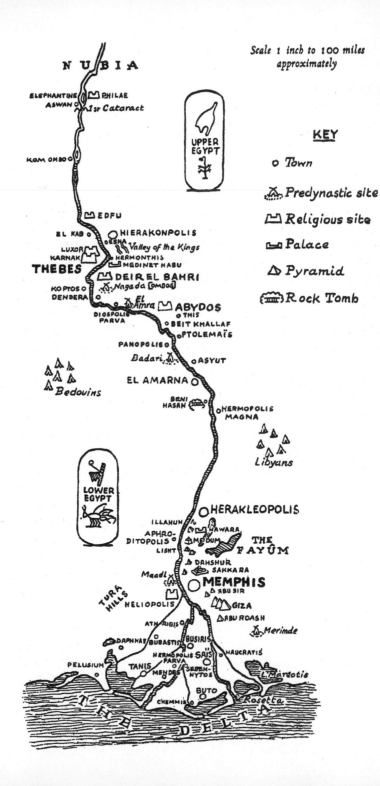

N U B I A

Scale 1 inch to 100 miles
approximately

ELEPHANTINE / PHILAE
ASWAN 1st Cataract

UPPER
EGYPT

KOM OMBO

KEY

○ Town

Predynastic site

Religious site

Palace

Pyramid

Rock Tomb

EDFU

EL KAB ○ HIERAKONPOLIS
ESNA
LUXOR Valley of the Kings
KARNAK HERMONTHIS
MEDINET HABU
THEBES DEIR EL BAHRI
KOPTOS ○ Nagada OMBOS
DENDERA EL
Amra ABYDOS
DIOSPOLIS ○ THIS
PARVA ○ BEIT KHALLAF
○ PTOLEMAÏS
PANOPOLIS ○
Badari ○ ASYUT
EL AMARNA ○

Bedouins

BENI
HASAN ○ HERMOPOLIS
MAGNA

Libyans

LOWER
EGYPT

○ HERAKLEOPOLIS

ILLAHUN HAWARA
APHRO- MEIDUM
DITOPOLIS THE
LISHT FAYÛM

DAHSHUR
SAKKARA
Maadi
MEMPHIS
ABU SIR
TURA
HILLS
HELIOPOLIS GIZA
ABU ROASH
ATHRIBIS Merimde
DAPHNAE BUBASTIS BUSIRIS
HERMOPOLIS SAÏS NAUCRATIS
PELUSIUM TANIS PARVA
MENDES SEBEN-
NYTOS L. Mareotis
BUTO
CHEMMIS Rosetta
THE
DELTA

CHAPTER I

The Nile

"The Egyptians,' wrote the Greek historian Herodotus, 'live in a peculiar climate, on the banks of a river which is unlike every other river, and they have adopted customs and manners different in nearly every respect from those of other men.' The civilization of ancient Egypt owed much of its character to the climate and curious configuration of the Nile valley. The human story of that splendid civilization must be unfolded against its natural background of river and rock, sky and sand. Any study of it must be prefaced with a brief outline of the environmental factors involved.

From its rise in the vast lakes of the African interior, Albert and Victoria Nyanza, the Nile flows four thousand miles to the Mediterranean. The last six hundred and seventy-five miles of the river, from the First Cataract at Aswan to the sea, constitute the land of Egypt. Egypt *is* the River Nile. On each side of the winding ribbon of water runs a narrow carpet of soil which supports a teeming population. The contrast between the soil and the barren desert is sharp and striking. For five hundred miles, from Aswan to the edge of the Delta, the river forces itself through a steep-walled cleft in the rocky plateau of the Sahara, a cleft never more than twelve miles wide. This five hundred mile stretch is known as Upper Egypt. While traversing Upper Egypt the river falls from a height of three hundred feet to forty feet. Near ancient Memphis the river suddenly broadens into the Delta, an area sixty miles wide at the Mediterranean seaboard. The environs of Memphis and the Delta comprise Lower Egypt. Lower Egypt, which is flat and marshy, differs in scenery and atmosphere from the arid severity of Upper Egypt. Lower Egypt is short and broad, Upper Egypt is long and narrow. The two divisions, or Two Lands, as the ancient Egyptians called them, are complementary. The Delta is a spreading bloom, fed by the Upper Egyptian stalk. In form the River Nile resembles the lotus from which the sun god was born.

In May the level of the river is at its lowest point and the soil of Egypt is parched and cracked. But in June the annual miracle of the flood or Inundation begins. The White Nile and its tributaries, the Atbara and the Blue Nile, are gorged with spring rains pouring down from the Abyssinian plateau. First comes a green wave laden with vegetable detritus, to be followed a month later by a red wave bearing a rich humus full of minerals and potash. The life-giving waters continue in spate until October, when they begin to recede. The soil is saturated with a fluid so fertile that two or three crops may be sown and garnered annually. After October the water is held in reserve by means of artificial canals and dykes. The Abyssinian mud gave the ancient Egyptians a second name for the Two Lands: the Black Land. The Black Land was all the blacker for its contrast with the Red Land, the sterile and pitiless desert whose deadly encroachment was always imminent. The ancient Egyptians identified the river and the soil with their best loved god, Osiris, while the desert was associated with his murderer, Seth.

The climate of Egypt is mild and radiant. As Herodotus noted: 'Perpetual summer reigns in Egypt.' Rain is almost unknown. The winds are cool and drying. Light is brilliant and constant, for the sun shines down in its full majesty and is seldom obscured. It was inevitable that the sun should be worshipped in conjunction with the river. The steady sunlight lent an air of solidity and stability to whatever it illumined, while its dry warmth ensured the preservation of all objects buried beneath the sand: monuments, papyri or

2. THE PRINCESS NEFERT
Fourth Dynasty

3. THE TEMPLE OF LUXOR

4. THE TEMPLE OF LUXOR
The papyrus columns of the Pharaoh Amenophis III

human bodies. The cult of the sun was a reassuring tribute to the principle of permanence. Its unchanging beams, coupled with the regular rhythm of the Inundation, encouraged the Egyptians to become a conservative, sedentary and contented people. The valley in which they lived was rich in natural resources and bordered by quarries and goldfields. The single raw material which was lacking was wood, with the exception of the soft and fibrous palm. Fortunately cedar and the Asiatic fir could be procured by trade from the nearby forests of Lebanon.

The Nile valley is a unique and enormous oasis, a garden in a wilderness. Even Lebanon is not readily accessible, save by sea. The ancient Egyptians, cut off by deserts to east and west from any civilized community of comparable size, evolved their own idiosyncratic customs and institutions with a minimum of outside influence. Ancient writers testify to the ingrown nature of the civilization which grew up on the pampered, attenuated strip of dark soil enclosed by desert wastes. It was Herodotus again who noted that Egypt was 'a gift of the Nile.' When wisely solicited, Haapi the Nile god could be generous: the oasis, the Egyptian lotus, would blossom and luxuriate. But Haapi was also capricious. He would brook no misuse of his yearly gift. If the inhabitants of his sheltered paradise were careless husbandmen, then their situation in their isolated valley was perilous indeed.

The ancient Egyptians farmed the Black Land with skill and energy. Every available foot of soil was under cultivation. For this reason the villagers were willing to set back their huts from the precious earth on to the edge of the demon-haunted desert. They knew only too well that they were dependent on Haapi's whims. A 'meagre' Nile would cause famine, an excessive Nile would damage the dykes and canals. The Nile dwellers early developed a close acquaintance with the habits of their river. They measured its rise and fall and entered the figures in a written record, a proceeding that may have contributed to the evolution of hieroglyphic writing. They learned that a 'good Nile' measured twenty-eight cubits at Aswan and twenty-four at Edfu. The priests of Memphis calculated that disaster would ensue if the river rose above eighteen cubits or fell below sixteen cubits as it entered the Delta.

Efficient supervision of the Nile was the first requisite of good government. Every landowner in Egypt was higher up-stream than another landowner, therefore it was essential that no one should pollute the waters. It was imperative that all dykes, canals and drainage systems should be in perfect con-dition at all times, for the neglect of a single individual could imperil the subsistence of hundreds. It was vital that no one should claim or take to himself water rights belonging to his neighbour. The most satisfactory agent for controlling both the river and the landowners was a powerful central government acting through a provincial administration in each nome or province. When central government was weak, local rivalries upset the entire system of water distribution.

Unfortunately there were serious obstacles to efficient centralized government, obstacles which each succeeding · dynasty was required to surmount anew. In the first place, active surveillance of a country seven hundred miles long was no easy matter, particularly when journeys upstream could only be made slowly against a strong current. The Nile was the highway of ancient Egypt, a land in which horses, wheeled vehicles and soil-wasting roads were unknown until the onset of the New Kingdom. In this respect the paramount influençe of the river was again manifest. The major problem which faced the Pharaoh was the location of his capital. It was neces-sary to choose a position which would dominate both Upper and Lower Egypt, and therefore it became the custom to rule from Memphis, near modern Cairo. Memphis gave equal access to both Upper Egypt and the Delta. In the New King-dom, however, the Theban Pharaohs preferred to rule from Thebes, a site convenient for the government of the expanding colony of Nubia, but inconvenient for the government of the

4

extensive Asian territories which they conquered. It therefore became necessary to entrust each of the Two Lands to the care of a separate vizier. At the end of the New Kingdom and during the Late Period it became equally necessary to go to the other extreme and establish the capital in the Delta. In both cases the geographical location was out of balance, but whereas the Theban Pharaohs remained at Thebes for religious and sentimental reasons, the kings who ruled from Tanis, Saïs and Bubastis were compelled to do so for motives of political strategy. The isolation of the Nile valley was coming to an end at the conclusion of the New Kingdom. The insular character of the Old and Middle Kingdoms, which represent self-contained phases of Egyptian civilization, was vanishing. Egypt had absorbed exotic tendencies from her huge empire and by 1400 B.C. Asia itself was awake and on the march. Egyptian monarchs were forced to install themselves on the borders or the shore of the Delta, now continuously subjected to assault from without. In this way the unity of the country was irretrievably damaged.

In a more immediate fashion, geographical considerations affected every phase of human activity in the valley of the Nile. The rectilinear appearance of the landscape of five hundred mile long Upper Egypt early impressed itself upon the Egyptian imagination. The river flowed with harsh symmetry through two strips of land, between the sheer cliffs and the spreading desert. This symmetry in Nature was accepted by the Egyptians as an intellectual and artistic principle. The clear-cut lines of river-bank and cliff, the knife edge where the cultivation met the desert, were reflected in the angular contours of Egyptian architecture. Ancient Egypt was less given to the soft round curve than to the incisive parallel. The steady sunlight and bold blocks of shadow induced a corresponding simplicity of architectural surface. In Lower Egypt, a mephitic and mysterious land of marshes and meandering streamlets, the more subtle landscape induced a rather more sensuous approach

ANCIENT EGYPT

to architecture, an approach detected in the sophisticated
artistry of the Step Pyramid. Without pressing the argument
for geographical determinism too far, it seems likely that the
ancient populations of the Two Lands, as revealed in their
history, can be differentiated from each other. Upper Egypt
belonged to the continent of Africa, Lower Egypt to the world
of the East Mediterranean. It is possible that the basic racial
strains of these areas, though predominantly fair skinned in
each case, were respectively African and Asian. The Upper
Egyptian, whose mentality was that of the highlander, was by
temperament hardy, quarrelsome and forthright. The Lower
Egyptian, the lowlander, was less bellicose but more inventive.
He was gay, clever, pleasure-loving, in contrast to the puritan-
ical and nationalistic Upper Egyptian. The Delta would also
enjoy constant intercourse with advanced urban communities
abroad, while the only foreigners to enter Upper Egypt were
stray desert wanderers, African tribesmen or Bedouin drivers
of Red Sea mule trains. To the shuttered gorge of Upper Egypt
may be ascribed the claustrophobic, inward-looking element in
Egyptian art and ethics. It is unwise to push the matter further,
but it must be remembered that the peasant, particularly during
the formative epochs of the Thinite Period and the Old Kingdom, was tied to his master's estate and permitted little freedom
of movement. Such phenomena as the pilgrimage to Abydos
only came into vogue with the democratic reforms of the
Middle Kingdom. The bulk of the people were confined to the
ceaseless routine of provincial agriculture, a condition that
would tend to perpetuate the different character of the twin
populations. In the Delta the incomprehensible dialect and
uncouth manners of 'a man from Elephantine' were a matter
for laughter, and vice versa. Economically and intellectually,
nevertheless, Upper and Lower Egypt were dependent upon
each other. It was impossible to sever the blossom from the
stalk or the stalk from the blossom. The populations of the
Two Lands were approximately equal, and so were the number

6

of acres available for cultivation. The twin kingdoms were the two halves of a well balanced whole. The total number of the inhabitants of ancient Egypt can only be guessed at, but a maximum of five millions would seem a reasonable figure.

CHAPTER II

The Pharaoh

The stylized portrait of Pharaoh which ancient sculptors and painters have left us is singularly impressive. The king sits in a hierarchical attitude upon a massive throne. His expression is impassive, his eyes gaze out into eternity. Upon his head is one of his many crowns, upon his brows is the sacred symbol of the Uraeus, upon his chin is the plaited false beard. In his crossed hands he bears the twin emblems of sovereignty, the crook and flail, counterparts of the orb and sceptre. This is the ideal portrait of the man-god of ancient Egypt, responsible for both the material and spiritual welfare of his subjects.

After the creation of the world the land of Egypt was ruled by a succession of divine dynasties. The first king was the sun god Ra-Atum himself, to be followed in turn by the members of his family. The rule of the gods was not free from troubles. There were incessant assaults from the powers of darkness, there were clashes between rival gods and between men and the gods. The most serious convulsion during this period was the fratricidal war between Osiris and Seth, which will be fully described in the next chapter. From this long and bitter struggle the forces of the murdered Osiris, led by his son Horus, emerged victorious. Horus, avenger of his father, was ever afterwards held to be the pattern of the good son, and it was Horus who at the end of his life bequeathed the throne of Egypt to the line of human Pharaohs. Every Pharaoh in dynastic times thus claimed direct descent from Horus. More, he became the actual reincarnation of the falcon god. It may be that the Lower Egyptian conquerors of Upper Egypt in about 4245 B.C. were led by the ruler of the Falcon Nome, with whose emblem Horus was identified. Even usurpers took care to bolster up their claim to kingship by urging the protection which Horus and his fellow gods exercised upon the monarchy. It became the duty of Pharaoh to watch over the estates entrusted to him by his father or predecessor in the way in which Horus had once watched over them for his father Osiris. When Pharaoh died he ceased to be a guardian, a Horus, and became an Osiris, while another vigilant Horus took his place on the throne of the Two Lands.

The enemy whose onslaughts Pharaoh resisted was not only the host of Libyans, Nubians, Bedouins and Asiatics who lurked on Egypt's physical boundaries, but also the spiritual enemy in the shapes of Seth and Apophis. The powers of darkness, though constantly vanquished, attempted ceaselessly to overthrow Egypt by blighting the crops, obstructing the flow of the Nile, causing floods or preventing the sun from rising. It was Pharaoh, himself a god, whose influence alone could combat these cosmic powers. He took upon himself, in his intermediary status between gods and men, the dual responsibility for the prosperity of his country. During the pre-dynastic period, when the dwellers in the Nile valley were shut away from any significant commerce with the outside world, the leader of the community must have been an awe inspiring figure, possessor of a wisdom and a magic power which upheld him in his position. Under the Old Kingdom the lustre of royalty remained undiminished for five hundred years, during which time Pharaoh, his family and his favourites were the sole persons permitted to ascend to heaven after death. The divine potency of the monarch remained a vivid reality in the minds of his people even when the widening horizons of the Middle and New Kingdoms showed them that the Pharaoh of Egypt was but one king among many. It can also be truly said that during the course of three millennia the throne of Horus was occupied by a succession of Pharaohs of outstanding character and ability. When the emperors of Persia and Rome adopted the cartouche and the titulary of the native kings, they were paying tribute not only to the divinity of the Pharaohs but also to the devotion with which they had discharged their age-old office.

The word Pharaoh is derived from the two words *per aa*, Great House. In the middle of the Eighteenth Dynasty the phrase was employed for the first time as an honorific manner of referring to the king himself, just as the Sultan of Turkey was called the Sublime Porte (Great Door) or the medieval Emperor of China was called the Grand Khan (Great Palace). For superstitious reasons it was not desirable to use the name of so powerful a person in a direct fashion: a polite circumlocution was preferred. In actual fact Pharaoh bore not one but five 'great names,' which he assumed on the day of his accession. The list of names and titles, known as the titulary, followed an invariable sequence. Suitably enough, it began with the *Horus name*. This name, by which the king was commonly known in early dynastic times, consisted of the particular personification of Horus which the king chose for his personal use on earth. The name was often enclosed in a rectangular frame representing a primitive form of the royal palace with a crowned falcon perched on top. After the Horus name came the *Nebty* or *Two Ladies* name, the two ladies in question being the vulture goddess Nekhebet of Upper Egypt and the cobra goddess Buto of Lower Egypt. The title was an ancient one, perhaps assumed by the founder of the First Dynasty to signify that the Two Lands were united in his person. The third name was the *Golden Horus name*, the significance of which is imperfectly understood. On the Rosetta Stone, dating from the Late Period, the Greek scribe employed the phrase 'Horus superior to his foes' to translate the Egyptian title. In the early period the monogram may have symbolized more particularly the victory of Horus over Seth, or even his reconciliation with Seth. Between the Golden Horus name and

10

the fourth name stood a title which reads 'He who belongs to the Sedge and the Bee,' symbols respectively of Upper and Lower Egypt. The title is thus translated 'King of Upper and Lower Egypt.' The fourth name was the *prenomen*, the king's principal name, employed upon his monuments and in his documents. From the time of Cheops onwards, with a few Old Kingdom exceptions, it was compounded with the name of the sun god Ra. Finally there came the *nomen*, preceded by the epithet 'Son of Ra.' The nomen usually consisted of the family name of the dynasty or the personal name of the king before his accession to the throne. The prenomen and nomen were enclosed in separate cartouches. 'Cartouche' is the French word for a cartridge, which in its elongated form the Egyptian object resembles. The actual Egyptian words means 'circle,' and under the First Dynasty the cartouche was simply the king's name inscribed within a circular clay seal. Some authorities prefer to describe it as a double thickness of rope with the ends tied together. There may be the symbolic suggestion that the Pharaoh whose name was inside the cartouche governed all that was 'encircled by the sun,' the outline of the cartouche representing the diurnal course of the sun across the heavens.

A full example of the titulary may now be given. The following are the names and titles of the great Tuthmosis III of the Eighteenth Dynasty:

Horus Strong-bull-arising-in-Thebes, *Two Ladies* Enduring-of-kingship-like-Ra-in-heaven, *Golden Horus* Powerful-of-valour-and-holy-of-diadems, *King of Upper and Lower Egypt Menkheper-Ra* (i.e. The-appearance-of-Ra-is-established), *Son of Ra, Tuthmosis-beautiful-of-appearance* (Tuthmosis, i.e. Thoth-is-born), beloved of Hathor, Lady of the Turquoise.

The reference to the Lady of the Turquoise was included in this particular example of Tuthmosis III's titulary because it was carved at Sinai by an expedition which brought back from the famous quarries a supply of that coveted stone.

Although Pharaoh tended to emphasize the prenomen, it is the nomen which Egyptologists have used to build up their sequences of kings. The manner in which Egyptologists render these royal names deserves a brief comment, for the newcomer to the subject is often bewildered by the wide variety of forms to be found in Egyptological publications. Thus the name Tuthmosis can be found in the form of Tethmosis, Thutmosis, Thotmosis, Thutmose, Thutmase, Thothmes, Thotmes, Tehutimes, Djehutimes and so on. To take another example, Sesostris occurs as Senusert, Senusret and Senwosret. The prime difficulty involved in rendering proper names is to decide whether to accept the Hellenized forms handed down by Manetho and other ancient writers or whether to attempt an approximate transliteration of the original Egyptian. Thus Tuthmosis and Sesostris are the Greek renderings of words which may originally have sounded dimly like Djehutimes and Senwosret. The safest rule would seem to be to use word forms which are clear, euphonious, readily pronounceable and supported by authoritative scholarship. Perverse, pedantic and uncouth word forms are to be avoided. No systematic usage can be agreed upon and the matter must remain one of personal taste and judgment. Anomalies are bound to occur. For example, the present writer, while employing the forms Tuthmosis and Sesostris, does not employ the Hellenized form Sethos for Seti on the ground that it is not so much in general use.

Turning now to Pharaoh's regalia as depicted by ancient artists, it will be seen that he wears a number of different crowns. There is a high conical hat of graceful shape which lends itself admirably to sculpture. This is the White Crown of Upper Egypt. There is a flat-topped cap with a tall projection at the back and a long feather curling forward. This is the Red Crown of Lower Egypt. Sometimes both these crowns of high antiquity were combined into the Great Double Crown. Rulers were prone to adopt the crown of the kingdom from which their own dynasty hailed. Kings who belonged to the Theban dynasties had a natural predilection for the White Crown. A crown which came into vogue in the New Kingdom was the Blue crown or War Crown, a beautiful piece of head-gear composed of blue leather studded with golden sequins.

Around the king's crown was placed the Uraeus or cobra symbol. The cobra was sacred to the goddess Buto, patroness of Lower Egypt. Buto, sometimes identified with the cow goddess Hathor, was represented in reliefs and paintings in the guise of a vulture flying above the head of the king. Since the vulture was also a personification of Nekhebet, patroness of Upper Egypt, the Uraeus was another symbol of the twin rule of the Two Lands. The king was represented in the Uraeus symbol by the sun disc, which was sustained by the wings of Nekhebet and protected by the fire-spitting tongue of Buto. The wings that enfolded the disc might alternatively represent the wings of the sacred falcon.

The crook and flail symbolized simultaneously the wooing and coercive nature of the Pharaoh's power. He persuaded, but also he compelled. The strange dualistic quality of Egyptian thought will be touched upon in the next chapter. Here we may note that the alternately harsh and gentle aspects of the king's personality were endorsed by his subjects. In a single passage we are told: 'He is exultant, a smasher of foreheads (cf. Pl. 26, 41), so that none can come close to him. He is a master of graciousness, rich in sweetness, conquering by love.' For three thousand years, from predynastic to Ptolemaic times, the king was frequently represented in the pose of a 'smasher of foreheads.' He strides forward, grasping in his left hand the forelock of a kneeling captive, while his right hand swings back the macehead which will beat out the man's brains. Yet there was also a tradition that the king could 'conquer by love.' When Osiris set out from Egypt on the conquest of the world he achieved his victories not by force of arms but by reason and argument and by an Orpheus-like use of music. The crook and flail were the implements of the predynastic cattle drover, and from earliest times Pharaoh was the good herdsman, vigilant for all mankind. He possessed the shepherd's fondness for his flock or herd, but he realized that it required to be goaded, whipped and led along by the nose. It is possible that the crook and flail, together with the two head feathers sometimes worn by royalty, were originally the emblems of an early Delta chieftain-god called Anzti whose form and functions were usurped by Osiris.

The childhood of Pharaoh was happy and carefree. The ancient Egyptians loved children and allowed them great latitude. As a small boy the crown prince ran about naked in the sunshine with his small brothers and sisters, like the off-spring of the humblest peasant. The child sported pretty ornaments and his head was shaven except for a single long side lock or Horus lock. As soon as he was old enough he was put in charge of a tutor, whose business it was to teach him reading, writing and the elements of arithmetic, architecture, astronomy and other arts and sciences with which he would later need a measure of acquaintance. Lessons were long and thorough. Once the years of childhood were behind him the boy became rapidly aware of the onerous duties awaiting him when he grew up. During his adolescence he served an appren-ticeship as an army officer, in company with the sons of noblemen and young foreign princes sent to Egypt to be educated. Under the Middle and New Kingdoms he took part in his father's campaigns or undertook campaigns of his own. He made frequent hunting expeditions, for male royalty set great store by regular massacres of animals and game. Forays were made into the desert to track down the rarer sorts of beast, which were despatched with spear or bow, on foot or from a chariot (Pl. 31). Regular military tournaments were held at which royal princes were expected to display exceptional skill with weapons and as charioteers.

The future Pharaoh was married in childhood to the most

14

suitable of his small sisters, half-sisters or cousins. When he was a man he was permitted to take as many additional wives and mistresses as he desired, but it was essential that his immediate heir should possess the strongest possible strain of royal blood. The spiritual potency of the king, on which the well-being of his subjects depended, was enhanced by the purity of his breeding. Theoretically the actual blood of the sun god had been transmitted by Horus into the royal veins. The priesthood took this conception very seriously. It frowned upon any watering down of the divine ichor in the Pharaonic blood-vessels by marriages outside the royal family. To safeguard the purity of the succession it was advisable that the king should procreate as many children as possible within what is called the forbidden degree. To this end he not infrequently married his own daughters. The religious warrant for incestuous marriage was the marriage of Osiris with his sister Isis, the fruit of which was Horus, Pharaoh's exemplar. It was Osiris and Isis who revealed the institution of marriage to mankind. It has been suggested that their union represents the substitution of the practice of endogamy for the practice of exogamy within the predynastic community. The substitution occured when the settlers in the Nile valley forsook a nomadic existence, established a cultural identity with one another and banned extra-clan marriage. The later brother-sister marriages of the royal line may thus have re-emphasized Egyptian society's awareness of its own nature. An entirely practical aspect of consanguine marriage, which may also have been practised in society at large, was the ease with which it enabled power and possessions to be transferred from one generation to the next. It is important to realize that ancient Egyptian society was originally matrilineal and that even in dynastic times the female line was of equal account with the male in certain respects, notably in tracing descent, inheritance and drawing up a will.

The data available with regard to the genetics of inbreeding among Egyptian royal houses are too exiguous to permit positive statements to be made. Marriages between close relatives were carried out in the case of individual royal families for a few generations only. A frequent lack of male or female children on one side of the family or the other caused such matches to be made in a haphazard rather than a systematic fashion. The number of families who succeeded in enjoying power for more than a century is small. The Thebans of the Eighteenth Dynasty alone were able to practise incestuous or semi-incestuous marriage for a space of two centuries and a half. It seems likely that Amenophis IV (Akhenaton) inherited serious physical deficiencies from his father, but this may have been due to the determined dissipation of Amenophis III rather than to any more deep rooted cause. Tutankhamon, the successor of Amenophis IV, died in adolescence from the common Egyptian complaint of consumption. His mummy proves that he lacked the abnormal physique of his predecessor. The Eighteenth Dynasty, physically and intellectually, was represented for more than two centuries by kings and queens of exceptional health and sanity.

In his capacity as ruler Pharaoh was able to proclaim—though not of course in French—'L'état, c'est moi.' His word was literally law. Justice was defined as 'what Pharaoh loves,' wrongdoing as 'what Pharaoh hates.' The king's slightest word was oracular, his most trivial pronouncement was ex cathedra. His rôle as secular ruler was inseparably combined with his rôle as god. He kept his people in good order by means of divine utterance: his statements were statutes in themselves. In theory he directed every phase of secular and religious activity. He was at the same time high priest and chief justice. Whoever acted as priest or official throughout the land acted as his deputy. The Pharaohs were as a general rule very hard workers, and in the world of Oriental plot and counter-plot in which they lived a sense of affairs came easily to them. Although he was held to be 'the divine man', in contrast to 'the mortal man' or vizier, the king usually contrived to transact a

16

vast amount of mortal business in a lifetime largely employed in elaborate ceremonial. Kings of weak character sometimes became complete prisoners of ceremonial, and indeed many of them appear to have succumbed to it. To survive the number of religious services the king was required to celebrate in the course of a single day called for a stout frame and a buoyant spirit.

It was the actual performance by the king of the daily liturgy that rendered efficacious the liturgies celebrated elsewhere in Egypt. In his legal capacity, the king was supposed to be accessible to all his subjects. He constituted a final court of appeal. The privilege of appeal to Pharaoh indicates his supremacy in the field of law, although it is doubtful whether many persons were possessed of sufficient temerity to bring their cases to his notice. Pharaoh remained a remote personage even in the comradely circumstances of a foreign campaign. The contemplation of this lonely and magnificent figure, burdened by the weight of his divine destiny, filled his subjects with dread. Approach to him was difficult. Perhaps no monarch in world history was so hemmed in by 'the divinity that doth hedge a king.' As crown prince he doubtless contrived to lead a reasonably entertaining existence, but once his brows were encircled by the sacred diadems, once he became a Horus upon his coronation day, he was a being dedicated and apart.

Pharaoh's court was by tradition a place of pomp and luxury. Many Pharaohs lived frugal and ascetic lives, but their palaces were always famous for their magnificence. It was fitting that a king and a god should be richer and more generous than ordinary men. The splendour of his surroundings displayed to advantage the splendour of the king himself. What the sociologist would call the significant display of the royal abode impressed upon native and foreigner the glittering majesty of the Pharaoh of Egypt. A visitor to the palace could expect to be lavishly entertained, and the king's expenses were not lessened by the number of retainers whom he supported, the majority

17

of them purely for purposes of prestige. To enhance the effect of Pharaoh's eminence his palace was not only constructed in the form of a temple, but was actually a temple itself. No opportunity was lost to emphasize the fact that the king was a god dwelling in the midst of men. It is likely that Pharaoh divided his time equally between his palace in Upper Egypt and his palace in Lower Egypt. Beside the Double Residence there existed a Double Treasury and a Double Granary, for the original independence of each of the Two Lands was never forgotten.

The royal palace was so superbly constructed and equipped that it was natural that it should become the prototype of the royal tomb. When the king died he did not utterly cede his position as king of Egypt. In the stone palace of eternity where his spirit dwelt he exercised a continued if diminished influence upon the business of government. He still maintained a living court, for his pyramid city or mortuary chapel was staffed by a well endowed line of priests who remained in his service for many generations. Because the king exerted this ghostly power over his former subjects it was necessary to provide him with 'a good burial.' The immense labour of building the Great Pyramid or excavating the hypogeum of Seti I in the Valley of the Kings was undertaken because the occasion was the burial of a god. A contributory reason may have been the sorrow with which the nation witnessed the passing of a monarch who had ruled it wisely and devotedly. To provide him with a fitting sepulchre was a mark of their affection.

The esteem in which the ancient Egyptians held their king may be judged from the words in which a high official spoke to his children of his royal master, the great Amenemhat III of the Twelfth Dynasty. 'He is the god Ra whose beams enable us to see. He gives more light to the Two Lands than the sun's disc. He makes the earth more green than the Nile in flood. He has filled the Two Lands with strength and life. He is the Ka (i.e. the guardian spirit). He is the god Khnum who fashions all flesh. He is the goddess Bast who defends Egypt.

18

Whoever worships him is under his protection. But he is Sekhmet, the terrible lion goddess, to those who disobey him. Take care not to defy him. A friend of Pharaoh attains the rank of Honoured One, but there is no tomb for the rebel. His body is thrown into the river. Therefore listen to what I tell you and you will enjoy health and prosperity.'

The significance and philosophical implications of the phrases in this admonition will become clear during the course of the following chapters.

CHAPTER III

The Priest

There is no field in which the intellectual processes of the ancient Egyptian seem more foreign to our own than in the field of religion. To us a religion signifies a well defined body of belief developed as far as possible according to the rules of logic. In religion as in our other mental activities we look for coherence and consistency, as soon as certain initial premises have been accepted. But the ancient Egyptian paid little attention to logic or consistency. He was only dimly aware of the conception of cause and effect that gives polarity to modern thinking. He was less concerned with whether an idea was right or wrong than with considering whether or not it could be used to balance another idea. The intellectual motivation of the ancient Egyptian was towards arrangement and symmetry, in religion as in art. The occurrence of an idea was a gift of the gods, and it could never be committed to oblivion as erroneous or incompatible with some general scheme. Once an idea came into existence it took on life and was indestructible. The ancient Egyptian went happily to work to find a place for it in the pattern of belief, inserting it at a point where it balanced harmoniously with some opposing or complementary idea. In philosophy and religion, as in art and architecture, the Egyptian delighted in organizing disparate elements into apparently homogeneous wholes. The myriad elements which composed his religion offered unique scope for the exercise of mental ingenuity. They could be arranged like pieces of mosaic into a thousand pleasing designs.

5. THE GODDESSES NEITH, ISIS AND SELKIT
From the tomb of the Pharaoh Tutankhamon

6. A CAT WITH GOLDEN EARRINGS
A personification of the goddess Bast

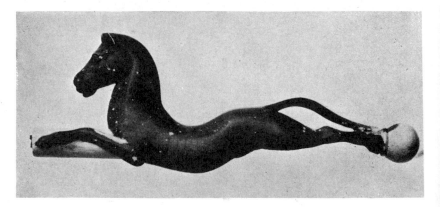

7. A LEAPING HORSE
A WHIP-STOCK OF THE EIGHTEENTH DYNASTY

The search for the truth—or for the single truths that together compose the universal truth—was unknown to the Egyptian. If you were to ask him about the nature of the universe, he would explain that the sky was supported on four pillars placed at each of the four cardinal points. This might appear a reasonable, if fallacious, supposition. He would then proceed to state that the four pillars might be, alternatively, the four legs of a cow. A cow? This is surely a curious complication? Yes: the legs of the cow along whose belly moved the sun, the moon and the stars. Or, he would continue, the pillars might also be the arms and legs of the sky goddess Nut, whose naked body was arched across the heavens. That is, if her body was actually arched across the heavens and not held in position by the air god Shu. On the other hand Shu, Nut, the pillars and the cow might have nothing to do with the problem. The sky might in fact be a flat inverted plate resting on the rim of the mountains to east and west of the Nile valley. All these explanations and others beside were possible to our ancient Egyptian. They all seemed feasible and aesthetically satisfying to him, for he was concerned more with the appearance than the essence of a notion. Different explanations could serve in different contexts. If you were in a scientific mood, you might plump for the plate. If you were feeling spiritually exalted, you might consider the goddess Nut. The existence of multiple explanations was reassuring: if one explanation was proved in the Next World to be false, it was probable that one of the others would turn out to be true. In this account of Egyptian religion, then, the reader must not expect a cut and dried discussion of a very perplexing and contradictory subject.

It seems safe to assert that the fundamental and abiding basis of the structure of Egyptian religion was the worship of local gods and goddesses. Altogether, including the foreign gods who were cheerfully admitted into the pantheon, over two thousand gods were worshipped in Egypt at one time or another. Many of them were minor variants of the principal deities or different forms of the same god. The worship of the local gods stemmed from the beginning of the predynastic period, about 6000 B.C., when numerous tribes came together in the valley of the Nile. The oldest gods were the gods of the nomes or provinces, worshipped in the form of deified nome ensigns in each small tribal capital. These nome gods preserved their identity to the very end of Egyptian civilization. From time to time, as a particular god became ascendant for political reasons, the nome gods changed their dynastic affiliations. They belonged first to one family of gods, then to another. Often they identified themselves with a prevailing national deity by adding its name to their own. Thus Amon and Atum, for example, became Amon-Ra and Ra-Atum. But the local god, despite tactical changes of front, remained the real god of his district throughout Egyptian history. No matter how bitterly the pontiffs of opposed cults assailed each other, peasant and nomarch paid unswerving allegiance to their provincial fetish. It is this constant grouping and regrouping in diplomatic alliances that produces much of the confusion which distracts the modern student.

A further cause for confusion is the fact that Egyptian gods were not categorized as good or bad. Seth was the slayer of his brother Osiris, but as the ancient patron of nomes in both Upper Egypt and the Delta he was assured of faithful devotion even after his overthrow. He held an honoured place among the warriors of the sun god and he was worshipped as a war god. As god of the desert, on the edge of which lived numerous villagers, it was prudent to cultivate his good will. He can therefore by no means be regarded as the Egyptian equivalent of the Christian devil. Horus himself, traditionally the good son, on one occasion cut off his mother's head in a fit of anger. The ancient Egyptian felt a warmer affection for his gods if they suffered from the same human weaknesses as himself. Popular tales were full of the treacherous, lecherous, drunken and quarrelsome activities of the gods. The gods were not always regarded as superior to mortals, and mortals could employ magical devices to bend the gods to their will.

We shall now attempt to give an account of the gods who, frequently from obscure and humble beginnings, became most prominent in the religious life of the Two Lands. Owing to their potency and prestige their fame spread from their native townships throughout the whole country. They were either associated with the local gods by actual identification or they became direct patrons of the local god or members of his trinity. Gods in Egypt tended to go in threes. Most temples were built with a main sanctuary and two subsidiary ones. Gods of similar nature or of local celebrity were in this way linked together. The triads usually consisted of a father, mother and son, following the example of the divine family Osiris, Isis and Horus. At Thebes the triad consisted of Amon-Ra, Mut and Khonsu. At Memphis it was Ptah, Sekhmet and Nefertem (later Imhotep).

The oldest of the great principal gods was RA, ATUM or RA-ATUM, god of the university city of Heliopolis, the City of the Sun. His cult early gave rise to the *Doctrine of Heliopolis*. Ra-Atum was a sky god, always depicted in human form, who created himself either by masturbation or by naming the several parts of his body. He arose out of Nun, the primordial waters. The eight parts of his body which he brought into being were grouped into four pairs of gods, two male and two female. These were the air god Shu and the moisture goddess Tefnut, the earth god Geb and the sky goddess Nut, Seth and Nephthys, Osiris and Isis. According to another version Ra-Atum begot Shu and Tefnut, who in turn begot Geb and Nut, who in turn begot Seth, Nephthys, Osiris and Isis. The outline of a theory of creation can be detected here. In the beginning of things are the dark waters, without form and void. Then the demiurge Ra-Atum introduces the germ of life. Air and moisture follow, to be succeeded by earth and sky. After earth and sky come creatures in human shape, the four gods who were the

23

earliest inhabitants of the land of Egypt. The nine Heliopolitan gods, with Ra-Atum at their head, constituted the Great Nine or Great Ennead, a body of gods much venerated at all periods. A Little Ennead, consisting of nine minor gods under the presidency of Horus, was also devised. Horus the falcon god was specifically identified with Ra-Atum under the name of Harakhte and was known as the 'Son of Ra.' He was personified as a vigorous youth who symbolized the rising sun. Ra was personified as the sun at its noonday zenith, while Atum was personified as a tired old man who represented the sun at its time of setting. Horus, the Lord of Heaven, possessed many additional titles and became the Apollo of the Greeks.

At Hermopolis in the Delta and Hermopolis Magna in Middle Egypt a different demiurge was worshipped. This was THOTH, whose cult gave rise to the *Doctrine of Hermopolis.* According to the Hermopolitan priesthood the initial act of creation took place at Hermopolis itself. Here Thoth brought into existence by means of calling out their names a set of gods who together laid the egg from which the sun was eventually hatched. These primeval gods consisted of four male frogs and four female snakes. Together they composed the Eight or Ogdoad, a canon which may have been the model for the Heliopolitan Ennead. Certainly both systems of theology were very ancient, preserving myths formulated by predynastic communities. Thoth, the Greek Hermes, was pictured as a man with the head of an ibis. He was vizier and scribe of the gods and controller of the seasons, the moon and the stars. He invented hieroglyphic writing, mathematics, the keeping of accounts, languages, magic, the legal system and even the game of draughts. He was married to the heavenly librarian Seshat, who inscribed on the leaves of the Tree of Heaven the record of every man's life. Their literary interests no doubt made them well suited to one another.

The protagonists of these two doctrines found themselves engaged during the Thinite epoch in ideological warfare with a third. During the First and Second Dynasties the Thinite kings tended to rule from Memphis, the most suitable administrative centre from the geographical point of view. The local god of Memphis was PTAH, and he grew in importance as his native city came to the forefront of affairs. The early Pharaohs encouraged the cult of Ptah for political reasons, for his shrine was at the centre of their sphere of influence. It was essential to their authority and their self-esteem that Ptah should be of greater importance than the fetishes of Heliopolis and Hermopolis. It was therefore asserted that he was more ancient than Atum himself, and his priests announced that he was coeval with the primordial waters of Nun from which Atum emerged. The *Doctrine of Memphis* taught further that Ptah created Ra-Atum by means of a profound effort of the mind. This spiritual process of taking thought was contrasted with the method of self-pollution employed by Ra-Atum. Ptah was the Mind of the Universe, the one god, self-conceived and self-existent. All gods and men were projections of his intellect. The falcon god Horus was his heart and Thoth, the god of wisdom, was his tongue: a clear indication that he annexed and superseded the deities of Heliopolis and Hermopolis. The cult of Ptah was a lofty philosophical idea which soared above the pragmatic fetish worship that comprised the bulk of Egyptian religion. Its abstruse and elevated nature precluded its popular acceptance, for the secular members of society continued to pay their devotions to more earthy divinities. Identified by the Greeks with Hephaistos and by the Romans with Vulcan, Ptah was the special patron of artists, artificers and men of letters.

At the end of the Thinite Period, although the capital remained at Memphis, the supremacy of Ptah was destroyed by the formal adoption by the royal house of the earlier sun religion of Heliopolis. The *Royal Doctrine*, based upon the Heliopolitan dogmas, was seen to approximate closely to the mythological basis of the Pharaonic dynasty. The sun priests now firmly established the notion that Ra-Atum was the first king of Egypt and that after him the sceptre had been wielded by members of their Great and Little Ennead in turn. They pointed out that because of his direct link with Horus the human Pharaoh possessed the blood of the sun god in his veins. They became the guardians of the royal succession and advisers on its purity, a fact which increasingly strengthened their influence upon the monarchy. The Royal Doctrine was maintained until the end of dynastic history. Pharaoh was always Horus, Harakhte, Son of Ra. Ra became so powerful during the latter part of the Old Kingdom that henceforward his name was propounded with that of every male god, Ptah, Thoth and Osiris alone being sufficiently strong to resist him.

The last of the great national gods of dynastic times was AMON-RA, the god of Thebes. Amon-Ra was almost entirely a political deity, without any elaborate formulation of doctrine behind him. Originally Amon was an insignificant god with a small shrine in the Sceptre Nome, whose god was Montu. He came to the fore during the First Intermediate Period (2300–2065 B.C.), the era of confusion between the fall of the Old Kingdom and the establishment of the Middle Kingdom. For some reason the nomarchs of Thebes, who had assumed the leadership of Upper Egypt, preferred him to Montu as their war god. He subsequently led them to victory against the Herakleopolitan chieftains of Lower Egypt and against the invading Bedouins. Following Heliopolitan doctrine they identified him with Ra. He formed a triad with the vulture goddess Mut and their son Khonsu. His cult grew steadily under the Theban Pharaohs of the Middle and New Kingdoms until his high priests became not only king makers but kings themselves. The armies which conquered Asia marched beneath his ensign and a major portion of the tribute and booty was expended upon his temples at Luxor, Karnak and Medinet Habu. Though he entered the lists rather late in the day,

Amon-Ra became by far the richest and most redoubtable of the gods of Egypt.

Ra-Atum, Thoth, Ptah and Amon-Ra were essentially aristocratic gods. They were manufactured or made prominent by speculation and cerebration or by the appeal which they made to a ruling caste. The great myths to which they were related or of which they formed selective portions were the immemorial myths recounting the life and death of Osiris. The Osiris myths were popular with every section of the community and in particular with all members of the poorer classes. The *Doctrine of Osiris* was so well known to every ancient Egyptian that there was never any need to record it in continuous narrative on papyri or temple walls. The longest account we possess is given by Plutarch in his *de Iside et Osiride*, but since Plutarch lived about 100 A.D. it is not surprising that he gave a garbled version of a complex corpus of myths which had been current for well over three thousand years.

Osiris was the best loved of the Egyptian gods. Pharaoh and his adherents might favour a more artificial and exclusive cult, but they could never ignore the wider and more forceful impact of Osirianism. It was inevitable that the worship of Osiris should make spectacular advances during such epochs of democratization as the First Intermediate Period. During the Old Kingdom ascent to heaven was a royal prerogative. The spirit of the dead Pharaoh flew up to the sky to be united with his ancestor, the sun god. The king, in his capacity as god, could extend this privilege to favoured officials outside the circle of his immediate family by granting them not only permission to build a tomb in the royal necropolis but also permission to use certain magical formulae that would enable them to ascend skywards. Other mortals were condemned to a hypothetical after life passed in a gloomy subterranean region. The Pharaonic monopoly of the pleasures of heaven fell into disuse with the collapse of the Old Kingdom. By the onset of the Middle Kingdom the secret formulae were revealed to all men, and every man was entitled to regard himself as united with Osiris when he died. Even under the Old Kingdom the attempt to suppress or minimize the traditional function of Osiris as the great god of the dead had been attended with uneasiness by the priests. In the Middle Kingdom all such attempts were abandoned and the paramount rôle of Osiris freely acknowledged. Again, by the Middle Kingdom Osiris had consolidated his position by assimilating or relegating to secondary importance all other early local gods of the dead, such as Sokaris, Khentamenti, Anubis and Wepwawet. An aspect of the funerary myth of Osiris which must be emphasized is the fact that he was the first mummy. His mummification either sprang from or resulted in the exaggerated respect paid to the preservation of the corpse. Osiris was resurrected after death, which led every Egyptian to hope for a similar event. There are no grounds for thinking, however, that Osiris was regarded as a personal redeemer in the sense in which Christians are said to view the resurrected Christ.

The hold of Osiris over the popular imagination was not confined to his importance to the individual in the next world. He was also a nature god, associated closely with the river and the rich soil of the valley. He was the principle of fertility, in opposition to the principle of sterility personified by Seth. Iconographically he is surrounded by lotuses, sedges, water and pastoral tokens. The splendid cycle of his life and death was a symbolic rendering of the progress of the seasons and the annual rise and fall of the Nile. When the peasants watched their crops springing up they rejoiced because the event signalized the rebirth of the god, whose body had fructified the seed as it lay winter long beneath the earth. When they cut and threshed the grain in the autumn they were re-enacting the murder and dismemberment of Osiris, and they uttered ritual cries of lamentation in sympathy with Isis for the cruel death of her husband. As god of every green and growing thing Osiris passed into the body of every man who ate them. The changing face of nature was reflected in the different phases of the myth. The story of Osiris was not something which had taken place in the remote past: it was something which took place every year in front of men's eyes. Thus Osiris was truly a living as well as a dead god, who explained the mysterious processes of nature. Osiris was also held to be a culture hero, the god who introduced agriculture and the arts of life into Egypt. The myths may in fact have been founded upon the career of some early leader of the predynastic community in the Delta, perhaps the shadowy figure known as Anzti. We noted in the case of the other great national deities how closely religion followed the exigencies of politics, and it is likely that legends of predynastic origin. contain hints about the interpretation of the archaeological story. The contention of Osiris and his son Horus with Seth appears to be based on the events of a real struggle for supremacy between Upper and Lower Egypt. This matter is to be more closely considered in Chapter VIII.

Diverse fragments of the Osiris legend are contained in the Pyramid Texts of the Old Kingdom and on a stele inscribed with a hymn to the god of Middle Kingdom date. Plutarch's version of the legend, to which may be added the accounts of Diodorus, Maternus and Macrobius, is substantially as follows:

Osiris was a wise king who civilized Egypt and made it the centre of a world wide empire. While he was away on his travels the administration of the country was in the hands of his wife and sister Isis. His younger brother Seth, the Greek Typhon, fell in love with Isis and determined to usurp the throne. He leagued himself with a queen of Ethiopia and seventy-two other conspirators. One Egyptian text states that Thoth was among his allies. Osiris was invited to a great banquet on his return from abroad at which a wonderfully wrought coffer was produced. Seth offered to present the coffer to the guest whose physical dimensions it fitted most exactly. One by one the conspirators stretched themselves out in the

coffer, but all were too short. At last it was the turn of Osiris.
He lay down inside the coffer and it was seen that it fitted him
—oddly enough—as though it had been measured for him.
Seth and his henchmen quickly flung themselves on the coffer
and clapped on the lid. The lid was nailed down and the box
swathed in lead. It was then cast into the Nile, where it floated
downstream past Tanis and out of the mouth of the Delta.
Finally it was washed ashore at Byblus, on the coast of Syria.
Here a tree, which was either a tamarisk or a persea, grew
round it and it became incorporated in the trunk. The tree was
later a fetish annually worshipped at Busiris in the Delta. It
was one of the amulets invariably placed between the wrappings
of a mummy.

The Syrian episode in the legend suggests that Osiris was
closely connected with Adonis of Byblus, the earlier Tammuz
or Dumuzi of Sumer and the later Dionysus of Greece. All
these gods were vegetation gods and culture heroes who perished
in their prime. The cycle of their lives corresponds to the cycle
of Osiris. It is possible that the word Osiris was the secret
name of Adonis of Byblus. Osirianism may have been brought
to Egypt in some predynastic migration from Syria, perhaps
the migration responsible for the Gerzean facies of the Badarian
culture of Upper Egypt. The tamarisk or persea tree was
eventually cut down by Malkander, king of Byblus, who
erected it as a pillar in his palace. Tree worship was an integral
part of the cult of Adonis and of ancient Asian agrarian
religions. It is hardly likely to have been indigenous in the tree-
less terrain of the Nile valley.

All this time Isis was searching frantically for her husband.
When at last she heard where he was to be found, she went to
Byblus and enrolled herself as the maidservant of Malkander's
queen Astarte or Ishtar—significantly the name of the consort
of Adonis. At length Isis revealed her identity and begged
Astarte to give her the body of her husband. She then brought
back the coffer and its contents to Egypt by sea. It may be

noted that the sea route between Egypt and Byblus was in regular use at the dawn of the dynastic era. The Egyptian colony at Byblus may be dated to about 2600 or 2500 B.C. Once in Egypt, the corpse of Osiris was immediately mummified by Anubis after directions supplied to him by Isis. Isis then took the mummy to a hiding-place in the marshes of the Delta, where she contrived to get herself impregnated by the resurrected but dead god. Her son Horus was born at Behdet or Hermopolis Parva and later resided at Buto.

But Seth too had been searching restlessly for his brother's body. He found it in Isis' absence, carried it off, dismembered it and scattered the pieces throughout the length of the land. Isis patiently sought them out and reassembled them. When Horus, whom she had managed to conceal from Seth during his boyhood in the swamps at Chemmis, came of age he set out to avenge his father's murder. This episode savours of the primitive vendetta or *lex talionis* which no doubt flourished in the predynastic community. The Pyramid Texts state that Horus fought an epic battle with his uncle during the course of which Seth tore out the eye of Horus and Horus hacked off the testicles of Seth. In the upshot the deadly quarrel was submitted to the arbitration of the earth god Geb, who established the claim of Horus as the successor of Osiris. In an earlier judgment Geb had awarded Lower Egypt to Horus and Upper Egypt to Seth, but now both kingdoms were placed beneath the sway of Horus. Here may be detected the translation into legendary terms of an actual conquest of Upper by Lower Egypt. It is noteworthy that all the major gods, with the exception of Amon-Ra, were gods of the Delta. There is also reason to think that the Delta dwellers of predynastic times were culturally more advanced at the outset than the tribesmen of Upper Egypt. It is therefore not unlikely that Osiris was a talented Deltaic chieftain whose successors conquered and civilized Upper Egypt, impelling at the same time widespread acceptance of Lower Egyptian religious dogmas.

Among the minor gods and goddesses who deserve mention are the following:

ANUBIS, the jackal-headed god of This and Cynopolis. Anubis, an ancient god, was the divine embalmer who shared with Osiris the titles of Prince of the West (i.e. where the dead dwelt) and Prince of Those-who-are-in-the-West (i.e. the dead themselves). It is probable that he was the original funerary deity of Upper Egypt who was displaced by the conquering funerary deity of Lower Egypt, Osiris.

KHNUM, the ram-headed god of Elephantine. He was held to have modelled the world and the forms of men upon his potter's wheel. This alternative creation myth, as we saw at the beginning of the chapter, would satisfy rather than confuse the ancient Egyptian.

MIN, the most jovial of all the gods. The cult of this Egyptian Silenus centred about Koptos and such caravan cities of Middle Egypt as Panopolis. He may in fact have been a foreign importation into Egypt. Min was the god of generation: the business of populating the Two Lands depended on him and orgies were celebrated in his honour. His statues and amulets, which are exceedingly common, represent him as a magnificently obese man with an enormous penis.

SEBEK, the crocodile-headed god of Kom Ombo and the Fayûm. A dreaded creature, he was the associate of Seth.

HATHOR, the great cow goddess, Lady of Heaven, Earth and the Underworld. She was much beloved and her cult extended from Nubia to Syria. Representations of her crescentic horns were common in the dynastic period. There are Hathor heads on the palette of Narmer. By nature Hathor was wise and gentle, helpful to both the living and the dead. She protected women during pregnancy and childbirth and was the confidante of lovers and lovely women. She was identified with nearly every goddess, entering as guest into a large number of triads. Many gods claimed her for wife or mother and she was the wet-nurse and wife of Horus.

32

As goddess of music and the dance the sistrum became her special emblem.

NEITH, Lady of Saïs, was the Diana of Egypt. A deity of predynastic hunting tribes, her insignia consisted of two feathered arrows crossed on a shield of cowhide. As a matter of course she was much venerated under the Twenty-sixth (Saïte) Dynasty.

KHONSU, a young warrior god, was worshipped in later times at Hermonthis, Edfu and Thebes. SOKAKIS was a predynastic falcon god associated with Ptah at Memphis and Osiris at Abydos. MONTU was the 'Mighty Bull' and Lord of Thebes, later overshadowed as a war god by Amon. SOPDU, pictured as a bearded man, was a Delta god who guarded the borders of the Delta from foreign invasion. HAAPI, god of the Nile, was seldom portrayed. He was thought to live in a grotto above the First Cataract and to be both male and female in person. WEPWAWET and KHENTAMENTI were wolf or jackal gods who acted as protectors of the dead. They were frequently confused, merged together and worshipped as a single deity. ONURIS, local god of This, was a war god honoured by the Thinite Pharaohs. Among minor goddesses NEPHTHYS, though wife and sister of Seth, was inseparable from Isis and devoted to Osiris. BAST was the cat-headed goddess of Bubastis who acted as guardian to the Delta. MAAT was the personification of justice and right dealing. MUT was the wife of Amon-Ra, the local goddess of Thebes. Among her many titles were Ruler of Karnak and Queen of All the Gods. It should be noted that although a god or goddess might be particularly associated with a certain city or nome, the cult might be fashionable in other localities. Hathor, for example, was goddess of four nomes, while in various guises Horus was lord of six nomes in Lower Egypt and six in Upper Egypt.

ANIMAL CULTS flourished with particular prominence during the Late Period. 'Who does not know,' asked Juvenal, 'what monsters are adored by demented Egypt?' Animals, birds, reptiles and insects were all considered to be embodiments of gods. They included the bull (Apis—incarnation of Ptah, Mnevis—incarnation of Ra, Buchis—incarnation of Montu), the ram (incarnation of Amon, Khnum and Harsaphes), the crocodile (Sebek), the ibis (Thoth), the ichneumon (Atum), the cat (Bast). It has been recorded that when the Ram of Mendes died the entire city went into mourning and the beast received a gorgeous funeral at state expense. Cemeteries of mummified creatures have been excavated. A notable example is the Serapeum of Apis at Memphis, where the 'reigns' of twenty-four sacred bulls between the time of Ramses II and the Ptolemaic period were meticulously recorded. Other necropoles include the cat cemetery at Beni Hasan, the crocodile cemetery at Kom Ombo and the ibis cemetery at Abydos.

Why did the ancient Egyptian portray his gods even from the earliest times in such curious forms? Only a small number of them were anthropomorphic. The vast majority were personages with the heads of beasts and birds affixed to the bodies of men and women. The great dynastic gods Atum, Ptah and Amon-Ra were all of human aspect, and it may be that all the semi-human and animal gods were of predynastic origin. Perhaps there was some kind of evolution from pre-historic animal forms through half-human to human forms. It may be asked whether the ancient Egyptian could possibly have taken his more freakish deities seriously. Was it really credible that he could worship in all solemnity a goose, a scorpion or a dung beetle? The answer is that he regarded these creatures as useful envelopes for the vital spirit of the god to whom they were dedicated. He had a concrete mind. He wanted his gods to assume a recognizable shape. Why then should he not worship a beetle, if a beetle was acknowledged to be one of the forms of Ra? The desire to imagine the object of worship in tangible form is common to most religions. The ancient Egyptian thought of the creator god Atum as a benevolent old gentleman, just as the modern Christian may imagine his own

34

creator god as a venerable and somewhat doddery personage. The falcon god Horus does not seem ridiculous in comparison with the swan-winged and anatomically absurd Archangel of Christendom. It should be remembered that the Egyptian could watch the impressive sweep of the falcon across the firmament, while the number of persons who have laid eyes on an Archangel is probably infinitesimal. The salient point is that the Egyptian believed in a fluid life force that could be poured at will into any suitable mould. This is the explanation of the fact that the sky could be the belly of a cow or the body of a woman, or why Pharaoh could be described in a single context as the sun, a star, a bull, a crocodile, a lion, a falcon and a jackal. The life spirit was protean: it transformed itself effortlessly into a multiplicity of shapes. A god would inhabit one fleshly envelope and then transfer to another, or dwell in both simultaneously. Sometimes a god would even share his abode with another god. There are representations of Horus and Seth, those apparently mortal enemies, occupying a single body. The Egyptian religion was the least rigid and arbitrary of religions.

In modern society the word religion is overlaid with heavy ethical overtones. Religion undertakes the evaluation of human actions into good deeds and bad deeds. It concerns itself with the health of that tender entity the soul. It denotes a certain conception of personal conduct. To the ancient Egyptian religion appears to have been a far less sensitive and subjective matter. The worship of the gods was of an impersonal quality, designed primarily to assure the worshipper of his place and participation in the great scheme of things. The ideas of sin and redemption as Christians recognize them appear to have played no part in Egyptian religion. The gods certainly awarded punishment, but rather because their rites had been neglected than because the worshipper had committed wicked acts. The gods were respected for their magical rather than their moral powers. The Egyptian was intensely concerned with proper social behaviour, which constituted the lifelong ideal at which he aimed. But social and anti-social behaviour were more secular than religious problems. The relationship of a man to his fellows, his superiors and his king was regulated by a code which owed more to traditional lore and accepted custom than to religion. There is little in Egyptian religious literature which could influence a man's conduct: the moral precepts which provided him with guidance are contained in collections of proverbs attributed to distinguished law givers, great Pharaohs and viziers. Religion was not a means whereby a man obtained divine advice concerning his manner of life, rather it was one of the ways in which society was made conscious of its corporate identity. The daily act of worship was intended to emphasize the common and not the individual character of the citizen. Egyptian religion was also practical in outlook. Whether you were a good man or a bad man it supplied you with a gratifying assortment of magical formulae guaranteed to get you by hook or by crook into heaven. Whatever sort of terrestrial existence you led, if you recited the rubrics correctly you would obtain everlasting bliss.

What kind of life did the ancient Egyptian envisage for himself in the NEXT WORLD? He regarded death as an unmitigated disaster and his earnest desire was that the next world should resemble the pleasant land of Egypt as much as possible. He wished to continue all the bodily activities which he was accustomed to perform when alive. 'May I eat in the heavenly fields,' he prayed, 'may I drink, plough and reap, fight and make love there. May my words be mighty and may I never serve as a slave but be always in authority.' The accounts of the next world preserved on tomb walls and in religious papyri are confused and contradictory. The scribes and artists followed religious practice in refusing to agree upon a single satisfactory version. Under the Thinite Period and the Old Kingdom, when the Royal Doctrine was in vogue, the Elysian Fields in which Pharaoh and his entourage passed eternity were situated in the eastern part of the sky. A preliminary and some-

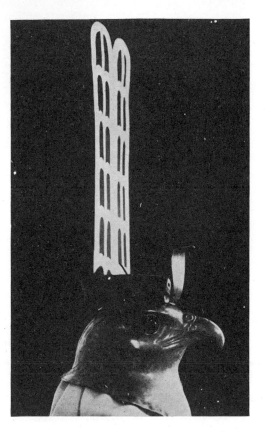

8. A GOLD MASK FOR A MUMMIFIED
HAWK, WITH EYES OF OBSIDIAN
From Hierakonpolis. Sixth Dynasty

9. A FALCON IN POLYCHROME FAIENCE INLAY
Late Dynastic

10. (*top*) THE FALCON HORUS   A jewel from the tomb of the Pharaoh Tutankhamon
(*below*) INLAID FAIENCE DECORATIONS FROM A COFFER OF LATE
DYNASTIC DATE (The ibis god Thoth is at bottom right)

what cursory examination in which the deceased person was declared 'true of voice' or 'justified' was enacted, after which the dead king or nobleman was welcomed into heaven by the Great and Little Enneads and took his seat among them. The dead man was entitled to claim a place in the boats of Ra, the day boat and the night boat. The boats, which represented the sun in its daily journey across the sky and its nightly journey beneath the earth, were manned by the most important gods. The gods, assisted by the new member of the crew in the person of the dead man, fought a nightly battle with the huge serpent Apophis, who tried unsuccessfully to devour the boat and thereby swallow the sun. This battle was an expression of the fear prevalent among many primitive communities that because the sun sets in the evening there is no corresponding guarantee that it will rise the following morning. Two model boats formed part of the standard tomb furniture of Egyptian burials. Apart from fishing and hunting, the Pyramid Texts and the Coffin Texts reveal little of the pursuits of the privileged in heaven under the Old Kingdom.

Religious works of the Middle and New Kingdoms show that the triumph of Osiris radically altered the conception of the life to come. Pharaoh still went to his heaven in the sky, but the people in general now inhabited a more commodious and better appointed Underworld. The Underworld ran parallel to the Nile valley and partly beneath it. It was separated from Egypt by a mountain range with a narrow gorge through which the sun and the spirits of the dead could enter. The dead person who wished to gain access to the Underworld had first to pass through a dark and fearful region haunted by fiends and monsters. Here the waverer was seized, tortured and at last devoured or cremated. Each division or nome of this black abode was governed by a separate demon. The dead man travelled in a boat which sailed beneath the cities of Egypt. He passed through a succession of pylons whose gates opened to him only when the appropriate password was quoted from sacred lore. At the end of this terrible journey he arrived at the blessed realm of Osiris, consisting of two Elysian Fields. Instead of the ancient location in the eastern corner of the sky, the fields were located in the western corner of the Underworld. The two fields, perhaps a reminiscence of the Two Lands, were the Field of Rushes and the Field of Offerings. Clothed in white raiment, the deceased would busy himself in all manner of agricultural occupations. The two sun boats were still at his disposal, one for sailing upstream and the other for sailing downstream, if he wished to visit the cities of Elysium. He would be reunited with his family and enjoy all the pleasures of the flesh. His new surroundings could never rival the amenities of the excellent land he had been forced to leave, but at least they were almost exactly similar in general appearance. If he wished to avoid the tiresome business of working in the fields, he could evade the heavenly *corvée* by calling upon the workmen who were 'buried' with him in his tomb. The workmen were represented by diminutive inscribed figures of stone, wood or faience called *ushabtis*: 'answerers' (Pl. 15). Contained in boxes, they were known as answerers because they came at their master's summons to perform his tasks for him.

Before the dead person was permitted to enter the Elysian Fields he was compelled to undergo the JUDGMENT OF THE DEAD. The ceremony is depicted in funerary papyri from the Eighteenth Dynasty onwards. It was no doubt an elaboration of the judgment of the dead king by Ra described in the Pyramid Texts. The judgment of Osiris which received recognition under the New Kingdom consisted essentially of the ceremony of the psychostasia or weighing of the heart. The ceremony took place in the Hall of Maat, goddess of Truth, presumably after the journey through the Underworld was concluded. In the middle of the Hall of Maat stood a large pair of scales, in one pan of which rested the heart of the dead man and in the other the feather of Maat (Pl. 34). The heart was chosen for judgment because it was held to be the seat of the intellect and the emotions. While it was being weighed its owner stood near it and abjured it not to inform against him. The process of adjusting the balance was performed by Anubis and the result noted down by Thoth, whose attendant baboon sat attentively on top of the scales. Maat herself watched the procedure, while a fierce monster called the Devourer, with the head of a crocodile, the forepart of a lion and the hindquarters of a hippopotamus, waited eagerly to tear the dead man in pieces if the judgment went against him. If the balance of heart and feather was equal (and since none of the papyri ever show it to be otherwise we may suppose that the ancient Egyptians were paragons of virtue) Thoth turned to the Great Company of gods who were present at the performance and declared the petitioner 'true of voice' or 'justified.' The Great Company, to whom the petitioner had made a preliminary declaration of innocence known as the Negative Confession, consisted of forty-two Assessors, each of whom was associated with a particular offence. Many of the Assessors can be identified as nome gods or town gods; they thus represented a tribunal drawn from the entire country. When the suppliant was declared worthy of immortality by Thoth, Horus took him by the hand and conducted him into the presence of Osiris. Osiris was not exhibited as playing the part of presiding judge in the proceedings: it was the Assessors who ratified the proclamation of Thoth. The great Prince of the West, wrapped in his winding sheet, was shown sitting in his shrine. Standing in front of him on a lotus plant were his four sons, behind him stood Isis and Nephthys. It should be noted that the forty-two 'sins' from which the suppliant stated he was free consisted almost entirely of offences against the law, primarily the law of property. Treason, deceit, boastfulness, false witness and sexual perversion were also mentioned. The 'truth' or 'righteousness' of which Maat was the personification appears to have been linked more closely to civil than to religious morality, in

our sense of the term. It was more important to stand before
the Assessors with a good record as citizen than with an
individual consciousness that one had done no wrong. The
word *maat* seems above all to signify civic regularity.

The precise form in which a man was to spend his time in the
Elysian Fields is difficult to determine. The spiritual manifesta-
tion which scholars are apt to translate as 'the soul' was the *Ba*.
The Ba was depicted as a stork or as a bearded human-headed
bird with a lamp in front of it. The lamp may be a reference
to a belief that every star was a Ba. There is no doubt that the
Ba was at once material and immaterial. It could take the actual
shape of its owner, but it could also assume the body of a bird,
an animal or a fish. It seems to have emerged from the corpse
at the moment of death and the texts are clear on the subject
of its place in heaven: 'Your Ba stands among the gods,' 'Your
Ba is a star, foremost among its brothers.' With the Ba was
associated the *Ka*, an entity closer to the physical body than the
Ba. The Ka was born with a person and remained earthbound
on his death. At the instant of death a man's Ka and his body
were united. The Ka lived in the tomb with the mummy, feeding upon the daily offerings and dwelling in the statue enclosed in the Serdab. If the offerings were withheld the hungry
Ka might wander abroad and eat filth, an act which would
endanger the existence in the next world of the Ba. The
mummy, too, must be kept undefiled, for if it were seriously
damaged or destroyed the soul would perish. The status of the
Ka is debated. The Egyptians themselves may have entertained
conflicting views about its nature. It may have been a man's
genius, his personality, his life force, his twin or double, his
guardian spirit. All these terms can be justified in various contexts. The use of the word Ka in such names as 'Ra-is-my-
Ka' suggests that it was somewhat akin to *mana*, the protean
life essence of Egyptian religious concept. The vital essence was
sometimes referred to as the Sekhem, which materialized itself
in a form resembling the Ka. The soul of a dead man as it

wandered through the Elysian Fields was often called the Akh, the 'effective spirit,' a translucent and shining ghost which reflected the achievements of its possessor when upon earth. The heart too was credited with a spiritual character, as the psychostasia demonstrates. It was put back in the body after the intestines were removed during mummification. A man's name was also of spiritual importance. Every care was taken to perpetuate it, since its obliteration would cause his memory to fade in the land of the living. The physical ties that bound the deceased person to the land of Egypt were of necessity to be retained if he were to survive in the next world. 'Let my name abide in your house,' runs an inscription of the Saïte Dynasty. 'Let my Ka be remembered after my life. Let my statue abide and my name endure upon it imperishably in your temple.'

The ceremonies performed in the temples bear traces of the rituals of both Ra and Osiris. A standardized daily service seems to have been performed from the Middle Kingdom onwards. The focal point of the service was the person of Pharaoh or the priest who deputized for him. Pharaoh's rising each day was a sacred occasion known as the *Rite of the House of the Morning*. The king was first laved with water brought from the sacred lake which was part of the ritual equipment of every temple and palace. The water, symbolizing the primordial waters of Nun, caused the king to be 'born anew.' He was then anointed, robed and invested with the royal insignia by two priests wearing the masks of Thoth and Horus. This token ritual was carried out in the sacristy as a preliminary to the *Daily Service*. After the laving and fumigation were completed, the two priests took Pharaoh or his proxy by the hand and led him into the sanctuary. Here stood the stone, wood or metal statue of the god, enclosed in the shrine or *naos*. The sanctuary was known as 'the sky,' and when the king broke the clay seal of the shrine to reveal the sun god he was 'opening the two doors of the sky.' The king prostrated himself before the shrine and woke the god by reciting the Hymn of

Morning Worship, addressed a few hours before to the king himself: 'Wake in peace, as the goddesses of the two crowns wake in peace!' The king purified the statue, took it in his arms, went through the motions of feeding it, robed it in coloured cloths, rouged its face and adorned it with the royal emblems. He then replaced it in the shrine and sealed the doors. He left the sanctuary walking backwards, effacing the traces of his footprints with a palm leaf. Appropriate formulae were recited at every stage of the strict ceremonial. The ceremonial became so well established that even Akhenaton did not dare to tamper too radically with it. In the heretical temples of the Aton there was no image of the god, but otherwise the daily procedure was unaltered.

The *Mortuary Liturgy*, performed each day in the mortuary chapels of tombs and temples on behalf of the dead Pharaoh or dead man, followed the pattern of the daily service. The image in this liturgy was replaced by the mummy or statue of the dead person. Particular attention was paid to the part of the ceremony known as the Opening of the Mouth, designed to restore to the dead person the use of his limbs and senses. The mummy or statue was placed on a small mound of sand, purified, clothed and offered food. Its mouth and eyes were anointed and the lips 'opened' with a metal instrument. In performing the mortuary liturgy the priest was repeating for the deceased the rites which Horus performed for his father Osiris. The *Mortuary Sacrifice* was an essential element in the worship of the dead. Bread, fruit, meat, beer and other kinds of food and drink were placed on a low altar to satisfy the needs of the Ba and the Ka, which subsisted on the spiritual substance of the offering. The offering was called the 'Gift-which-the-King-gives' in recognition of the direct intercession with the gods which the king and the king alone had power to make. The term was also a relic of the days of the Old Kingdom when the king actually made a royal gift of food to his dead favourites. The Ba and the Ka came through the false door to receive the funerary offering. Worship of the dead was obligatory because a man's ancestors, like former Pharaohs, still maintained an interest in the fortunes of their successors. The dead controlled the destinies of the living, but they were also dependent on the goodwill of the living for the prayer and the sustenance which sustained them in the next world. This aspect of religion was therefore a reciprocal arrangement, each party possessing a measure of power over the other. It was not uncommon for a disappointed worshipper to threaten a dead wife, husband, uncle or brother with a suspension of devotion in the same manner in which he sometimes threatened the gods. Animals were often sacrificed in connection with the mortuary sacrifice and libations of blood, milk and the revivifying water of the Nile were compulsory.

The first of two major ceremonies of which Pharaoh was the protagonist was the *Coronation*. It was on his coronation day that he became a Horus. The ceremony opened with prolonged purification by two priests in Horus and Thoth or Horus and Seth masks. The king was then presented to his people and his official titles proclaimed, after which he was twice crowned, once for Upper and once for Lower Egypt. Under the Thinite dynasties an additional rite of 'going round the Wall' was enacted. The Wall in question was the White Wall of Memphis, traditionally built by Menes, founder of the First Dynasty. The Pharaoh went in solemn procession round the Wall or a model of it behind the standard bearers of the nomes. 'Going round the Wall' was a feature of early celebrations of the *Heb-Sed Feast*, which was also of predynastic origin. The Heb-Sed was a royal jubilee performed as far as can be judged at arbitrary intervals. Ramses II celebrated as many as five. The feast was designed to restore to the monarch his greatness and his physical strength and also to prolong his life. 'You are renewed and you begin again,' the gods promised Seti I on the day of his jubilee. 'You become young like the infant moon god, you wax continually like him from season to season, like

43

Nun at the beginning of his time. You renew your births by repeating the Heb-Sed feast.' Clad in a winding sheet, Pharaoh mimed the life and death of Osiris. After the symbolic death the king rose again in his pristine vigour, as Osiris had done after his resurrection. An essential part of the ritual was the erection of the Osiris pillar, a totem carved to resemble the lopped trunk of the tree which grew round the god's coffin on the shore at Byblus. Sometimes an obelisk was substituted for the wooden pillar, indicating a solarization of the rite. The king also took part in many minor ceremonies, such as the rite of Building the Temple. The business of stretching out the measuring cord and laying the corner stone was entrusted to Pharaoh, who afterwards consecrated the edifice by processing round it, rapping twelve times on the door and purifying the naos with fire. A similar ceremony was carried out in connection with the construction of palaces, pyramids, fortresses and even irrigation works. Representations exist of the king cutting the first sod of a new canal. A priest was called upon to perform a curtailed version of these rites at the consecration of a private tomb or ordinary house.

Festivals and religious junketings were of frequent occurrence in ancient Egypt. Every god was assigned his particular feast days. Among the most spectacular feasts were the Feast of Horus at Buto, the Feast of Min at Esna and the Feast of Amon-Ra at Thebes. The Feast of Amon-Ra took place at the beginning of the New Year and lasted twenty-four days. The greatest of all these festivals was the annual performance of the Mysteries of Osiris at the sacred city of Abydos. The mysteries were first given under the Pharaohs of the Twelfth Dynasty, who bowed to the inevitable in their recognition of the popular resurgence of the ancient Osirian myths. The necropolis of Abydos was considered hallowed ground even in the pre-dynastic era, but during the decades which heralded the onset of the Middle Kingdom the joint patrons of the necropolis, Anubis and Wepwawet, were supplanted by Osiris. At first

Abydos ranked as the god's second city after his original home at Busiris in the Delta. With the growth of a legend that the head of the god was buried there, Abydos came to the forefront of the holy sites of Egypt. It became everyone's ambition to make the pilgrimage to Abydos to participate in the mysteries and to set up a small commemorative stele in the necropolis. Rich men frequently left orders that their bodies were to be transported by river to be interred near 'the staircase of the great god at Abydos.' The mysteries were cast in the form of an eight act drama. The rôles in the passion play were assigned by the king to high officers of state, the part of Horus, the 'darling son,' being coveted as a signal honour. The whole cycle of the life, death, mummification, resurrection and enthronement of Osiris was portrayed in a pageant which occupied many days. The local population and the influx of pilgrims joined in the proceedings as extras. The mysteries opened with a tableau in which Wepwawet, whose name means the Opener of the Ways, prepared the stage for the entrance of Osiris. A section of the populace, arrayed as Seth and his followers, pretended to oppose the landing at Abydos of the magnificent barque which bore the body of the god. Another section of the populace, impersonating the supporters of Horus, drove them off. After one of the principal actors in the character of Thoth had looked for and found the body, the statue of Osiris, decorated with gold, electrum, lapis lazuli, malachite and all manner of precious stones, was conveyed to a desert shrine in a triumphal progress known as the Great Outgoing. There the mummification and resurrection of the god were performed and the statue brought back to its final resting place in the splendid temple. These culminating rites were accompanied by an epic battle between forces representing the armies of Horus and Seth, during which a large number of noses were bloodied and heads were broken. Similar mysteries were performed in honour of Osiris and his family at Heliopolis, Buto, Busiris and Letopolis. Herodotus watched the ceremony at Bubastis,

45

Busiris and Saïs, while at Philae the mysteries were still enacted in the fifth century A.D.

The precise manner in which the PRIESTHOOD was organized is unknown. Pharaoh himself was chief priest. The priests, whose name in Egyptian signifies Pure Ones, were divided into two large general classes consisting of Prophets and Ordinary Priests. The temples were staffed with recognized cadres: Chief Prophet, Deputy Prophet, Prophet, Priest, Deputy Priest and so on. There were specialist priests of many kinds, including lector priests, orators and mortuary priests. Priestesses were ranged in a hierarchy of their own, the duties of female priests being confined in the main to the provision of music and dancing on religious occasions. Sacred concubines and sacred prostitutes existed at all times, particularly in conjunction with the cult of Min. Members of the priesthood combined other activities with their religious functions. Since reading and writing were almost entirely a monopoly of the priests, who administered the schools and kept the libraries, it is not surprising that they supplied the majority of politicians, doctors, lawyers, undertakers and other professional men. Their privileges were numerous, including exemption from manual labour and freedom from taxation. They also possessed the right of asylum. When not officiating, priests wore ordinary dress, though they shaved their heads and carried a special wand of office. According to rank and special duties, when officiating they wore a variety of masks, pectorals, elaborate wigs and animal cloaks.

CHAPTER IV

The Aristocrat

After Pharaoh, the most powerful man in the state of ancient Egypt was the VIZIER. In the small compact courts of the Thinite Period and the Old Kingdom the vizier and other high functionaries were kinsmen of the monarch. In later times, when a comparable degree of centralization was impossible, the vizier was chosen from among the ranks of the nobility or the priesthood. Under the New Kingdom the complexity of administration led to the appointment of a vizier for Lower Egypt at Memphis and a vizier for Upper Egypt at Thebes. The territories over which they held sway extended respectively from the Delta to Asyut and from Asyut to Elephantine. It was not uncommon for the vizierate to pass from father to son in talented families, though hereditary succession was encouraged only in cases of genuine merit.

The responsibilities of the vizier were onerous. In agricultural matters he heard all territorial disputes within two months, or three days in the case of his own city. He checked the census reports of cattle, noted supplies of feeding stuffs and inspected reservoirs. He superintended all tree-felling and dyking activities. The nomarchs of his province submitted a detailed report to his office every four months at the beginning of each of the three Egyptian seasons. Reports were also compiled with regard to rainfall and the condition of the Nile. All administrative documents required his seal, while as official archivist a document could be consulted only with his consent. He selected the staff of the royal household and despatched all palace messengers. The tax authorities sent their accounts to

47

him and he issued the receipts of the royal storehouses. He recruited the royal bodyguard and took charge of all arrangements for the king's progresses. Every morning he went to the Residence to be received by Pharaoh. After enquiring about the royal health, he reported on affairs of state. In this he was assisted by his close colleague the chancellor, who had previously received a detailed statement from the head of every department.

The vizier was also chief justice, and tomb inscriptions of Eighteenth Dynasty holders of the office give a broad picture of the ancient Egyptian legal system. Each city appears to have possessed a council of elders, known as the Saru under the Old Kingdom and the Kenbet in later times. The Kenbet was an advisory body which delegated the business of policing and punishment to an active tribunal called the Zazat. The terms of reference of these local organizations were narrow, since all serious cases were referred to the Great Kenbet at Memphis and Thebes. The most senior court of all was the court of the vizier. Here the great man sat enthroned among his executives, his Director of the Cabinet, his Keeper of the Things-which-come-in and his numerous scribes. The entrance chamber of the hall of judgement was always crowded. 'Audience is not given to the man at the back before the man in front,' runs an inscription. In other words, one had to take one's place in the queue. The verdicts handed down in this august courtroom were of great moment, for the Egyptians, in the manner of a conservative and law-abiding people, based their laws on precedent. In delivering judgement the vizier was less concerned with ideal justice than with interpreting the will of Pharaoh, whose mouthpiece he was. No less than the criminal who stood before him, the vizier was the humble servant of a god. Pharaoh was the real chief justice as he was the real chief priest, and it was only because he was unable to attend to administrative detail in person that he was willing to delegate authority. Any unorthodox or independent expression on the part of the king's deputies was out of the question. The end of a set of instructions delivered by Tuthmosis III to the Vizier Rekhmara on his assumption of office contains the injunction: 'When a man is an official he should act according to the rules laid down for him. Happy is the man who does what he is told! Never swerve from the letter of justice, whose tenets are familiar to you. Look at what happens to a presumptuous official: Pharaoh sets the timid above the presumptuous. Act therefore in accordance with the rules laid down for you.'

Despite his enormous powers the vizier was taught to recognize his insignificance in relation to his master. It is probable that he consulted the king with regard to all difficult decisions. In particular no man could be put to death without the king's express permission. The instructions of Tuthmosis III, which may represent a traditional charge to a vizier upon his installation, include many amusing and revealing passages. 'To be vizier requires not mildness but firmness. You must not take sides with the Saru or Zazat or make any man a slave. When a petitioner comes from Upper or Lower Egypt you must look thoroughly into his case and act in such a way that he has his rights. Remember also that an official must live with his face uncovered (i.e. his life must be an open book). The wind and water report all that he does. Look on your friend as a stranger and a stranger as your friend. An official who acts in this way will hold his post a long time. Do not send away any petitioner unheard and do not brusquely reject what he says. If you refuse him, let him know why you refuse him. A man with a grievance likes his tale of woe to be heard sympathetically even more than he wants it put right. Do not fly into a rage with a man wrongfully. Fly into a rage only when rage is necessary. A real magistrate is always feared. If he is feared it makes court procedure more impressive. But if people are positively frightened out of their wits by him, it can do his reputation a great deal of harm. People won't say of him: ''There's a fine fellow!'' You will be respected in your profession if you act strictly according to the dictates of justice.'

Many of these hard-working administrators became famous in after years. Amenemhat, vizier of the last Mentuheteps, became the founder of the Eleventh Dynasty. Two famous viziers of the Middle Kingdom were Mentuhetep, vizier of Sesostris I, and Sehetepibra, vizier of Amenemhat III. Under the Eighteenth Dynasty, Weser and Rekhmara sprang from the same Theban family. Rekhmara is said to have liked to rise before dawn to roam the streets of Thebes. Perhaps the tax returns, the tree-felling accounts, the latest despatches from Syria or the recent scandal in the harîm conspired to give the poor man insomnia. Several viziers were worshipped as gods by later generations. They include the Old Kingdom sages Kagemni and Ptahhetep, to whom were attributed celebrated collections of wise sayings. The great Imhotep (p. 147) was the original of the Greek god Aesculapius, and at Memphis he was incorporated in the triad of Ptah as the son of Ptah and Nut. He was represented as a seated priest holding an un-rolled papyrus scroll upon his knees (Pl. 25). The Saïtes, who deified Imhotep, also deified another architect and philosopher, Amenhetep, friend and vizier of Amenophis III. Amenhetep erected many of the mighty monuments of his master, including his huge palace at Thebes and the Colossi of Memnon. He played the part of an enlightened Maecenas, and on his death the grieving king ordered a temple to be built to him at Deir el-Medina.

A functionary whose importance fell not far short of that of the vizier was the CHANCELLOR. Known as the Director of the Seal, he was in charge of the complicated economic affairs of a civilized country which transacted its business according to a rudimentary system of barter. It was the chancellor who determined the amount of tax and saw to its collection. The Treasury or royal storehouse must have borne a strong resemblance to a pawn shop, since every tradesman and artisan paid his taxes in kind. In one papyrus such ill-assorted objects as corn, dates, flour, cakes, fish, worked wood, dressed hides, balls of frankincense, eyeblack and wigs are listed on the same inventory. Since much of the garnered material was perishable it needed prompt action to collect and clear it. The contents of the storehouses not only represented taxes, calculated on the basis of the height of the Inundation and the yearly agricultural yield, but also the structure of the wage system. The owners of provincial estates no doubt arranged their wage scales according to individual wealth and generosity, but it was the chancellor's task to determine the remuneration to be paid to workers on royal estates. He also presided over the economic affairs of the temples, which controlled the largest area of land after the king. In view of the innumerable exemptions and allowances to which the priesthood was entitled, administration of religious finances can have been no easy matter. The great number of funerary estates and pyramid cities held in mortmain must have presented a special economic difficulty. In addition to his civil duties the chancellor also performed the task of paymaster-general to the army and navy.

The VICEROY OF NUBIA was a small Pharaoh in his own right. His office was created in the Eighteenth Dynasty when the colonization of Nubia had been carried as far as Napata on the Fourth Cataract. Egyptian influence also extended into the semi-independent territory which lay between Napata and Meroë, near the Sixth Cataract. This area was part of the homeland of the Nubian rulers of the Twenty-fifth (Ethiopian) Dynasty. The viceroy, known as the 'royal son of Kush,' was head of an organization modelled on the political machinery of the capital. His jurisdiction was mainly exerted in the field of civil policy, the military arrangements remaining in the hands of the general staff. It was always necessary to mount strong garrisons in Nubia, perpetually threatened as it was by attacks from the tribesmen of the African Interior.

The OFFICERS OF THE COURT were legion. Around the king were ranked a group of intimate advisers known as the

Honoured Ones. Admission to this small circle was permitted only to men who had served the king with distinction over a long period of years. The Honoured Ones were maintained at court at the king's expense, but the greatest of their privileges was to receive a grant of a tomb and tomb furniture from their master. The king supplied linen, oils, wood and the fine stone of which tomb and sarcophagus were made. He also allotted the Honoured One a tomb plot near his own last resting place. The Honoured Ones, among whose number the royal family were automatically included, possessed other laudatory titles, such as King's Friend and Unique Friend. At court the councillors often occupied specific posts. These included the Lordship of the Secret of the Royal House (i.e. custodian of the crown jewels) and the Lordship of the Secret of All the Royal Sayings, who issued state invitations to the king's presence. The formidable protocol of the court was in the hands of numerous chamberlains and majordomos. The king's person was attended to by a Director of the King's Dress, who commanded a host of functionaries which included the Valet of the Hands, the Director of Oils and Unguents and the Keeper of the King's Wigs. The personal staff maintained by the queen and the ladies of the royal harîm was of course even more elaborate. The royal kitchens showed a similar regard for precedent. The three royal meat-carvers preceded the cakemaker, who in turn preceded the soufflé-maker and the jammaker. It should be remembered that palace kitchens supplied not only an extravagant abundance of food for the living but also countless 'Gifts-which-the-King-gives' for the benefit of the dead. Outside the immediate circle of the Pharaoh existed the chiefs of innumerable ministries. Granaries, herds, the irrigation system, arsenals: all were administered by an appropriate division of the civil service, responsible to the chancellor and the vizier. A man of considerable note at court was the clerk of the works, whose task it was to erect new buildings and maintain old ones in a good state of repair.

One of the best aristocratic 'autobiographies' which have come down to us is that of a courtier of Pepi I of the Sixth Dynasty, inscribed in his tomb at Abydos. It is so complete and so typical of its class that it deserves to be quoted at some length. The courtier in question, whose name was Weni, was employed successively on the royal estates, in the bedchamber, the pyramid city, the courts, the army and the civil administration. Weni was a successful professional courtier, a man who climbed the ladder from obscure origins to high office. There is more than a suggestion that he was something of a sycophant and a toady, but the grovelling tone in which he recounted his achievements for posterity was the socially accepted one. He took an overwhelming pride in his complete subservience to the royal will. 'Happy the man,' as Tuthmosis III enjoined Rekhmara, 'who does what he is told.' It was in interpreting the will of Pharaoh that the ancient Egyptian found true contentment. Weni gives the impression that he hardly enjoyed an individual existence of his own. He was entirely the king's creature. The word 'autobiography' is advisedly placed between inverted commas, for the inscription is redolent of the impersonality with which all inscriptions of this class are imbued. No ancient Egyptian ever reveals himself to us in a frank and vivid light. Like his fellows, Weni was a deeply conventional person: conventional in his career, in his habits of mind and in his mode of expressing himself. The characteristic bombast and self-praise serve to thicken the phraseology beneath which the personality of the writer lies concealed. The inscription, considerably shortened, runs as follows:

'I was born and brought up in the reign of King Teti. My first post was that of a superintendent of the royal tenants, but King Pepi made me a groom of the bedchamber. I was then promoted to the rank of King's Friend and made supervisor of the king's pyramid city. The king next elevated me to a judgeship, for he loved me with his whole heart, more than any other of his subjects. I discussed state secrets in the sole company of the vizier. I dealt in the king's name in matters relating to the harîm and the six great courts of justice, for I was dearer to the king than any other noble, dignitary or subject. I begged his sacred Majesty to bring me a sarcophagus of white limestone from Tura, whereat he ordered the chancellor to set sail with mariners and labourers to fetch it for me. It arrived with its lid, a door, a false door, lintels, foundations and an offering table. The king had never done anything of the kind before for any other subject. He did it because I pleased him. When I was a judge I was promoted Unique Friend and a chief superintendent of the royal tenants, over the heads of four other superintendents. I did exactly what the king wanted, on escort duty, in planning royal progresses, in waiting attendance. I continually took care to act in such a way that the king would praise me. When secret proceedings were taken in the harîm against the queen, the king brought me in to hear. There was nobody else there: just me. There was no vizier or nobleman: just me. When it came to recording the case in writing, I did it with one other judge. And I started life as a mere superintendent of tenants! Before the king called me in no one had previously had an opportunity to hear secrets of the royal harîm. This was because the king had a higher opinion of me than he had of all his other officials, councillors and servants.'

Weni was appointed to lead a punitive expedition against the Libyans and Bedouins. He headed an expeditionary force drawn from the nomes of both Upper and Lower Egypt. The army was officered with all manner of influential people, but it was Weni who took charge of it and led it to victory (although he began life as a miserable superintendent of tenants). He was evidently a resourceful general, despite his somewhat sheltered experience hitherto in the royal harîm. He seems to have penetrated into Southern Palestine on a daring razzia. At the end of Pepi's reign Weni occupied the enviable sinecure of Royal Sandal-bearer (see figure behind monarch on reverse of palette of Narmer (Pl. 26)). On the accession of Merenra

54

11. THE PRIEST AND ROYAL SCRIBE HESIRA
A carved wooden panel from his mastaba at Sakkara
Third Dynasty

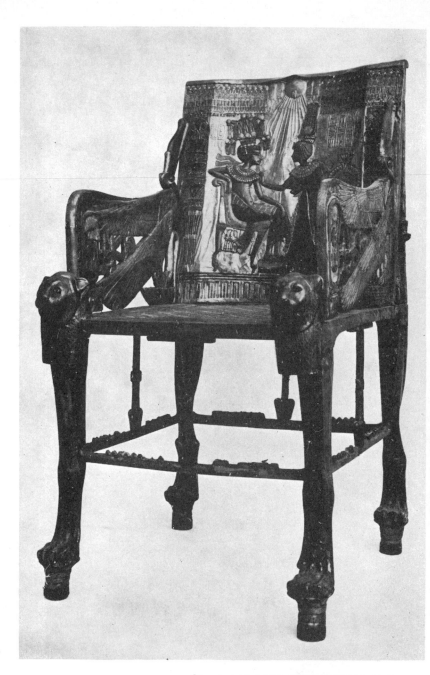

12. THE CHAIR OF THE PHARAOH TUTANKHAMON
The Pharaoh is shown with his wife Ankhesenamon

he was made governor of the nomes between Elephantine and Aphroditopolis, an appointment which had lapsed under the previous dynasty and was now specially re-created for him. His last acts in a lifetime spent in unsparing service of the monarchy were journeys to the alabaster quarries of Alabastronpolis to procure materials for Merenra's pyramid, which still stands at Sakkara. Though we may call Weni and his fellow courtiers conventional in outlook, the civilization of the Nile valley bore witness to their courage, ability and strength of character. Their concern to conform to a rigid code was based on the superstitious belief that 'the King's Friend rests in peace as an Honoured One, but there is no tomb (and consequently no after life) for the man who rebels against the king.' But there was also the realization of a more mundane truth: that the welfare of a country with the peculiar physical conformation of Egypt depended on the sense of responsibility and self-restraint of its leading citizens. Whenever the loyalty of the nobility to Pharaoh was relaxed or obscured by self-interest, whenever men could not be found to endure the discomfort of provincial governorship and foreign service, the land fell on evil days. Not long after the death of Weni the Two Lands were to have a terrible lesson of what befell when Honoured Ones and priests entertained a contempt for their sovereign and followed their own selfish ends.

Weni is an instance of the civilian turned soldier who was the common type of military leader during the Old Kingdom. A few GENERALS who made a professional career of arms existed, but they were appendages of court life. Thus we hear of captains of the guard and chiefs of the archers and the infantry. With the well-organized imperialist campaigns of the Middle and New Kingdoms the army and navy took on a new importance. The king was commander-in-chief, but the army corps and the fleet were in the hands of regular soldiers and sailors. Warfare became a lucrative trade, for not only were successful officers rewarded with bounties, splendid ceremonial weapons and gold necklaces known as the 'gold of valour,' but they also received grants of land from the royal estates. When not on active service or with their regiments they were given token posts in the service of Pharaoh or the nomarchs. As it often does in countries building or maintaining an empire, military service became hereditary in many families. During the Old and Middle Kingdoms the army was recruited at need from the nomes, each of which raised a levy of between five hundred and a thousand militiamen for specific campaigns. Nubian mercenaries were employed in great numbers. The navy came into prominence during the campaigns against the Hyksôs at the end of the Middle Kingdom. If the invader baffled the Egyptians with the newly introduced chariot, the Egyptians were able to trouble the Hyksôs with the unfamiliar tactics of the naval sortie. A naval officer called Ahmes left an account in his tomb at el-Kab of his part in the final dramatic thrust down the Nile under Ahmosis that finally dislodged the Asiatics. He was present at the destruction of the enemy base at Avaris, and for his part in the campaign he received the gold of valour,' women, slaves and a tract of land. Under the New Empire two large armies in four divisions named after Amon, Ptah, Ra and Seth were permanently stationed in Upper and Lower Egypt. The names of a number of outstanding soldiers are known from the later period. One of them, Ahmes Pennekhbet, was a member of the same warlike family at el-Kab as Ahmes the mariner. For his services against the Hyksôs and the Asiatics during the early years of the Middle Kingdom he was awarded armlets, bangles, rings, sceptres, two golden axes, two silver axes and further decorations in the shape of six flies and three lions of gold (Pl. 40). A tough old general called Amenemhab was the lieutenant of the greatest of all Egyptian warriors, Tuthmosis III. On the walls of his tomb at Thebes Amenemhab recorded a series of terse observations on ten of his campaigns with Tuthmosis that read like extracts from despatches. On one occasion in the country of Naharina on the Euphrates he saved his master's life. He relates that the king was indulging in his favourite sport of elephant hunting when he unexpectedly encountered a herd of a hundred and twenty of these beasts at a watercourse. The number is probably the exaggeration of an old soldier. It was only the pluck of Amenemhab which brought Tuthmosis out of danger.

After the reign of Tuthmosis III the Asian Empire was preserved with varying fortunes under the military Pharaohs Horemhab, Seti I, Ramses II and Ramses III. All were bold tacticians and were well supported by their staff officers. It became necessary, however, to stiffen the armies of the later New Empire with an increasing leaven of mercenaries, due to external pressure on Empire and homeland exerted by widespread folk movements in Asia and the East Mediterranean. Ramses III, who fought the Libyans and Sea Peoples in three bitter campaigns, was later obliged to enrol 'tens of thousands' of them in his sea and land forces and settle them in colonies in the Delta. This ominous expedient contributed to the ultimate seizure of power by the Twenty-second (Libyan) Dynasty two hundred years later. Kings of the Twenty-sixth (Saïte) Dynasty introduced into their armies a body of Greek mercenaries whose able generals elevated it to the same position of a state within the state that the Libyan generals had done for their own expatriates. The Greek mercenaries were the advance guard of the host of Ionian, Carian, Athenian, Samian and Milesian colonists who quickly became the richest and most effective section of the community.

The NOMARCHS who constituted the provincial aristocracy were the descendants of the chieftains who ruled the pre-dynastic tribes of the Nile valley. The nomarch was both the material and spiritual leader of his own small province, which corresponded roughly to our own county. He was at once administrator, judge and high priest of the local cult. Under the Old Kingdom the power of the nomarchs was subordinated entirely to the power of the court, but when the centralized

.state of the Pyramid Age began to disintegrate during the Sixth Dynasty the nomarchs seized the opportunity to set themselves up as independent rulers. The princely necropoles which are scattered along the length of the River Nile date originally from this period. They are particularly in evidence in Upper Egypt, wilder territory than Lower Egypt and remote from the seat of royal surveillance. Hitherto the office of nomarch had been a royal appointment. Now it became hereditary. Provincial barons manifested less and less desire to dance attendance at court and were content to live on their estates, where they became petty dynasts in their own right. Inscriptions in their elaborate tombs show an unaccustomed absence of servility in their relationship with the king. 'I claimed from King Pepi II,' states the nomarch of the Twelfth Nome at Hierakonpolis, 'the honour of obtaining a sarcophagus, funerary wrappings and oils for my father. I asked the king to make my father a prince, and the king made him a prince and awarded him the Gift-which-the-King-gives.' The nomarchs enticed leading artists and artisans away from the royal residences and set them to work on their own tombs and in their sumptuous little courts. They began to indulge in squabbles over boundaries and made territorial encroachments at the expense of weaker neighbours. Dynastic alliances were contracted which sometimes resulted in a single nomarch assuming the leadership of more than one nome. In the upshot the impotence of the court during the closing decades of the Old Kingdom, coupled with the isolation on their own domains of great barons jealously guarding their own prerogatives, resulted in a fatal weakening of authority. It is probable that the self-denying spirit of the ruling class which created the splendour of the Old Kingdom was at last bred out into sloth, conceit and a craving for luxury. The disasters which befell Egypt during the First Intermediate Period arose in the main from civil riot and foreign invasion, but it is possible that another immediate cause was the fomenting of civil war between rival nomes. The

58

Theban and Herakleopolitan nomarchs headed confederations of Upper and Lower Egyptian nomes respectively. The Theban war leaders were possessed of great military ability, and it fell to their lot to establish the Middle Kingdom. They were quick to realize that their chief supporters in the victorious struggle were also the chief threat to their own security and to stable government. By a subtle policy of alternate cajolery and severity the sagacious Pharaohs of the Twelfth Dynasty sapped the independence of the provincial nobility. Boundaries of nomes were strictly defined, hereditary succession was discouraged and families were divided against themselves by appointing the sons of nomarchs rulers of a portion of their father's territory. Under the semblance of restoring order the king absorbed the nomes into an integrated system of government. The peasants and artisans who had won themselves a measure of respect by their desperate exertions during the First Intermediate Period were granted certain fundamental rights that enabled them to be critical of the rule of their local nomarch. From the rank of feudal barons the nomarchs were reduced to the status of country squires. Sesostris III somewhat harshly quelled a tendency on the part of the nomarchs to reassert themselves during his absence on Asian service, and from his reign onwards the imposing necropoles of the provincial nobles fell into disuse. It was nevertheless a welcome recrudescence of some of the old warlike spirit of the nomarchs which liberated Egypt from the ensuing Hyksôs invasion of the Second Intermediate Period. The Middle Kingdom began and ended with the triumph of a small company of Upper Egyptian barons. Under the New Kingdom the conquering nomarchs seemed to sense the advantages of cohesion with their Theban war lords. They abandoned the concept of individual political action which they entertained during the Old Kingdom. Never again were they to enjoy the personal autonomy they once knew, but their office was retained and respected until the end of the dynastic era.

CHAPTER V

The Architect

The ancient Egyptians were by temperament a cheerful people, yet they are chiefly known to us by the gloomy preparations which they made for death. Because of their appetite for the sun-saturated life of the valley of the Nile, the dark prospect of death filled them with the deepest foreboding. It was a man's ambition to live a span of a hundred and ten years in his earthly house, but the tomb, the 'House of Everlasting,' was to be his final and permanent abode. Therefore he lavished much care upon it in his lifetime. Whereas his earthly habitation was built of brittle plaster and friable brick, his tomb was manufactured of perdurable stone or hewn in the living rock. Little trace of dwelling-houses has remained. Even Pharaoh was accustomed to build his palace of brick and his 'House of a Million Years' of stone. The design of the tomb originated, however, in the design of the house, and if we derive a disproportionate amount of evidence about ancient Egypt from the tomb we are fortunate in that all phases of terrestrial existence were painstakingly recorded there. Models, statues, frescoes, reliefs, stelae, wooden panels: all were employed to recreate in the house of the dead the atmosphere of the house of the living. The furnishing and decoration of the tombs of the wealthy provide a picture, complete to the last detail, of life in the Nile valley. It is therefore to the tomb that we shall first turn our attention.

Before dynastic times the tomb was a mere pit or hollow in the sand, square or oval in shape. Wrapped in a reed mat, animal skin or linen shroud, the body lay on its side in a flexed posture, decked with a few personal adornments. Jars of food and drink were supplied to sustain the dead man during his journey to the Next World. His weapons were buried with him, ready for service in the endless quest for food which would recommence as soon as he reached his destination. Occasionally these pit graves are lined with clay, matting, wooden boards or mud brick. No trace of the superstructure of the pre-dynastic grave has survived. Probably it consisted of nothing more elaborate than a mound of sand. If a sandstorm arose or jackals were abroad the bodies of the dead were liable to be exposed or dismembered, and the aristocracy decided early to spend a proportion of its wealth in ensuring the perfect pres-ervation of its corporeal remains. The notion that survival after death depended on the preservation of the body appears to have developed early. For the common people the custom of pit burial lasted down to Roman times.

At the beginning of the dynastic era a form of tomb known as the MASTABA began to appear. The word mastaba is a term used by the modern Arab to describe the bench commonly present outside his house, which the ancient tombs faintly resembled. One of the earliest mastabas is the tomb at Sakkara attributed to Aha, second dynastic king of Egypt. Here the predynastic pit has been expanded to a subterranean structure of five rooms, while above ground is a large brick superstructure containing no less than twenty-seven storage cells. In these cells were placed the food and weapons pre-viously placed in close proximity to the dead man. The superstructure was enclosed within two stout walls and the whole edifice coated with white lime stucco. Mastabas of this type were modelled on dwelling-houses. Already a man's tomb was regarded as a house where he actually lived after death. In mastabas of the Second and Third Dynasties even a closet was sometimes included among the storage cells, and in the offering-room which soon became a feature of this type of tomb a niche was provided through which the soul of the

61

deceased could enter and leave at will. This niche was the precursor of the false door. Below ground a large central hall now appeared, reached by a deep central shaft which was filled with rubble immediately after the burial and sealed with a heavy slab of stone. Thus the twin problems which vexed the nobleman during the entire dynastic epoch were apparent at the outset: how to build an ostentatious monument and at the same time conceal the precious corpse inside it from the depredations of time, thieves and the elements. These two mutually self-contradictory problems were never solved or reconciled. The more the body was laden with jewellery and consigned to a pompous sepulchre the more eager and ingenious the professional tomb robber became. The deeper the body was thrust into the earth, into a cliff or into a man-made stone mountain, so much the farther it was removed from the preserving warmth of the sun and the more subject it became to decay.

During the Fourth Dynasty many nobles began to construct their mastabas of stone. Stone was a material hitherto reserved for the exclusive use of the king, probably because of the technical and economic difficulties of quarrying and transport at this early date. The stone employed for fine facing work was the famous limestone from Tura in the Mokattam hills, used also on the casing of the royal tombs round which the mastabas of the courtiers were systematically grouped. A courtier continued to render service even after death and was therefore buried near his master's tomb. It was every courtier's ambition to be buried as close to Pharaoh as possible, for such proximity conferred inestimable spiritual benefits. Two thousand years after the erection of the pyramids of Giza, the Saïte noblemen of the Twenty-sixth Dynasty elected to be buried among the surrounding mastabas of Fourth Dynasty date. The royal tomb enclosed within a network of mastabas, the daily rituals observed in temples endowed by Pharaoh: an entire court complex was in this strange manner preserved from one generation to another. Preserved in theory, that is, for endow-ments were often appropriated by later monarchs and the temple liturgies became more honoured in the breach than the observance.

Fourth Dynasty mastabas usually consisted of a single under-ground room with a recess for the stone or wooden coffin. There was often a small pit which was possibly intended to hold the viscera removed during mummification. Later the viscera were contained in canopic jars. A massive portcullis blocked the entrance to this room. The superstructure of the mastaba now contained a diminutive and frequently entirely inaccessible room called the serdab, an Arabic word signifying a cellar. Inside the serdab stood the statue of the dead person looking through a narrow slit on a level with its eyes. There was no door or window in the serdab: only the slit through which the statue, abode of the soul, gazed at the worshippers in the chapel with its painted or crystal eyes. The Third Dynasty tomb of Hesira is decorated with magnificent reliefs on wooden panels fitted into the walls (Pl. 11), but under the Fourth Dynasty it became the fashion to adorn the tomb with intricate reliefs carved in stone and afterwards coloured. The practice continued under the Fifth Dynasty, and the mastabas of Ptah-hetep and Ti at Sakkara are noteworthy for their superb murals. The mastaba of Ti contains two serdabs. In these tombs and the tombs of the Sixth Dynasty, which consist of as many as thirty rooms, the great magnates of the Old Kingdom are portrayed at their daily occupations: dressing for the day, supervising the work of their estate, hunting, fishing, dis-pensing justice, worshipping the gods, relaxing with their families and their friends. These murals were not intended merely to provide posterity with testimony to the opulence and power of the nobles who commissioned them, but also for the cogent magical purpose of securing for the dead man the con-tinuance of these pleasant pursuits in the Next World. Fresh provisions were brought regularly to the mastaba and laid on the altar in the offering-room in the east side of the super-structure, the side nearest the beloved River Nile over which the dead spirit watched from the false door. The mastaba survived the calamitous fall of the Old Kingdom and remained the standard type of upper-class sepulchre during the Middle Kingdom. But from the Fourth Dynasty until the end of the Middle Kingdom a new type of tomb was adopted by the royal house: the pyramid.

The PYRAMID evolved from the mastaba during the Third Dynasty, perhaps under the influence of the sun cult of Helio-polis. We saw that Aha of the First Dynasty was buried in a replica of his earthly palace, where he would pass an earth-bound eternity. The pyramids of the Pharaohs of the Third Dynasty show that this conception was giving ground to a new idea: that the dead Pharaoh could now ascend to heaven. A spell written on the walls of one of the pyramids of the Fifth Dynasty announces: 'A staircase to heaven is laid for Pharaoh, that he may ascend to heaven thereby.' At first the pyramid was constructed like a gigantic series of steps leading upwards into the sky, but when the steps were filled in and the four faces of the pyramid presented a smooth appearance to the beholder a secondary idea which lay behind the building of these monu-ments was emphasized. The pyramid was also the symbol of Ra, a magnification of the small pyramidal stone called the *benben* which reposed in the temple of Ra-Atum at Heliopolis. The *benben* probably represented the 'hillock of eternity' whereon the creator Ra-Atum first made his appearance. Where better could Pharaoh, the Son of Ra and his reincarnation upon earth, consign his body than within the 'hillock of eternity'? The *benben* and the pyramid were also emblematic of the cone of the sun's rays as they poured down upon the earth. The *benben* was probably gilded to resemble the golden cone of sunshine, and at the top of every pyramid rested a gilded pyramidion in imitation of the sacred *benben*. From the beginning of the Fourth Dynasty to the collapse of the Old Kingdom three hundred years later every Pharaoh was buried under the symbol of Ra. The sole exception was Shepseskaf, last Pharaoh of the Fourth Dynasty. Shepseskaf, perhaps in defiance of the priests of Ra, built himself a mastaba at Sakkara. His opposition to religious despotism appears to have been as ineffectual as that of Akhenaton twelve centuries afterwards.

The word pyramid is tentatively derived from a Greek word meaning 'wheaten cake,' possibly because the Greeks and Egyptians made cakes of pyramidal shape. The first of these remarkable edifices was the STEP PYRAMID at Sakkara. It was built by the celebrated vizier Imhotep for Zoser 'the holy' of the Third Dynasty, whose reign may be dated about 2778 B.C. Zoser reigned at first from Upper Egypt, home of the conquerors who united the Two Lands, from whom he was descended. At Beit Khallaf, north of Abydos, he raised a huge brick mastaba. It was at Abydos that Pharaohs of the First and Second Dynasties were interred in simple house-like structures. Later Zoser transferred his capital to Memphis, and under the influence of the priests of Heliopolis he instructed Imhotep to build him a pyramid at Sakkara, thirty miles away. He had in any case decided to build a second mastaba in Lower Egypt in order to possess a tomb in each of the Two Lands. This mastaba or cenotaph was accordingly constructed a short distance away from a large conglomeration of First and Second Dynasty mastabas. But this second mastaba was destined to undergo a series of epoch-making transformations. First a second mastaba was built on top of it, then a third on top of the second, until a total of six was reached. All diminished in size, thereby giving rise to five steps or terraces. The entire mass was thereupon cased in fine Tura limestone. The many rooms and cells in the pyramid were sunk into the limestone beneath its base, growing in corresponding complexity with the superstructure. At the foot of a wide central shaft of the type encountered in the early mastabas was a tomb chamber of pink granite from Aswan in Upper Egypt. This chamber was blocked by a granite plug. Around the four sides of the chamber, at a distance of seventy feet, ran four long galleries intersected by a maze of subsidiary galleries, some with beautiful blue-tiled imitations of reed mats on their walls. The tomb chamber was completely rifled in antiquity: the fate of the tomb of every Pharaoh with the exception of Tutankhamon. Imhotep may have built his series of mastabas one on top of the other to try and counter the prevalent method used by tomb robbers in breaking into this kind of tomb: digging down from the top. He failed, as every subsequent architect was to fail in this grim battle of wits.

The importance of Imhotep's masterpiece from the point of view of Egyptian architecture did not lie only in the two hundred foot high pyramid itself but also in the nexus of buildings which surrounded it. The pyramid occupied an almost central position amid a complex of courts and smaller structures. There was a mastaba-like Great Tomb, square and with a curved roof. Its purpose is unknown, but it may have housed Zoser's viscera or played some part in rituals enacted in the adjacent Great Court. It possessed subterranean chambers decorated with more reed mats in blue tiles. There was also a Hall of Colonnades, an Osiris Court, a Heb-Sed Court with ten large shrines and numerous smaller ones, a serdab with an accompanying Serdab Court, a Mortuary Chapel and two courts called the Courts of the Northern and Southern Palaces. These names, which were invented during excavation, are largely hypothetical. The entire pyramid complex was enclosed within a great wall measuring a mile round its periphery. The wall was composed of alternating recesses and projections, and there were fourteen large bastions each carved with an imitation of closed double doors. In one of these bastions, situated near the Great Tomb and giving on to the Hall of the Colonnades, the single actual door existed. The wall was faced with gleaming white Tura limestone. Crenellated walls of this design are present in many of the earlier mastabas. It occurs for example in the inner wall of the mastaba of the Pharaoh Aha, which

66

13. THE STEP PYRAMID

14. THE PYRAMIDS OF GIZA

15. USHABTI FIGURE
Eighteenth Dynasty

stands at no great distance from the Step Pyramid. But the bastions and gateways of the enclosure wall of the Step Pyramid suggest that the wall was copied neither from previous tombs nor from Zoser's palace, but from the renowned 'White Wall' which was built around Memphis by the first Pharaoh, Narmer. Thus whereas Zoser's royal predecessors passed eternity in a modest house, the dead Zoser enjoyed a larger domain within a positive fortress.

The most striking single feature of the Step Pyramid and its cluster of buildings is the sophistication of their architecture. There is a suavity, a delicacy, a vitality about them which was all too rarely recaptured in later times. They possess a sensuous quality not readily associated with Egyptian architecture as a whole. The haphazard manner in which the complex of the Step Pyramid evolved is not reflected in the pyramid complexes of the succeeding dynasty, despite their characteristic changes of plan. The pyramid complexes of the Giza group are arranged with an implacable symmetry which mirrors the despotic nature of Fourth Dynasty rule, whereas the Step Pyramid appears to be the product of a less stringent political order. It is noteworthy that the masonry and structural workmanship of the Step Pyramid are not of the first order. The charm of the architecture is all on the surface. But this surface is superb, particularly in the case of the slender columns with exquisite pendant-leaf capitals that make a favourable contrast with the thick and squat columns with clumsy capitals of later epochs. Imhotep devised ribbed, fluted and papyrus columns, saddle capitals and many other architectural innovations. The Step Pyramid is the world's first great monument in stone. Why it should be so remarkably advanced in technique remains a mystery: it would have been thought that Imhotep's achievement required long experience of the handling of stone. It must be noted, however, that the buildings of the Step Pyramid are careful literal translations of wooden buildings into a more enduring medium. The Egyptian woodworker must have acquired a marvellous dexterity in the use of wood at a time when the supply of timber was still for some reason plentiful. All the traditional forms in wood or mud brick were faithfully reproduced in stone. Reed mats, reed curtains, bundled papyrus, the appearance of construction in timber: every aspect of the royal palace was fixed for ever in the new and imperishable material. There is even a faithful representation in stone of a half-open door. The Pharaoh's tomb was to be a permanent copy of the surroundings in which he had passed his life. The Step Pyramid is one of the glories of ancient Egyptian architecture. In its selfconscious artistry, its plain surfaces, its columns unscored by a mass of hieroglyphs, it rivals and resembles the simplicity of Athenian architecture.

All the pyramids of the Old Kingdom were situated close to Memphis, from Abu Roash to Meidum. They lay on the west bank of the river, the bank nearest the setting sun. High ground with a sound rock foundation was preferred, but the site was always chosen as close as possible to the river, down which the blocks of quarried stone would be floated. The bedrock was levelled, a rough mound being left in the middle to form part of the core of the pyramid. A survey was next undertaken by means of cords or wooden rods and the corners of the pyramid orientated by astronomical observation on the four cardinal points. Gangs of labourers were formed under individual foremen, while away in the Mokattam hills and distant Aswan the long copper chisels of the quarrymen were already hewing out the first raw blocks.

After the construction of the Step Pyramid the business of exploring the possibilities of the new form was begun in real earnest. The Layer Pyramid and the Unfinished Pyramid, both near Giza, have survived only in a fragmentary state, but they have been tentatively ascribed to Zoser's obscure Third Dynasty successors, Kha-Bau and Nebka. The BENT PYRAMID at Dahshur, which may be the next pyramid in the sequence, is on the contrary in an excellent state of preservation. Much of its original casing of Tura limestone is still intact, whereas in all other cases the glittering facing that added immeasurably to their impressiveness has been stripped away by the house and mosque builders of our own era. The Bent Pyramid is so called because its architect, after he reached the half way mark, suddenly seems to have changed his mind and decided to finish off his work as quickly as possible. The top half of the pyramid is constructed at a much flatter angle than the bottom half. The pyramid has two separate entrances, a unique feature, while a technical innovation is the corbelling of the vaults of the two chambers to which these entrances lead. The lower chamber is below ground level, the upper chamber is inside the lower courses of the pyramid. Of the buildings which once surrounded the pyramid few traces remain.

The PYRAMID OF MEIDUM, which now exists in a sadly truncated condition, seems to have been initially a step pyramid which in successive transformations became eight steps high. A decision was then taken to encase the whole edifice in Tura limestone and turn it into a true geometrical pyramid, but the decision was never fully executed. Traces of a mortuary chapel, a causeway and a valley temple, which were also faintly detected in the Bent Pyramid complex, surrounded the Meidum Pyramid. This standard pyramid complex will shortly be described in relation to the Giza group. With the Meidum Pyramid is usually associated a large pyramid at Dahshur which was three hundred and twenty-five feet high. The Dahshur Pyramid was originally known to archaeologists as the Northern Pyramid and the Meidum Pyramid as the Southern Pyramid of the great Snofru, first Pharaoh of the Fourth Dynasty. There would be nothing unusual in the fact that Snofru chose to erect an imposing cenotaph for himself in addition to his proper tomb, in the manner of Zoser's cenotaph at Beit Khallaf. Recent discoveries in the Bent Pyramid suggest, however, that the Bent Pyramid belongs to Snofru and not to Huni, the last Pharaoh of the Third Dynasty, to whom it was formerly ascribed. The Meidum Pyramid is ascribed with fair certainty to Snofru, whom inscriptions record as the possessor of two pyramids. At the present moment, therefore, the builder of the Northern Pyramid is unknown.

At Giza, on a rocky plateau, stand the three pyramids which ranked among the wonders of the ancient world. They were built by Cheops (Khufu), Chephren (Khafra) and Mycerinus (Menkaura). The PYRAMID OF CHEOPS was originally no less than four hundred and ninety feet high. Its base covers an area of thirty-one acres: an area in which Westminster, St. Paul's and the cathedrals of Florence, Milan and St. Peter's could comfortably be grouped. Napoleon once sat down beneath its shadow and calculated—wistfully perhaps—that the mass of stone contained in it would build a wall round France ten feet high and one foot thick. It is estimated that the pyramid in fact contains two million three hundred thousand blocks of stone, each averaging two and a half tons in weight. Some of the blocks weigh as much as thirty tons. The interior of this stone mountain is threaded with corridors, the main Ascending Corridor giving access to the earliest, abandoned tomb chamber popularly called the Queen's Chamber. The Ascending Corridor then rises through the corbelled Grand Gallery, a hundred and fifty-three feet long, to the King's Chamber. The King's Chamber is a large granite room in which the sarcophagus that once contained Cheops' body still rests. The roof of the chamber is composed of seven huge granite slabs, spaced one above the other. From the chamber two narrow vents pierce through the core of the pyramid to the outer air, to permit Cheops' soul to obtain access to his body. The exterior casing of the pyramid was a miracle of stone-cutting: the lower courses, which are all that remain, are set with joints measuring one ten-thousandth of an inch wide. How was such a tremendous edifice constructed? It was erected with no more complicated apparatus than palm-fibre ropes, wooden sledges and levers, earthen ramps and copper chisels. Herodotus, who visited Egypt in the fifth century B.C., was told that the causeway was built first and occupied ten years. Cheops' labour force of a hundred thousand men then devoted twenty years to the pyramid itself. Some authorities incline to regard the Great Pyramid as a memorial to a megalomaniac. But Cheops was no ordinary man: he was the greatest Pharaoh of a great dynasty, and he was also a god. We should not expect the tomb of a god to be like the tomb of a mortal. It is equally possible that Cheops was an astute administrator who made the construction of his tomb a method of averting unemployment during the slack season which always occurred at the peak of the Inundation, when the whole of Egypt was under water. For the major part of the year the king would utilize a small corps of specialist labourers, but at the time of full flood he would call on the services of a large portion of the population which would otherwise be unable to earn wages and secure food. During the Inundation the rafts bearing the stone for the pyramid would be able to float farther up the causeway, closer to the scene of operations, and additional hands would be needed to land large quantities of quarried material. We saw in Chapter II that it was necessary to give the king of Egypt a 'good burial.' The funerary cult of the builders of the Giza pyramids was continued down to the time of the Macedonian conquest, which hardly suggests that in the memory of the people they were abhorred as tyrants.

Near the causeway of Cheops' pyramid there came to light in 1925 the only intact tomb chamber of the Old Kingdom so far discovered. A wonderful collection of objects was unearthed. There was a canopy, a bed, two chairs and a carrying chair, all sheeted in gold. There were alabaster vessels, a copper basin, copper tools, gold knives and razors, three gold vessels and a gold manicure instrument. There was a toilet box with cosmetics contained in eight little alabaster pots, and a jewel case with twenty silver anklets inlaid with lapis lazuli, carnelian and malachite. Inlaid gold hieroglyphs on the ebony panels of the carrying chair carried the fourfold inscription: 'Mother of the King of Upper and Lower Egypt, follower of Horus, guide of the Ruler, favourite whose every command is carried. out for her, daughter of the god (born) of his body, Hetephras.' The excavators had found the tomb of Snofru's wife and Cheops' mother. But although they found the alabaster sarcophagus, they did not find the queen's body. Her viscera were in the canopic chest, but the sarcophagus was empty. Yet the tomb was manifestly undisturbed by robbers. What is the solution of the problem? It may be that the queen was buried near her husband at Dahshur, where not long afterwards the tomb was broken open and her body stolen. Her son thereupon caused her funerary equipment and the melancholy remainder of her relics to be conveyed to Giza, where they were reinterred near his own tomb at the foot of a simple shaft unmarked by any visible monument. There they lay undetected for forty-five centuries beneath the level sand.

The bodies of Cheops' queens may have rested nearby in the three miniature pyramids which adjoin the eastern side of the Great Pyramid. A short distance away stands the pyramid of his son Chephren. The PYRAMID OF CHEPHREN stands on higher ground than the Great Pyramid and the angle of its four faces is steeper, so that despite its smaller dimensions at the base it appears to be taller than its companion. Since the lower courses of Chephren's pyramid consist of red granite, it may have been his intention to rival his father's monument in harder material where he could hardly hope to match it in bulk. A fine polished marble sarcophagus was discovered in its tomb chamber.

Near Chephren's valley building is the GREAT SPHINX, a knoll of rock transformed by Chephren's workmen into a lion with a human head. The head, which served as a practice target for Arab riflemen in the nineteenth century, is now sadly battered. It still wears the remains of a royal headdress and a false beard. The entire figure was probably at one time coated with plaster and realistically painted. The colossus is

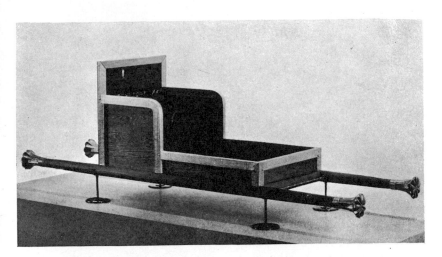

16. THE CARRYING-CHAIR OF QUEEN HETEPHRAS
Reconstructed from original material

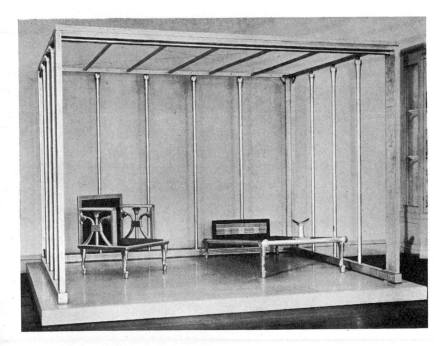

17. THE CANOPY, THE CHAIR AND THE BED WITH HEAD-REST
OF QUEEN HETEPHRAS
Fourth Dynasty

18. THE PHARAOH MYCERINUS
standing between the goddess Hathor and the goddess of the Jackal
Nome

two hundred and forty feet long and sixty-six feet high. Between its paws originally stood a statue of Chephren, now completely mutilated, and Tuthmosis IV placed there an inscription recording the fact that he had freed the Sphinx from sand in accordance with instructions given to him in a dream. The lion was considered by the sun priests of Heliopolis to be a keeper of the gates of the Underworld.

The third of the Giza pyramids belongs to Mycerinus, who succeeded Chephren and was probably his brother. The PYRAMID OF MYCERINUS is considerably smaller than its fellows, being originally only two hundred and eighteen feet high. It was left uncompleted. Mycerinus too desired to case his pyramid in red granite, and again only the lower courses were finished. The roughness of much of the casing and the discovery of fifteen unfinished statues of the Pharaoh in the pyramid precinct testifies to the hurried completion of his memorial. In the valley building, however, many fine pieces of sculpture were found (Pl. 18).

The valley buildings were small temples which stood either on or near the river bank at the end of the causeway. They were part of the pattern of the Fourth Dynasty pyramid complex. The body of the dead Pharaoh was brought in the royal barge from his palace to the valley building, which served as a ceremonial landing place. The journey by river symbolized the Osirian journey and the journey of the soul to the Underworld. The idea of a journey by water to the Next World played an important part in the mythologies of many peoples in the ancient world, among whom may be numbered the Greeks, Celts and Vikings. After long preliminary rituals were completed in the valley building, the body was carried along the causeway to the mortuary chapel, abutting on the pyramid itself. The ceremonies in the valley building, which included embalming, purification and the rite of Opening the Mouth, may have taken a year or more to carry out, and further ceremonials were enacted in the mortuary chapel.

The pyramids of the next three dynasties were built at Abu Sir and Sakkara. They were smaller than their grandiose forerunners, although in the main they followed the established Fourth Dynasty plan (see Pl. 21). In addition to pyramid complexes the Pharaohs of the Fifth Dynasty built small causewayed SUN TEMPLES of aberrant design. In the Pyramid of Unas, last Pharaoh of the Dynasty, and in all four pyramids of the Sixth Dynasty, the walls of the burial chambers were inscribed with spells which modern scholars have assembled into a collection known as the Pyramid Texts. Pepi II of the Sixth Dynasty, who reigned according to ancient records for ninety-four years, executed a pyramid complex on a large scale, but the ill-fated rulers of the Seventh Dynasty left only one unfinished pyramid. The pyramids of the opulent Fifth and Sixth Dynasties are remarkable for their profuse reliefs, reliefs of a less severe nature, if of rather lower artistic excellence, than those of the Fourth Dynasty.

When the dynasts of Upper Egypt succeeded once again in fusing the Two Lands into one, after the disastrous First Intermediate Period, the prosperous Mentuhetep II of the warrior Eleventh Dynasty constructed a remarkable funerary temple of fresh and unconservative conception at Deir el-Bahri near Thebes. The rulers of the Twelfth Dynasty returned to the old capital at Memphis and resumed the tradition of pyramid building. Their pyramids are of intricate design but inferior workmanship. There is evidence in these Middle Kingdom Pyramids that the Pharaohs who built them felt a deepening desire to protect their mortal remains from desecration. The powerful Amenemhat III devised an extraordinary maze of passages leading to dummy chambers with trick doors in the ceiling. His twenty-two foot long burial chamber was cut and polished from a single gigantic block of yellow quartzite. This block weighed a hundred and ten tons, and on top of it was placed a forty-five ton slab of rock. All to no avail.

After the Middle Kingdom the country once more relapsed

for a time into an unhappy condition of anarchy and invasion. Although pyramids appear to have been built sporadically until the middle of the Eighteenth Dynasty, they went out of fashion for royal burials. The pyramidal form, hallowed by association with Pharaoh, was thereupon seized upon by the aristocracy. At Deir el-Medina in western Thebes pyramid tombs were built on a domestic scale throughout the New Kingdom. They combine the shaft of the mastaba with a diminutive cone. About 720 B.C. the rulers of Nubia conquered Egypt and forthwith began to absorb Egyptian culture at first hand. The renowned Ethiopian Pharaoh Piankhi built himself a pyramid at Napata, deep inside Nubian territory, where the Kings of Nubia were buried. Nearly a hundred stone pyramids of quaintly provincial proportions were afterwards erected there. The practice continued when the Nubian capital later moved to Meroë. The Nubians indulged in the custom, foreign to the nature of the Egyptians, of immuring alive horses and retainers in their burials. The Egyptian master was accustomed to command the labour of his serfs in the Next World, but he was content to use paintings, models and *ushabti* figures for the purpose.

In the Eighteenth Dynasty, when pyramid burial was abandoned, royalty made a determined effort to foil the tomb robbers by retiring to the VALLEY OF THE KINGS and cutting their tombs in the cliffs. The valley lies behind the mountain barrier on the west bank of the Nile, opposite Thebes. It runs behind Deir el-Bahri into the lonely Libyan desert. The idea of the rock tomb was not in actual fact a new one. There are examples as early as the Fifth Dynasty, the tombs of the nomarchs of Elephantine at Aswan being of elaborate plan. The most famous rock-cut sepulchres before the Eighteenth Dynasty are the tombs of the rulers of the Oryx Nome at Beni Hasan, which may be considered the finest of all Middle Kingdom tombs. Some date from the unsettled period of the Eighth Dynasty, when this talented family first began to assert itself, but the majority date from the Twelfth Dynasty. The tombs in the Valley of the Kings, where the Pharaohs were buried for four hundred years, were of much more ambitious conception. Starting with a three-roomed sepulchre built by the architect Ineni for Tuthmosis I, they steadily increased in size until Ramesside times. In the Eighteenth Dynasty a standard design was established, consisting of an entrance with a steep descending stairway, a small antechamber and a large pillared hall with storerooms opening off it. At first the main preoccupation was to secure secrecy. The tombs of Tuthmosis I, Tuthmosis II, Amenophis II and Queen Hatshepsut are located in sombre and inaccessible folds in the hills. The entrances are hidden under the sand. Nevertheless the robbers were once again equal to the occasion, and in the Eighteenth and Nineteenth Dynasties all pretence of concealment was abandoned and reliance placed once more on secret passages and formidable sarcophagi, as in the Middle Kingdom pyramids. The Ramesside Pharaohs lengthened and broadened the rock-cut tomb, reaching an apogee in the tremendous hypogeum of Seti I, which is nearly five hundred feet long. The decision of Tuthmosis I to construct a tomb without a visible superstructure had a far-reaching consequence: it instigated the independent evolution of the temple. It had previously been obligatory to build the mortuary chapel as close to the pyramid as possible, and in the Old and Middle Kingdoms the mortuary chapel was a mere extension of the pyramid. To break with so venerable a tradition must have occasioned much heart-searching, but eventually the step was taken: the mortuary chapels of the Pharaohs who lay in the Valley of the Kings were built on the bank of the River Nile at a distance from their tombs. The soul of the dead king had now to travel a long way and to surmount a mountain barrier before it could receive the funerary offerings made to it in the mortuary chapel. The mortuary chapel rapidly grew into the size of a temple and finally lost its funerary function altogether.

At Deir el-Bahri, beside the pyramid of Mentuhetep II, stood the great Eighteenth Dynasty TEMPLE OF HATSHEPSUT (Pl. 22). The temple was the work of the queen's vizier Senmut, a man whose architectural gifts resembled and were not inferior to those of Imhotep. Hatshepsut required him to build an imposing monument which would enhance her disputed claim to the throne, and Senmut hit upon a design which lent grace and distinction to the grandiose intention of the building. He sent an expedition to the land of Punt on the Red Sea to procure myrrh trees, while on his airy terraces he disposed palm trees, sacred persea trees and papyrus beds. One of his colonnades was devoted to carved pictures of the expedition to Punt, another to representations of the allegedly divine birth of the queen. Other prominent features of his lovely building were a Hall of Amon, a mortuary chapel and chapels to Hathor and Anubis. An avenue of sphinxes led the devotee to a long ramp up which he walked to the first wide terrace. A second ramp led to the upper terrace, originally ornamented with a long row of columns each fashioned into a huge statue of the queen. Her vengeful nephew Tuthmosis III shortly afterwards cut them down to the shape of ordinary columns.

Tuthmosis III's own mortuary temple at Thebes, like those of other monarchs of his dynasty, was dismantled by rulers of the Nineteenth and Twentieth Dynasties who pillaged the materials for temples of their own. Such acts of vandalism were by no means rare on the part of Egyptian kings. A minor method of appropriating the memorials of their ancestors was the substitution of their own cartouches for those of the original owner of any temple, tomb, obelisk, sarcophagus or statue which they coveted. Among the major mortuary chapels of the Nineteenth and Twentieth Dynasties were the TEMPLE OF SETI I at Abydos, begun by his father and finished by his son Ramses II, and Ramses II's own RAMASSEUM. The Temple of Seti is full of the most delicate limestone reliefs, while the Ramasseum is a glowering monstrosity in the worst possible

architectural taste. At Medinet Habu stood the great PALACE-
TEMPLE OF RAMSES III.

These temples demonstrate features common to all New
Kingdom temples. They were all 'august places of eternity'
based on the palaces of Pharaoh himself. Pharaoh, whose daily
life followed a divine routine, inhabited both palace and
temple in his dual capacity as god and representative of the
gods. Or like Ramses III he combined palace and temple into a
single structure. Sometimes the original ground plan of the
New Kingdom temple was smothered by a multitude of subsidiary buildings, since temples grew by accretion from one
dynasty to the next. Additions and renovations were always
undertaken on a lavish scale, often out of all proportion to the
requirements of architectural harmony. At Karnak, for example,
successive Pharaohs of many dynasties vied with each other in
the erection of massive pylons. There were nevertheless four
essential elements of the temple of New Kingdom inspiration.
The first was the pylon or gateway, usually approached from
the Nile by means of an avenue of guardian spirits in the shape
of lions or sphinxes. The pylon consisted of two great towers
with a double gate between them. The temple was aligned on
an east–west axis, and the eastern tower of the pylon symbolized
the eastern horizon and the western tower the western horizon.
The east–west division was emphasized throughout the entire
temple and was even reflected in the daily ritual, when the
barque of the sun god was carried from the eastern to the
western side of the forecourt as the sun passed the zenith. At
daybreak young Horus Harakhte rose directly above the central
axis of the temple, over the gateway whose twin towers were
dedicated to Isis and Nephthys. At midday Horus stood
directly overhead, his beams pouring down upon the sanctuary.
The pylon contained sockets for masts of cypress or cedar
sheathed with precious metals, from which floated banners.
In front of the pylon stood a pair of granite obelisks. Obelisks,
which were small gilded pyramidions raised heavenwards on

immensely elongated pedestals, were also emblematic of the sun god. Behind the pylon lay the second element of the temple, the spacious forecourt, enclosed in a boundary wall or *temenos* and with a colonnade running round one or more of its sides. Here were celebrated the public sections of the temple liturgy. Behind the forecourt came the third element, the hypostyle hall. This hall contained two or more aisles of columns of large circumference, clustered close together. Light filtered in from a clerestory high up in the roof. The fourth element of the plan, the dark sanctuary of the god, was situated beyond the hypostyle hall, sometimes with a smaller and even murkier hypostyle hall between them. In cases where a temple was dedicated to a pair or triad of gods there were smaller sanctuaries adjoining the main one. The general effect of walking along the central axis of an ancient Egyptian temple, proceeding from gateway to sanctuary, was to traverse the hot, bright forecourt filled with the clamour of the outer world to plunge through thickening gloom into the chill, the shadow and the hushed mystery of the dwelling-place of the god.

At Thebes stood the two greatest New Kingdom temples, both dedicated to Amon-Ra. The TEMPLE OF LUXOR (Pl. 3, 4) may have been built by Amenophis III as a judicious piece of religious bribery. Since his mother was an Asiatic princess, the priesthood had it in its power to prove troublesome with regard to the impure strain in the royal blood. Luxor was possibly part of the price the king paid for sacerdotal appeasement. The temple is still well preserved, a noteworthy feature being the double row of fifty-foot papyrus columns leading to Amenophis III's pylon. At the end of this singular avenue Ramses II added a second forecourt and another pylon, before which were placed two obelisks and six colossal statues of the Pharaoh. The chief abode of Amon-Ra was not, however, the Temple of Luxor but the TEMPLE OF KARNAK, the largest religious building in the world, although Egypt once boasted an edifice called the Labyrinth which was even larger than Karnak.

The architectural history of this famous temple extended from its modest foundation in the early years of the Middle Kingdom to the end of the Ptolemaic era two thousand years later. Preliminary work was accomplished by Amenophis I, Tuthmosis I and Hatshepsut, who sent Senmut to Aswan for a pair of obelisks. Like the portrait columns at Deir el-Bahri, these obelisks were later dealt with by Tuthmosis III, who walled round the bases of these monuments of his detested aunt when he made his own additions to the temple. Amenophis III carried on the construction, and it was Ramses I who began the gigantic hypostyle hall which was completed by Seti I (Pl. 20). This hall is of staggering proportions. Between its fourteen rows of papyrus-bud columns are two central rows of twelve columns with open papyrus capitals. These gargantuan drum columns are sixty-nine feet high and nearly twelve feet in diameter. The temple possesses nine pylons in all, handiwork of successive Pharaohs. The largest of them was built by the celebrated Nubian warrior Taharka. At the height of their prosperity, under Ramses III, the temples of Amon-Ra at Thebes possessed ninety thousand slaves, half a million head of cattle, four hundred orchards, eighty ships and fifty workshops. They commanded the revenues of sixty-five selected townships in Egypt and the Asian Empire.

When Amenophis IV, the so-called 'Heretic King' Akhenaton, rebelled against the subservience of his father Amenophis III to Amon-Ra, he abandoned Thebes to found an entirely new capital at Tel el-Amarna in Middle Egypt. Here he reared the GREAT TEMPLE OF ATON, dedicated to the sun disc whose worship he set in rivalry against the cult of Amon-Ra. The plan of the Great Temple was not as revolutionary as might have been expected. The normal pattern of courts and pylons was followed, the only unorthodox feature being the open sanctuary, ablaze with sunlight. The oppressive gloom of the sanctuaries of Amon-Ra was abjured. The beams of the Aton penetrated into every corner of the spacious temple, banishing

80

19. THE TEMPLE OF KARNAK
The avenue of sphinxes

20. THE TEMPLE OF KARNAK
The hypostyle hall. A model

21. THE PYRAMID AND PYRAMID PRECINCT OF THE
PHARAOH SAHURA AT ABU SIR
A model
Fifth Dynasty

22. THE TEMPLE OF QUEEN HATSHEPSUT
AT DEIR EL-BAHRI
A model
Eighteenth Dynasty

the claustrophobic terror of the Theban fanes. Ultimately the priests of Amon-Ra prevailed, and after the death of the exhausted heretic his capital was abandoned to the surrounding desert. The great brick temple with its whitewashed walls decayed. The stone cathedrals of Amon-Ra survive to the present day, but the ground plan of the Great Temple of Aton has been recovered only from paintings in el-Amarna rock tombs.

Ramses II, the imperial Pharaoh who reigned a little over a century after Akhenaton, was a man of very different stamp. If brick and rubble be characteristic of Akhenaton, the rock-cut TEMPLES OF ABU SIMBEL are characteristic of Ramses. We have mentioned his Ramasseum, but it is the rock temples which are the outstanding achievement of this indefatigable artificer. Ostensibly dedicated to Hathor and Horus Harakhte, they are Ramses' tribute to his own greatness. The temples are situated on the west bank of the Nile far beyond the Nubian border, seven hundred and sixty miles from Memphis. Outside the larger of the temples are four colossal statues of the seated Pharaoh each sixty-five feet high. The temple itself extends a hundred and eighty feet into the rock behind a hundred foot high pylon hewn out of the cliff face. As if this extra-territorial effort were not enough, farther downstream at Sebna and Garf Husein the same king caused to be carved from the rocks two more temples in honour of Ptah and Amon-Ra.

During the Ptolemaic and Roman periods a great number of temples were built. The homage paid to the ancient gods suffered no diminution. The temples of the final phases were conceived on a smaller scale than those of the New Kingdom, but with enhanced decorative effects. The Ptolemaic temples are self-consciously classical in appearance, and in comparison with their forerunners they give an impression of an effete imagination. The reliefs which cover them from pylon to sanctuary are vapid, too ornate and over-naturalistic. The temples have the advantage of being in many cases magnificently preserved. Among them may be singled out the TEMPLE OF KOM OMBO, the TEMPLE OF DENDERA, and the TEMPLE OF EDFU.

We have little direct information about the earlier PALACES of ancient Egypt. It is possible to infer a certain amount of information from the tombs which were copied from them. The early palaces were walled round in the universal manner of the chieftain's stronghold, and key cities were also protected with fortifications, bastions and towered gateways. In the Eighteenth Dynasty both Akhenaton and his father Amenophis III built palaces which have been thoroughly investigated by modern archaeologists. The palace of Amenophis III at Thebes, designed for him by his friend Amenhetep, was a veritable township, with private workshops and an exceedingly commodious harîm. The palace-temple of Ramses III at Medinet Habu was fronted by a tower gateway of unique appearance, perhaps a reminiscence of his Syrian campaigns.

Predynastic HOUSES were mere windbreaks, tents or wattle and daub huts. Valuable evidence of these and other early dwellings can be gleaned from an examination of hieroglyphs, since the little picture-signs were evolved at an early period of the history of the Nile valley. The predynastic house was surrounded by a fenced-in compound, and a substantial palisade of sharpened stakes would transform the house of the king or a rich noble into an imposing fortress. Early in the Old Kingdom handsome houses of wooden frames with a mud-plaster exterior were being built. They possessed a forecourt, portico, pillared hall and private quarters. By the Middle Kingdom an outside staircase leading to a simple loggia on the roof was devised, and the two-storey mud-brick house began to come into vogue. Wealthier citizens sometimes boasted three-storey houses, but the three-storey house was rare. At all periods the normal house consisted of a single storey. During the New Kingdom the house of a nobleman or rich merchant often contained as many as thirty rooms. The visitor mounted a short flight of ornamental steps to a portico, passed through a vestibule into a small pillared hall and thence into the large pillared hall which was used for communal purposes. The master of the house occupied his own suite of rooms in a private part of the house, and there was separate accommodation for his guests, his family and his women. Bathrooms, anointing-rooms and closets were of advanced technique. Within the enclosure wall of the villa were carried on the activities of the estate, and also within the wall were to be found the dwellings of the nobleman's personal servants. The exterior of the house was whitewashed or left plain, while the walls and pillars of the interior were gaily painted with floral motifs. The Egyptian passion for flowers was also shown in the carefully tended groves and flower-beds in which the villa was set. The horticultural enthusiasm of the Egyptians was very marked, and the austere outlines of many of their monuments as they appear or are reconstructed today were originally humanized by many rows of trees and ranks of glowing blossom (Pl. 44).

In conclusion a few comments on ancient Egyptian archi-tecture as a whole are called for. The heading of this chapter is 'The Architect,' but it will have become apparent that the Egyptian architect was not the freely creative individual that is our own conception of an architect. The profession of architect in ancient Egypt was not even a distinct vocation. The Egyptian architect was first and foremost a court func-tionary, and he was frequently engaged in other occupations than architecture. In designing a building he possessed no creative will of his own but interpreted the will of the king, who in turn was the interpreter of tradition. Tradition was the rock on which the state was founded: to depart from it was to court calamity. The architect, like Pharaoh, was therefore not only the slave of tradition, but its willing slave. On occasion we catch a glimpse of unfettered imagination, as in the Step

Pyramid or the 'proto-Doric' Temple of Hatshepsut, but a return is always rapidly made to socially sanctioned forms. The fragility of these individual masterpieces was alien not only to tradition but to the canon of architectural art which the Egyptians admired. What the Egyptians as a race strove for in their public works was massiveness, height, bulk: sheer vulgar bigness, if you like. Their stone buildings were explicitly designed for impressiveness and durability. A palace, a temple or a tomb was 'an eternal work,' 'a castle of eternity,' 'a palace of eternity,' a 'house of everlasting.'

The architects of ancient Egypt were innovators. Like most innovators, many of the things which they executed for the first time were as good as later imitations of them. Their most inventive period, however, was the intensely formative epoch which preceded the Pyramid Age. Thereafter the patterns of behaviour of Nilotic life became too firmly established to permit any marked amount of intellectual latitude, and the earlier lines of enquiry were ignored or unexploited. There was always some good reason, nevertheless, for the abandonment of a promising idea. The delicate saddle capitals of the Step Pyramid, for example, were not adopted in later buildings because they were purely decorative: they made no contribution to the religious symbolism of the edifice. The papyrus column, on the other hand, contained an overt religious reference. The outer columns of the hypostyle hall were topped with columns representing the closed papyrus bud, to show how nature slept before the rising and after the setting of the sun. The middle columns of the hypostyle hall were topped with fully open papyrus buds, for when the sun god was overhead his beams were productive of life and energy. Similarly the smooth columns of the Step Pyramid and the Temple of Hatshepsut were not incorporated in architectural practice. They flouted the principle that a column was not primarily intended to be a decorative object but a surface on which to engrave the praises of the king and the gods. Once the great rectilinear traditions of architecture were perfected, early in the dynastic era, little further impulse towards experiment was felt. It is undeniable that aesthetic opportunities were thereby neglected and that badly needed improvements in technique were not put in hand. Bad foundations and faulty construction were common. The Egyptian architect and engineer focused his attention too closely on the end in view and too dimly on the means whereby he could achieve it. It may be a remarkable feat to raise a huge monument with the most primitive tools, but there are grounds for thinking that the Egyptian architect could have secured the same effects in a more economical fashion if his attitude as a craftsman had been more objective.

In the final count the fascination of Egyptian architecture—and its justification—is that it accomplished what it set out to do. Egyptian architects wanted to erect the tallest, broadest, most solid structures the world would ever see: and they succeeded. The monuments of the Nile valley were projected as symbols of triumphant power. No considerations of prettiness were permitted to obscure that object. The spectator is compelled to accept their handiwork for what it is. Their monuments stand foursquare. They literally dwarf criticism. They are the marks inflicted on nature by a race of giants, on the scale of stupendous entities brought into existence by nature herself.

CHAPTER VI

The Craftsman

THE SCRIBE

The scribe would be outraged to find himself included among the humble company of craftsmen. He followed a superior calling, he occupied a position of responsibility. The office of Royal Scribe was among the highest to which a courtier could aspire. The great Amenhetep, son of Hapu, was proud to describe himself as 'King's Scribe,' the word scribe being synonymous for counsellor and friend. Many a boy of lowly origin climbed to a position of authority by the exercise of the scribal office. His peasant father, ambitious for a gifted son's advancement, would bring the lad to the attention of his local nomarch or even the vizier himself. A strenuous course of study at one of the priestly colleges would follow. Here discipline was strict and beatings frequent, for it was recognized that 'a boy's ears are on his backside.' When his education was completed the fledgling scribe was appointed to the staff of some civil or religious functionary, where his starting position would be somewhere in the region of Tenth Secretary. If he were assiduous and endowed in equal proportions with ability, charm and cunning, he would rapidly become the recipient of his master's confidences, his fears, feuds and jealousies. It would then be only a short time before he began to grope his way through the anterooms of the royal residence.

On Plate 24 a scribe is shown seated in a respectful and attentive attitude. On his knees is a roll of papyrus on which he will write with his rush pen. Papyrus paper was manufactured

86

23. THE PHARAOH TUTANKHAMON
Ushabti figure

24. THE SCRIBE KHNUMBAF

25. THE VIZIER AND
ARCHITECT IMHOTEP

26, 27. THE SLATE PALETTE
OF THE PHARAOH NARMER

Reverse   Obverse

from the sedge-like papyrus plant. Fresh green stems were taken and cut into suitable lengths. The rind was stripped off and the slivers of pith laid crosswise upon one another. The pith was then pounded into a flat sheet and finally pressed and dried. Other materials were occasionally employed for documents, for example parchment, vellum, leather rolls and wooden boards. The scribe's inks can be seen in our statue on the wooden palette that he holds in his left hand. They are in the form of small, round, dry cakes. The cakes were like modern water colours, the pen being moistened at intervals with a light gum. Black and red are the most usual colours found on palettes, though blue, yellow, green and white were all occasionally employed. Since this particular scribe lived under the Old Kingdom, he would write characters closely resembling in appearance the characters engraved on monuments. He would most commonly write from right to left. Hieroglyphs often occur on monuments written vertically and from left to right, but as a rule this is for special reasons of symmetry: the hieroglyphs and human figures on each side of a door tend to face inwards, thus achieving a visual balance (Pl.46).

The Greeks, accustomed to the sight of interminable inscriptions on the walls of temples, called the writing in which they were couched *hieros* and *glūpho*: sacred and sculptured. The full formal HIEROGLYPHIC WRITING was used throughout the whole of ancient Egyptian history for monumental purposes. It is found as early as the First Dynasty and as late as the third century A.D., a span of over thirty-five centuries. As in Mesopotamia and the Indus Valley during the fourth millennium B.C., writing seems to have come into existence largely for the pragmatic purpose of keeping commercial records or establishing ownership over an object by means of a seal imprint. The earliest hieroglyphs occur on seal impressions, stone vases or clay and wooden boards. For everyday purposes a contracted form of hieroglyphic which could be written at speed soon became a necessity. A more flowing method of writing the hieroglyphs known as HIERATIC was therefore devised for secular documents. In the Middle Kingdom religious texts on papyrus continued to be written in full hieroglyphic, but at the beginning of the Late Period they began to be written in hieratic, and henceforward the hieroglyphs were reserved for tomb paintings and monuments alone. The word 'hieratic' is the Greek word *hieratikos*: priestly. Two hundred years after hieratic, the shorthand version of hieroglyphic, came into general use, a shorthand reduction of hieratic itself was introduced. This was the very rapid DEMOTIC (Greek *dēmōtikos*: popular). The connection of the parent hieroglyphic with hieratic and demotic became extremely tenuous, and the scribe who penned the cursive characters was no longer consciously aware of their pictorial basis.

In the beginning the underlying concept of hieroglyphic writing was to show the object referred to by means of a little picture of it. Between the First and Third Dynasties this primitive method was elaborated by putting in front of the little picture a number of alphabetic signs to convey its actual sound. These alphabetic signs were themselves originally pictorial signs: the letter *k*, for example, was adopted from an object which was pronounced as *k*. In technical language, what happened was that an ideogram was preceded by a number of phonograms, a simple sense-sign or sight-sign by an appropriate number of sound-signs. First the object was spelled out, then it was drawn at the end. To give an example of the process as it would occur in English, let us select the word 'bat.' In the early stage of writing, the object, a cricket bat, would simply be drawn. A little later the three phonetic characters *b-a-t* would be written and the cricket bat added at the end. But there is a difficulty: the word 'bat' also signifies the flying animal. In writing this word, with the same sound but a totally different meaning, the signs representing *b-a-t* would still be employed and the new meaning made clear by drawing the animal as the ideogram. If the word 'bat' were used as a

88

verb, in the sense of batting in a cricket match, a small human figure with a cricket bat in its hands would constitute the ideogram that followed the phonetic *b-a-t*. In the slang sense of 'to bat someone on the head,'' the human figure would be wielding a club above its head with an unmistakable intention.

To the ancient Egyptians the ideogram was the important element. They regarded writing as an extension of drawing, and although they went a certain way towards appreciating the convenience of an alphabet they remained indissolubly wedded to their first conception of communicating the sense of an object by delineating it. It was left to the Semites to abandon the clumsy device of the ideogram and rely solely on a convenient number of phonetic symbols. The Egyptians had essentially pictorial imaginations. The early hieroglyphic inscriptions are masterpieces of miniature painting in which birds, plants, animals, buildings and persons are all gaily represented. They form a veritable museum, a piquant archaeological record of the flora, fauna and human habitation of the Nile valley in late predynastic and early dynastic times (see Pl. 11). The Egyptians were devotees of the concrete object: they did not traffic in speculations or abstractions. They were not metaphysicians but practical men. Just as they failed to appreciate the fundamental principles underlying their building, engineering, mathematics, astronomy or medicine, so they failed to interest themselves in the principles and possibilities of hieroglyphic writing. It would hardly be going too far to say that the ancient Egyptian dreaded theorizing and abstract thinking. He felt at home only with what he could experience with his five senses. Even his attitude to so nebulous an experience as death or survival after death was practical and positive. It is therefore not surprising that the Egyptian language contains no words of a truly abstract nature. Such an idea as 'to be angry' terminates with the ideogram of a baboon, notable for its wrathful gibbering, or 'to tremble' terminates with a river-bird distinguished by the delicate shaking of its wings.

An idiosyncrasy of Egyptian orthography is that the vowels were not regarded as the basic phonetic element of the word and were therefore left unwritten. Again the overriding influence of the ideogram is evident. The phonetic signs were merely intended to serve as a clue in the identification of the drawn object, and for this purpose the writing of the consonants was deemed sufficient. In any case, in a system with such complicated characters as Egyptian a certain amount of compression was plainly necessary. All Egyptian words have therefore been described as consonantal skeletons. The name of the crocodile god whom we call Sebek was spelled *s-b-k*, the town we call Dep was spelled *D-p*, the word for desert was spelled *d-sh-r-t*. In some other Semitic languages, with which linguistic group Egyptian has certain affinities, the vocalization of the verbs is effected, and its absence in Egyptian, Hebrew, and Arabic has been a trial to the philologist. In modern transliteration the values of the vowels are commonly replaced with an entirely conventional *e*, although these values can in some cases be ascertained to some extent through Coptic. COPTIC was a vocalized manner of writing the inflected Egyptian tongue developed by the Christian descendants of the ancient Egyptians (Greek *aiguptos*: Egypt). It was the literary language of the Egyptian monks from the third to the sixteenth century A.D., when it succumbed to Arabic. It represents a sadly corrupt stage of writing the ancient tongue with an admixture of Greek.

The decipherment of the hieroglyphs became a lost art soon after their eventual disappearance. It remained a subject for speculation until the nineteenth century, its unfathomable nature giving rise to the legend of the inscrutable wisdom of the ancient Egyptians. In 1822 the brilliant young Frenchman CHAMPOLLION hit upon the mixed phonetic and pictographic character of the signs and was soon able to translate the less complicated texts. The guide to the reading of the ancient language was the use of bilingual or trilingual inscriptions of the Late Period wherein the mysterious hieroglyphic inscription was parallelled by Greek or Coptic. In this work the discovery of the Rosetta stone in 1799 was a valuable stimulus. On the Rosetta stone the copy of a decree in celebration of the first commemoration of Ptolemy V Epiphanes was set out in hieroglyphic, demotic and Greek. Since the time of Champollion the scientific study of Egyptian language and literature has made magnificent progress, thanks to the devoted efforts of a succession of gifted scholars in all countries.

The language of which the hieroglyphs were the written expression could hardly have been expected to remain static during the entire course of dynastic history. Its changes were immeasurably slower than the changes which took place in our own language from Chaucer through Shakespeare to the present day, but they were radical none the less and can be traced. The classic period of their literature and language was considered by the Egyptians to be the Middle Kingdom. It was the literary conventions of this period that the nostalgic Saïtes chose to revive after a lapse of fifteen hundred years. By the zenith of the New Kingdom, however, the classic modes were considered archaic. It was still correct and stylish to use Middle Egyptian from a literary point of view, but Middle Egyptian no longer bore any relation to the spoken tongue. A linguistic revolution took place. Classic composition was relinquished and the current vulgar tongue employed instead, resulting in a more fluid style and a greatly enlarged vocabulary.

Religious writings form the bulk of the literature of the period known to Egyptologists as OLD EGYPTIAN (First to Eighth Dynasties). Some official documents survive, but the walls of tombs supply the greater part of the material. In the MIDDLE EGYPTIAN phase (Ninth to Eighteenth Dynasties) the papyri are more abundant. The classic literature has largely come down to us in careful copies made by later scribes. There are several long Middle Egyptian stories, including the famous *Tale of Sinuhe*, the *Tale of the Eloquent Peasant* and the *Tale of the Shipwrecked Sailor*. Books of 'instructions,' or wise maxims uttered by renowned sages, were popular. The four most important of these collections of proverbs were attributed to the viziers Ptahhetep and Kagemni, the father of Amenophis I and the father of the Pharaoh Merikara. The influence of Egyptian wisdom literature on the Book of Proverbs, the Book of Psalms and the Book of Deuteronomy was extensive and has been often demonstrated. Also of Middle Egyptian date is the papyrus Westcar, which preserves stories about the Pharaohs of the Old Kingdom. A group of texts called 'pessimistic' describe the distractions of the First Intermediate Period. Among the few poems preserved from this period are hymns in praise of the mighty Sesostris III. The style of Middle Egyptian literature is exact, concise and sensitive, distinguished by charm and humour. The literature of the LATE EGYPTIAN phase (Eighteenth to Twenty-fourth Dynasties) is marked by a deepening note of grimness and mordancy. The style is more forthright and less given to fantasy than in the preceding period. Among the stories of the Late phase are the *Tale of the Doomed Prince*, the *Tale of the Two Brothers*, the *Tale of Truth and Falsehood*, the *Tale of Horus and Seth* and the fascinating *Voyage of Wenamon*. These tales contain many brutal and ironic scenes. A reaction against the harsh realism of the prose stories may be detected in the beautiful stanzas which Akhenaton addressed to his sun god. There is also a cycle of lyrical love poems resembling the Song of Songs. A number of hymns to the Nile, to Pharaoh and to the gods, of a more stereotyped nature, also exist, and the cult of the epic was encouraged by the vainglorious Ramessides. Since the scribes did not write out poetical texts in regular stanzas, and because of our imperfect knowledge of the quantities of the vowels, little is known of the nature of Egyptian prosody. The real quality of the prose works is also concealed from us. It must be admitted that from an absolute viewpoint the literature of ancient Egypt is not remarkably exciting except to the specialist. Egyptian literary canons were evidently far removed from our own, but even if we could understand them it is likely that we would find them stilted and artificial.

The voluminous RELIGIOUS LITERATURE of the ancient Egyptians consists in the main of three great recensions or collections of spells, carefully assembled by modern scholars into regular volumes. These are in turn productions of the Old, Middle and New Kingdoms. Firstly come the PYRAMID TEXTS, inscribed on the walls of royal pyramids of the Fifth and Sixth Dynasties. The tomb chambers of the King were covered with these spells, many of predynastic origin. The living creatures which occur in the hieroglyphic writing were maimed or scored through by the scribes in order to ward off any baleful influence which they might exert over the dead man. Secondly we have the COFFIN TEXTS, inscribed in a conventional sequence on the interior and exterior of the wooden coffins of the First Intermediate Period and the Middle Kingdom. Third in the series is the so-called BOOK OF THE DEAD, more accurately entitled the BOOK OF COMING FORTH BY DAY. Under the New Kingdom spells from this recension were written on papyrus for inclusion in the tombs of the wealthy. The spells, many of which are of amazing puerility, were meant to secure for the dead man access to the Next World and the preservation of his spirit from the manifold dangers which would beset it. The Book contains some ninety 'chapters' in all. Many copies of the work were written in an exquisite hand and illustrated with fine vignettes. The rolls of papyrus may range from lengths of a hundred and twenty feet to a miserable scrap on which a spell or two have been inscribed for the benefit of a poor man. Other important religious books include the *Book of Gates*, the *Book of What-is-in-the-Underworld* and the *Book of Opening the Mouth*.

MATHEMATICS, like the writing of hieroglyphs, was given over more to practical than theoretical considerations. Our knowledge of all Egyptian sciences is restricted by the fact that the basic formulae were closely guarded by their priestly practitioners and never committed to papyrus. Teaching in Egyptian schools and universities was for the most part oral, and it is certain that Egyptian mathematics were more extensive than surviving documents suggest. Like so much else in Egyptian intellectual life, mathematics were probably perfected by the Pyramid Age and made little progress thereafter. The decimal system of numeration, employing separate digits and multiples of a hundred up to a million, was in existence as early as the First Dynasty. The device of zero was not discovered, and even the Greeks themselves did not hit upon it. Complex fractions were easily manipulated, with the disadvantage that the only fractional numerator was 1. Thus $\frac{3}{8}$ was expressed as $\frac{1}{8}\frac{1}{8}\frac{1}{8}$. Two-thirds, however, appears to have been a fundamental concept. Arithmetical progression by fractions and elementary geometrical progression were comprehended. Surface calculation was made on the properties of the triangle, the rectangle and the trapezium. The great Rhind papyrus in the British Museum contains many problems devoted to the properties of the rectangle, the triangle and the circle. It is doubtful whether the volume of the truncated pyramid or the formula for the area of a hemisphere were known, as some modern writers have claimed. The Egyptians applied their mathematical knowledge to practical affairs with extraordinary ingenuity. The papyrus Anastasi I, for example, contains a series of the building problems concerning the transport and erection of colossi, obelisks and enormous blocks of stone which the Egyptians solved with conspicuous success in practice.

ASTRONOMY also appears to have reached its full development by the Pyramid Age. Intense observation of the heavens was already carried on in predynastic times, and by the founding of the First Dynasty the Egyptians had already constructed a practicable calendar. The invention of the calendar has been hailed as the greatest scientific achievement of the Egyptians. The heavenly bodies were divided into three categories: the

Unwearied, the Imperishable and the Indestructible. The Unwearied stars were the planets, which move without surcease across the sky. The Egyptians early identified Jupiter, Saturn, Venus, Mars and perhaps Mercury. The Imperishable stars were the circumpolar stars. In early times it was believed that the Heavenly Fields in which the king passed eternity were situated in the region of these stars. The Indestructible stars were the fixed stars, thirty-six of which were chosen to preside over the thirty-six dekans or ten-day periods contained in the Egyptian year.

The constellations were mapped out and given such names as the Crocodile or the Hippopotamus. The Great Bear was known as the Ox Leg. It is possible that a reference to the phenomenon of the eclipse is contained in the myth of the moon god Thoth restoring the eye of the sun god Horus after the battle with Seth. The precise significance of the myth is unknown. The twelve signs of the Zodiac were introduced into Egypt by the Greeks, who in turn derived them from those more competent mathematicians and astronomers than the Egyptians, the Babylonians. The pseudo-science of astrology was practised in the Nile valley at all periods.

THE SCULPTOR

The first large scale works of sculpture which have survived from ancient Egypt date from the reign of the Pharaoh Khasekhemui of the Second Dynasty. The artists of predynastic and early dynastic times confined themselves to the decoration of slate palettes or ivory panels, and often their work was of marvellous dexterity. The promise of Fourth Dynasty sculpture is foreshadowed in a statue of Zoser from the Step Pyramid. Under the Pharaohs of the Pyramid Age the art reached a point which many art historians and Egyptologists believe it never afterwards surpassed. Single statues, pairs and groups have been excavated from Fourth Dynasty tombs in great profusion. Many were found in the enclosed serdab of the

95

tomb or mortuary chapel. The sitter is represented in a dignified, quiescent pose, an attitude of serene confidence and undisturbed calm of spirit. Sometimes he stands and steps
forward with quiet assurance (Pl. 18). The subject is presented
in the prime of life, in the full flush of bodily strength and
beauty in which he hoped to spend his days in the Next
World. Or he may be represented by a series of statues sculpted
at different periods of his life, in youth, middle life and old
age. Strangely enough, even when allowances are made for
differences in appearance at separate stages of life, there are
sometimes odd discrepancies between several portraits of the
same man or between his statue and his mummy. It would
appear that the statue of the deceased might in some cases
have been manufactured originally for someone else. It may
even have been bought ready made from a commercial artist,
like a modern tombstone, or have been usurped from an earlier
owner by the simple expedient of erasing his cartouche. It was
of supreme importance that the name of the deceased should
be clearly engraved on his statue. The soul, on visiting the
tomb, identified its earthly habitation by the label rather than
by the appearance.

There is another reason why Egyptian statues should not
always be assumed to be literal portraits. The custom was to
flatter the subject, to portray him for eternity in an ideal
guise. Akhenaton—no lover of tradition—bequeathed to
posterity a famous and very startling statue of himself as he
really was, in all his deplorable sick ugliness. Yet beside this
freakish essay in portraiture can be placed 'official' heads of the
same Pharaoh which represent him as a comely and attractive
young man.

Egyptian statuary of all periods is carved from a wide variety
of stone. The sculptor and stone-cutter were keenly appreciative
of the inviting raw material with which the Nile valley and
its environs supplied them. Alabaster, basalt, red, white and
green breccia, diorite, granite, limestone, marble, porphyry,

quartzite, sandstone, schist and serpentine: all were employed for statues, sarcophagi and reliefs. Statues were often painted to make them appear as lifelike as possible. The skin of a man was represented by red, the skin of a woman by yellow. Special attention was paid to the imitation of the eye. In the more elaborate examples opaque white quartz was used for the cornea, rock crystal for the iris, ebony for the pupil and copper for the socket. The final result was frequently lifelike to the point of the uncanny (Pl. 2).

The bold technique of the Fourth Dynasty was slightly softened during the latter part of the Old Kingdom, when art became a luxurious adjunct to court life. The old rigour re-emerged triumphantly with the Middle Kingdom, in certain statues discovered at Thebes and Deir el-Bahri. In the rude strength of the portraits of the warrior Pharaohs of Thebes can be seen the rediscovered virility of Egyptian society. The care-worn faces of Mentuhetep II and Sesostris III, as delineated by the Theban artists, give a moving impression of their sense of responsibility and stern self-sacrifice. The Middle Kingdom sculpture of Memphis, on the other hand, reflects the easy and enervating influence of Deltaic life. In contrast to Upper Egyptian sculpture of the Middle Kingdom, the Lower Egyptian sculpture of the period suffers from insipidity. It was unfortunate that the sculptors of the New Kingdom, although their royal patrons were from Thebes, chose to model their style largely upon that of the Memphite school, with the result that subsequent statues lack the honesty and immediacy of impact of the Middle Kingdom masterpieces. The standard of technical excellence nevertheless remained as high as ever. A brief deviation into the ranker forms of naturalism was initiated by Akhenaton, but his assault on artistic tradition was less radical and ultimately less damaging in the case of the sculpture than it was in the case of the painter. The sculptor, perhaps because of the nature of the material in which he worked, rapidly reasserted his faith in the old heroic forms. The painter, whose medium was more sensitive and less arbitrary, never seemed to regain full confidence after the Amarna interlude in the validity of the ancient modes. It may be that in the case of painting the Amarna experiment was justified, for it certainly produced frescoes imbued with a novel spirit of space and vitality (Pl. 30). In the case of sculpture the freedom of the Amarna episode was false and illusory. Under the Saïte dynasts a renaissance of Old and Middle Kingdom art took place. The reliefs and statues of the earlier periods were reproduced in a relentlessly mechanical fashion. The Saïte artists exhibit, none the less, a polish and ingenuity which has rarely been equalled.

The attitude of the Egyptian sculptor to his work was similar to that of the Egyptian architect. Statuary was executed for a specifically religious purpose. The seductions of aesthetics were relegated to a secondary rôle. There is a tendency among scholars to discount the aesthetic content of Egyptian sculpture altogether, but this view is certainly too severe. Despite his unwillingness to make what he would have regarded as feverish and frivolous experiments, the Egyptian sculptor no doubt considered his handiwork in much the same light as his counterpart in the modern world. He conceived a challenging and lofty idea which called for his whole skill if it were to be realized in stone. He was interested in the texture of his material. He experienced the legitimate pride of the craftsman in work well done. Where he differed utterly from the modern sculptor was in the apparent indifference he felt concerning the fate of the statue on which he lavished months, perhaps years of labour. His statue was not exposed for public admiration. It was shut up in a serdab, walled up for eternity where no eye could ever appreciate it. Or it was relegated to the tenebrous interior of a hypostyle hall. His choicest reliefs were executed, through the lack of co-ordination between architect and crafts-men notable in the early history of building, on dismal and inaccessible sections of the curtain wall of the temple or at the

28. A DIORITE STATUE OF THE PHARAOH CHEPHREN,
SHOWING THE PHARAOH PROTECTED BY THE FALCON
From Giza
Fourth Dynasty

29. THE PHARAOH TUTANKHAMON
The funerary mask

top of a high column. For all we know the ancient sculptor did not always acquiesce willingly in this treatment of his work, but it must be remembered that the Egyptian sculptor was not intent, like his contemporary counterpart, on expressing his own unique individuality. Individuality, the pampered darling of Western civilization, was not of any consequence to the ancient Egyptian. The aspiration of every member of Egyptian society was to suppress this troublesome individuality and strive towards corporate contentment and cohesion. The majesty of ancient Egypt was due in no small measure to the fact that the whole was greater than the sum of its parts. We would nevertheless be wrong to assume that because we do not know the name of any outstanding sculptor none therefore existed. No doubt there were great and revered masters, and the productions at which we marvel were not the productions of tyros or prentices. The men who carved them were first the pupils and afterwards the tutors of a leading school of artists. A block of fine stone was not manhandled by huge gangs of men to be wantonly hacked about by an untrained amateur. We would probably be correct in assuming that Egyptian sculptors, like artists everywhere and at all times, possessed their special *mystique*. A great work of art is not produced unconsciously or by accident. It is produced by a profound and protracted effort of the emotions, the intellect and the will.

The conventions employed in sculpting a relief were the same as those employed in the art of painting. These conventions will be discussed in the next section, and we shall devote ourselves here to some concluding remarks on sculpture in the round. The Egyptian sculptor appears to have seen his block of stone at all stages as a cube. He squared off the front and side faces into the grid which gave him his anatomical proportions, then he worked back the three faces until they came together. As in painting, Egyptian sculpture was essentially the art of profiles. The fourth face of the cube was frequently left intact as a back pillar, often with the first raw chisel marks upon it. The sculptor was aware from the outset that his statue was intended to harmonize with an architectural setting. With or without the back pillar, the statue would in any case be placed against a wall or column. When the subject was seated, the severe lines of the throne or chair emphasized the cubic preoccupation of the sculptor, who in addition was careful to preserve the form of the cube by chipping away as little stone as possible. This economy in cutting served a utilitarian as well as an artistic purpose, for it enabled the sculptor to turn more quickly to other commissions. The bare, flat planes, devoid of supererogatory detail, give Egyptian sculpture a massiveness and impressiveness which the more florid architecture of the country rarely succeeds in achieving. The finest Egyptian statues have an impassive power that makes them the best and truest embodiments of the philosophical outlook of ancient Egypt.

THE PAINTER

The tempera frescoes executed on the walls of tombs, religious buildings and private houses were sometimes painted directly on clay plaster, but in the great majority of cases on a specially prepared ground of gypsum or chalk plaster. The plaster was mixed with a binding solution of gum or glue and applied to the wall, where it formed a fine smooth surface. The paint was not an oil paint but a distemper, the dry pigment being mixed with water and some kind of adhesive of the nature of size. Brushes were manufactured from sticks of fibrous wood, crushed at one end into stumpy bristles. Nine distinct colours were employed: black, blue, brown, green, grey, red, white and yellow dating from the early dynasties, pink being introduced under the New Kingdom. Colours were in general manufactured from local minerals. Varnishes were commonly used, sometimes to cover a whole fresco and sometimes to cover certain select colours. At their best the colour-

30. A PAINTED WALL FRESCO OF TWO PRINCESSES
Amarna period

31. THE LEATHER HUNTING EQUIPMENT
OF A NEW KINGDOM NOBLEMAN
A gauntlet, two dog collars, two arrows, a quiver and quiver-lid

32. THE PHARAOH TUTANKHAMON

This ushabti figure shows him wearing the Blue Crown and bearing the crook and flail

ings of Egyptian frescoes match the vivid, glowing and un-equivocal hues of the Nilotic landscape.

Before he began work on a new fresco the painter planned out the available space into a series of registers. The human figures and inscriptions to be drawn were plotted into rigid vertical and horizontal patterns. Every wall was treated as a self-contained entity, and to each was allotted by tradition its particular subject. The cubic principle of sculpture applied also to painting. The accepted images were square patterns and square hieroglyphs on square walls punctuated by square door-ways. When his general plan was clear, the painter ruled off small squares in red or black paint to serve as guide lines for the proportions of his figures. These proportions were in-variable throughout dynastic history until the Saïte epoch, when a different grid was introduced. In the earlier grid the knee occurred at the sixth and the shoulders at the sixteenth square, while in the slimmer Saïte figures the knee fell at the seventh and the shoulders at the nineteenth square. Apprentices were so well trained that in many cases they were able to judge the proportions by eye to within a fraction of an inch without having recourse to the grid.

The feature which is immediately apparent in Egyptian painting is the extraordinary treatment of the human figure. The head is represented in profile, yet the eye is presented full face. The torso is turned square to the spectator, while the legs are twisted into profile. The posture is plainly a physical im-possibility, but it persists throughout the whole long history of Egyptian art. Presumably, then, it was not adopted through ignorance and perpetuated by laziness. The Egyptian artist in fact possessed a wonderfully accurate eye. His paintings of birds, animals, fish and plants are testimony to his powers of minute observation. The Egyptians certainly realized that to draw figures in their customary manner was anatomically incorrect. There were sporadic attempts, particularly in the Amarna period, to establish a realistic canon, and there are many impromptu sketches on fragments of plaster or potsherds which reveal a less ascetic approach to figure painting. The perversion of posture was deliberate. It did not disturb the Egyptian as it disturbs us.

What the Egyptian wanted to do was to draw every element in his picture in such a way that it would be instantly recognizable. Therefore, he argued, it should be exhibited in its most characteristic light. A torso is more evidently a torso if both shoulders are in view. A face seen from the three-quarter angle is less of a face than when it is seen in profile. Legs are more leg-like if they step sideways rather than take a pace of uncertain length towards the spectator. The Egyptian made no studies of hands in the manner of Dürer. The quality of essential 'handness' was revealed when all five fingers were shown fully extended. Projection, foreshortening, perspective, all the delight in *trompe d'oeil* and illusory appearance, were rejected. Egyptian art was not a sensuous but an intellectual undertaking. Was not Pharaoh ten times as important as the wretched mortal grovelling before him ? It was therefore logical to make the king ten times as large as the supplicant. Were not five hundred captives more accurately and strikingly represented by painting the entire five hundred of them, rather than by showing five and pretending that the other four hundred and ninety-five were standing somewhere behind them ? Therefore the captives must be placed in ten registers of fifty, one above the other. An artist should be literal and exact. He should ring round every shape with a good firm contour. The ancient artist was not painting a picture for his private amusement or his patron's insouciant pleasure: he was compiling a record, engrossing an account, writing an earthly and heavenly income-tax return. It is probable that the hard outline and isolation of objects in Egyptian painting were encouraged by environment. In the Nile valley everything was bathed in a clear, unwavering light. The studies of fleeting cloud and shadow effects in which our own artists have revelled for many centuries were precluded. Shadows were probably omitted not only because they were illusory but also because of the superstitious fear which many peoples feel for them.

One more aspect of Egyptian painting must be noted: its static disposition. The Egyptians were for the most part a sedentary people. With the exception of a handful of imperial adventurers, they were by nature stay-at-home. They lived out their lives quietly within the narrow confines of their valley. Movement was not of interest to them, it entered little into their experience. Excessive movement was also threatening to the equipoise, the inner core of calm, which was the central concept of society. The persons who figured in their frescoes, furthermore, were meant to be fixed there for all eternity, and no doubt this solemn reflection influenced the artist while he was at work. What prevented the artist from transmitting the natural gaiety of the Egyptian character was the sombre weight of traditional modes.

It cannot fairly be claimed, in conclusion, that Egyptian painting anywhere achieves the grandeur of Egyptian sculpture. The concrete nature of the ancient Egyptian's imagination, his desire to see and feel, would find more satisfaction in the exercise of the plastic arts than in the necessarily distorted and artificial medium of painting. For this reason the delicately cut reliefs, which stand half-way between painting and sculpture, are in general more impressive than works on a purely flat surface. The high standard of technical achievement of these reliefs may be taken for granted. Painting is the subtle art of cheating visually, and the Egyptian was by temperament too literal to practise it successfully. Again, his opportunities to exercise any talent he may have possessed for composition were inhibited by the fact that his frescoes were stereotyped set-pieces on conventional themes. Where the Egyptian painter scored a real triumph, however, was in his passionate, vibrant use of colour.

THE DOCTOR

The doctors of ancient Egypt were famous throughout the ancient world. Homer praises them in the *Odyssey* and Herodotus relates that the Persian emperors Cyrus and Darius set great store by their Egyptian physicians. Medicine was one of the oldest professions in the Nile valley. The earliest surviving medical papyri, which are of Middle Kingdom date, claim to be copies of works written in the Old Kingdom, and authorship is in some cases credited to Thoth and Imhotep. Like astronomy and other intellectual pursuits, medicine appears to have been studied first in Lower Egypt. The ancient shrines of Ra-Atum at Heliopolis, Neith at Saïs and Anubis at Letopolis are spoken of as early centres of the science.

The connection with Anubis, god of mummification, was always close and would suggest that medicine and embalming were related. Although the doctors kept the embalmers supplied with customers, it appears that the process of mummification was a jealously kept trade secret not revealed even to members of the medical profession. It seems scarcely credible that ignorance of anatomy should exist in a land where mummification was practised on such a scale, but such appears to be the case. It is noteworthy that the hieroglyphs which represent the various parts of the human body were derived from observation of the bodies of animals. Respect for the human corpse precluded any systematic development of the art of dissection.

The Egyptians apparently numbered hypochondria among their many ailments. Herodotus records the existence of innumerable specialists. 'Each doctor treats only one disease,' he states, 'and the whole place is crammed full with doctors. Some are oculists, others deal with head complaints, others are dentists, others deal with stomach trouble.' He goes on to say that the Egyptians 'take care of themselves with purgatives and emetics and clear themselves out for three days running once every month.' The clearing-out operation was performed with the aid of that alarming engine the clyster, which was held to be a gift of the gods. It seems that a party of savants was perambulating on the banks of the Nile when they caught sight of Thoth, in his customary form of the ibis, gravely filling his long beak with water and inserting it in his anus. The scholars were inspired to go and do likewise.

There were many methods by means of which doctors effected their cures. If the trouble was external the patient stood a fair chance of recovery. Breaks and fractures were cleverly set. The practice of amputation and the use of splints, bandages and compresses were well developed. Internal disorders were an entirely different matter. Here the physician was reduced to reciting spells and prescribing such potions as woman's milk with oil and salt or goat's milk with honey. It was thought that life depended on a series of vessels which started from the heart. In these vessels ran air, water, blood, semen, urine and faeces. There was no suggestion of any anticipation of the discovery of the circulation of the blood. No distinction was made between veins, arteries, muscles and nerves. On the other hand, there is evidence that the Egyptians became highly skilled diagnosticians, with a clear understanding of the effects upon the system of many wounds, blows and fractures. Internal diseases were considered to result from the obstruction or hardening of the vessels, and relief was attempted by means of plasters and liniments.

Of the numerous medical papyri which have been preserved the longest is the Ebers papyrus. The original roll contains a hundred and ten large columns in which are set out details of illnesses and the nature, amount and method of administration of the drugs to be used for treating them. Magical spells and formulae are freely interspersed with rational prescriptions. The Edwin Smith papyrus is perhaps more remarkable than the Ebers papyrus because it is almost wholly surgical in character. It lists with admirable objectivity a large number of external ailments and constitutes a strict scientific treatise on the treatment of wounds and fractures. The sixth papyrus in the Chester-Beatty collection, which is devoted to proctology, resembles the Edwin Smith papyrus in its attempt to adopt a detached and clinical attitude towards its subject-matter. The thirty-four sections of the Kahun papyrus which have survived are the relics of what was once a thorough manual of gynaecology. This branch of medicine was particularly well advanced, for there was ample scope for study in a country where a woman bore her first child at the age of twelve and seldom produced less than six or seven all told. Women formed an important section of the physician's *clientèle*, and it was a recognized part of his stock-in-trade to provide courses of beauty treatment. The banishing of wrinkles, the removal of scurf and the cleansing and smoothing of the skin all fell within his province.

The powders and concoctions of the physician were composed of a variety of plants, seeds, piths and such fruits as dates and figs. Many of the plants were grown in the herb gardens of temples. Tuthmosis III, whose army included a corps of surgeons, sent back to the temple of Karnak botanical specimens culled during the course of his Asian campaigns. Plant juices and the fat or blood of a large number of animals were incorporated in suitable liquid vehicles. Among the drugs whose properties were recognized for the first time by the ancient Egyptians a medical authority lists hartshorn, castor oil, mandragora, cumin, dill and coriander. Medicaments plainly borrowed from Egyptian sources are said to occur in the works of Pliny, Dioscorides, Galen, and in the Hippocratic Collection. The Greeks frankly acknowledged, in this as in other fields, the debt their own men of science owed to Egypt. The Romans, Arabs and Persians also availed themselves freely of Egyptian medical lore. The Egyptian doctor was undoubtedly the first great pioneer of serious medical investigation.

106

THE UNDERTAKER

After the doctor, the undertaker. The practice of mummifying was carried on by a special guild which received its charter by law. The members of the guild were chary of writing down their professional secrets, and the bulk of our knowledge is derived from Herodotus and the later Greek historian, Diodorus Siculus. The word mummy is derived from the Arabic word *mûmîyah*: bitumen. The modern Arabs possessed an erroneous idea that the black appearance of the majority of mummies was due to immersion in bitumen.

When the bodies of predynastic and early dynastic persons were buried in a shallow pit grave, it was noted that the natural juices drained off downwards and prevented putrefaction. The body was perfectly and naturally preserved in the warm dry sand. Later, however, the hazards of robbers and nocturnal animals combined with a growing urge for display to lead towards the erection of mastabas and pyramids. The body was now hidden away far from the warm sun in the cold depths of the tomb. Bodies now tended to decay, and the art of mummifying was devised to deal with the problem. The invention of the process was credited to Isis, who employed it to preserve the remains of her murdered husband. The actual business of mummification was carried out by Anubis. Diodorus called mummifying 'the remedy which confers immortality.'

The viscera of queen Hetephras were wrapped in linen bandages soaked with natron, which suggests that her missing body was also treated in a similar fashion. Simple swathing in sheets impregnated with some kind of preservative may have been the custom during the Thinite epoch and the early years of the Old Kingdom. The earliest attested mummy was a mummy of the Fifth Dynasty. It was destroyed when the Royal College of Surgeons was bombed in 1941. At first mummifying was entirely a royal prerogative, but with the growth of the Osiris cult it was extended to the nobility and the wealthier citizens. It was not adopted to any marked extent by poorer folk until Ptolemaic times, when Diodorus records that the three prices on the undertaker's tariff were a talent of silver (£250), twenty minae (£80) and a few miserable drachmae. The three methods of embalmment were described by Herodotus four centuries earlier. In the most expensive burial the brain was first macerated and then skilfully extracted through the nose by means of a specially designed iron hook. Then an incision was made in the abdomen with an 'Ethiopian stone' wielded by the *parischistes*. The office of *parischistes* was as odious as the office of common hangman is in our own times. When he had made his deep cut, the *parischistes* fled away with the other undertakers in pursuit. The pursuit and the ritual cries which they uttered resemble the acts performed at the sin-eating ceremony which took place until a few years ago in Celtic countries. Through the incision in the abdomen the intestines were removed, treated with chemicals and placed in the four canopic jars. Each jar in the canopic chest was under the protection of one of the four sons of Horus, whose heads were carved on the jars from the New Kingdom onwards. These four deities and the body in its case or sarcophagus were in turn watched over by Isis, Nephthys, Neith and Selkit, four of the oldest and most revered of the goddesses (Pl. 5). The heart was put back in the body, for it was the seat of the intellect and emotions. The mummy could not be resurrected without it, and its owner would require it for the judgment which preceded his entry into the Heavenly Fields. The cavity in the abdomen was then packed with rolls of linen or sawdust and aromatic spices. The contours of the shrunken corpse were restored to the plumpness of life by additional internal packing. Either before or after the process of packing the body was dried by immersion in natron, whether in a bath or by some method in which the natron was used in its dry state being a matter of controversy. The drying of the body took at least seventy days. The next stage was the washing of the corpse, after which it was anointed with precious and fragrant ointments, such as cinnamon and myrrh.

The complicated business of bandaging was now undertaken. Strips of linen saturated in gum were wound systematically round the body, preserving as closely as possible the physical outline. At intervals the swathing was interrupted to place charms between the folds. The most favoured charms were the large green heart scarab, with an inscription which implored the heart not to inform against its master at the psychostasia, the red Isis fetish and the white Osiris fetish. Scraps of papyrus with magical formulae and extracts from religious writings were also inserted, or the texts were inscribed on the bandages themselves. Each finger and toe was bandaged separately. The mummy of Tutankhamon was wrapped in no less than sixteen layers of fine linen.

The climax of the process was reached under the Eighteenth Dynasty. Resinous pastes were applied to the exterior of the body to emphasize the contours, artificial eyes were often used, and toenails and fingernails were held in place by means of thread or metal stalls. The priest-kings of the Theban Twenty-first Dynasty were also skilful embalmers, but afterwards a gradual decline set in. Until mummifying died out, at the dawn of our era, less and less attention was paid to the actual preservation of the remains, the external appearance becoming all-important. Gaily painted bandages and geometric swathing were the fashion. From the Twenty-first Dynasty onwards the intestines were wrapped separately and put back in the body with accompanying wax images of the sons of Horus. In Roman times the prevailing method was simply to coat the corpses with resin or pitch, which rendered them so hard and brittle that the Copts and Arabs were accustomed to snap them in pieces for use as firewood, with a sound described as similar to the breaking of test-tubes. At various times sacred animals were also mummified.

THE METAL-WORKER

The most important metal to be used in ancient Egypt was copper. The chief source of the metal was Sinai, and Sinaitic ores were smelted well back in the predynastic era, about 4000 B.C. Other sources of copper were located in Nubia and at a number of sites in the eastern desert between the Nile valley and the Red Sea. Before the introduction of the bellows in the Eighteenth Dynasty smelting was carried on by mixing crushed ore with charcoal in a shallow pit and forcing a draught through the smouldering mass by means of a blowpipe. Soon after the introduction of smelting the predynastic Egyptians learned how to melt the copper in clay crucibles and shape it in stone moulds. The edges of cutting tools were skilfully hammered to maximum toughness and then trimmed and ground. It is doubtful whether the edges were ever hardened by the process of re-heating known as annealing. Copper remained the staple material for tools used in agricultural and architectural work. Like all metals, it was scarce, and the peasantry relied principally on stone implements throughout dynastic history. In the New Kingdom the process of adding a proportion of tin to copper to obtain bronze was introduced from Asia. Quantities of tin were imported and bronze gradually superseded copper in the workman's tool kit. Statuettes and weapons were cast by the *cire perdue* process. In this process a model of the object is first manufactured by hand or in a mould. It is then coated with clay to form a case or mould. The clay mould is baked, which causes it to harden, and during the baking the beeswax runs away through small vents. Molten bronze is next poured into the empty clay mould. When the metal is cool and set, the clay jacket is broken off and the object emerges complete.

The fragments of iron which occur in early contexts in Egypt all appear to be meteoric. It may have been the hurtling to earth of meteors that persuaded the Egyptians that the bodies of their gods were composed of iron, the 'ore of heaven.' According to one theory the roof of heaven was composed of this metal. A few small iron objects occur in the tomb of Tutankhamon, notably the dagger blade that fits so badly into its elaborate hilt. These objects were probably all meteoric in origin, or were made from a bar of iron presented to the Egyptian Pharaoh by some Asian monarch. The Aryan kings of Mitanni appear to have been the first people to appreciate the possibilities and exploit the manufacture of the new substance, to be followed shortly afterwards by the Aryan kings of Hatti. We know that a Pharaoh of the Eighteenth Dynasty begged a Hittite king for a supply of iron and received only a single dagger. The secret of obtaining the fierce temperature required to produce iron was closely guarded, and despite their curiosity the Egyptians were unable to smelt it until the Twenty-first Dynasty, long after it had come into use elsewhere. In the ancient world the control of all types of metal was always a royal monopoly. Iron enjoyed a great prestige in antiquity, particularly among peoples who were late in acquiring it.

Gold was obtained in prodigious quantities from predynastic times onward. It came chiefly from Nubia and the eastern desert, but does not appear to have been present at Sinai. The demand for it was insatiable. Gangs of labourers were lashed on the whole year round in order to hammer at the quartzite veins in the granite quarries where the metal occurred. Vast amounts of it were obtained in tribute from the conquered provinces, and it served to buy and perpetuate diplomatic alliances. In the Amarna letters we learn that an early king of Assyria, Ashurnadinakhi, received a remittance of twenty talents of gold from Amenophis III, 'the same amount that was sent to the king of Hanigalbat.' From the same source we are informed that Tushratta of Mitanni wrote to Pharaoh as follows: 'Send me so much gold that it cannot be measured. Send me more gold than you sent to my father. In your land, my brother, gold is as common as dust!'

Gold was both cast and cold hammered. It was cut and shaped into plaques, foil, leaf, wire, rivets and nails. Silver was scarcer than gold and was therefore reckoned of greater account. It was evidently extremely hard to come by, for very little of it was found even in the tomb of Tutankhamon. The sources of supply are obscure, but much of it probably arrived in Egypt in the form of tribute. Electrum, a natural alloy of gold and silver, was available in small amounts in Upper Egypt and Nubia. It was known as 'white gold' and highly prized.

THE STONE-WORKER

Whatever eminence the Egyptians may have lacked as metallurgists they handsomely made up for in their adroitness in working stone. From the earliest times all manner of stone was handled by the masons with serene mastery. Soft stones could be readily cut with the chisel, but hard stones would respond only to more forceful methods. In quarrying operations the block of stone was first detached from the parent mass by means of wedges. Wedge slots were cut and the wooden wedges hammered home. It is possible that the Egyptians knew the ingenious method of inserting wedges of dry wood, wetting them, and then waiting for the subsequent expansion of the wedges to split the rock. The detached block was reduced to a rough manageable shape by means of pounding it with dolerite mallets. It is unlikely that the workmen wore away their precious copper chisels on this preliminary hewing out. Copper saws were sometimes employed, no doubt in combination with some satisfactory abrasive. The exact nature of the abrasive is debated. It may have been emery, pumice or quartz sand.

Sledges, rollers, levers and thick fibre ropes were used to manipulate and transport the blocks of raw stone, which were hauled into position up ramps of rubble before they received their final shaping. The use of the pulley, which would immeasurably have lightened the labour of building, was certainly unknown. Faint traces of mortar can be detected in many instances, but it has been suggested that in many cases the mortar was not a bonding agent but a thin mud slurry on which the blocks could be slid into place from their sledges or cradles.

For boring out the central core of the superb stone bowls and vases which were manufactured from the earliest times, tubular copper drills were used. It has been maintained, on insufficient grounds, that cutting jewels were sometimes placed round the edge of the drill tube. A kind of elementary brace and bit was also in operation. For fine work a large range of delicate copper tools was on hand.

The first *ushabti* figures were fine examples of the stone-cutter's art. These figures are representations of a dead man, generally about five or six inches high. Sometimes they were actual portraits of the deceased. They first became a regular item of tomb furniture in the Middle Kingdom, when they may have been simply a kind of miniature of the dead person. It was not long before they were regarded as slaves of the deceased, servants who would perform for him the menial tasks which would fall to his lot in the Next World. Accordingly the little mummy figures were now portrayed with agricultural implements on their backs, usually hoes and picks. In the New Kingdom large sets of *ushabtis* were placed in wooden chests or clay pots in the tomb chamber, each set possessing one or more figures intended to represent task masters armed with whips. The *ushabtis*, or 'answerers,' were engraved with magical texts. A common formula runs as follows: 'O *ushabti*, if the name of Osiris (Name of dead person) is called in the roll for work in the Heavenly Fields, for such tasks as tilling the soil or carting sand, speak up for him in his place and shout: "Look! Here I am! I am doing it!"' In the Middle Kingdom the tiny figures were frequently of white limestone or brown serpentine. Wood was used on rare occasions. After the Middle Kingdom *ushabtis* were commonly made of glazed pottery, but royalty continued to commission stone and wooden figures which were triumphs of skill (Pl. 23, 32).

The Egyptians were the first people in the world to work stone on an intensive scale. Since time was no object to the ancient Egyptian craftsman, the pieces he produced were of the first quality. The Egyptians also constructed the earliest and the largest stone structures in existence.

THE WOOD-WORKER

Carpentry reached an astonishing level of achievement during late predynastic and Thinite times. It may have been that wood was still sufficiently plentiful in the predynastic period to allow wood-working to come to perfection. Or perhaps the very rarity of wood resulted, as it did in the case of gold, in the careful development of suitable methods for handling it. Cedar and cypress appear to have reached predynastic Egypt from abroad, while ebony, juniper, fir, yew and oak were all imported in dynastic times. The persea, sidder, sycamore, fig, tamarisk and willow were all indigenous to the Nile valley, though in relatively small quantities (Pl. 43).

By the beginning of the Old Kingdom, halved, mitred and concealed joints, tenons, mortises, dovetailing and even the manufacture of plywood were standard items in the craftsman's repertoire. The inlaying, veneering and marquetry work of ancient Egypt rivals the best work of its kind ever produced.

The Egyptian carpenter was constructing elaborate boats of advanced design in the predynastic era. By the time of Snofru he was building boats of a hundred cubits (a hundred and seventy-two feet) long. Rafts were constructed which were capable of floating downstream over six hundred tons of stone. The raft which Weni designed to float material from the quarries in Upper Egypt to Sakkara was a hundred and three feet long and fifty-one feet wide. He claimed that his labourers built it in seventeen days. Many different types of craft were in existence (Pl. 38).

THE COSTUMIER AND COSMETICIAN

The art of spinning flax or fibre was well established at the
outset of the dynastic era (Pl. 39). It is therefore probable that
the more important members of society were already accustomed to the long robe of fine stuff, at least for ceremonial
occasions. The loin-cloth was apparently the more usual gar-
ment, however, and in dynastic times royalty and the nobility
retained it when sitting for their formal portraits. In the
dynastic period the loin-cloth worn by the upper classes developed into a short skirt or peaked kilt. Slaves, labourers,
peasants and artisans wore the loin-cloth throughout Egyptian
history.

In the Old Kingdom the long robe was a single length of
cloth. The men wore it draped from the shoulder and reaching
to the calf, while in the case of women it was tight-fitting and
reached to the ankles. Wigs and ornaments were worn in the
Old Kingdom. From the Middle Kingdom onwards men
adopted a closely fitting tunic for wear beneath the robe. In
the New Kingdom the linen was of superb texture, gauffered
and with accordion pleats. Wool was in use in small quantities
throughout Egyptian history, but was considered unclean from
a ritual point of view. Herodotus records that 'nothing
woollen is brought into the temples or buried with them.'
Cotton, already spun in India when the first dynasts ruled in
Egypt, did not appear on the Nile until the Roman period.
Silk was introduced by the Persians of the First Persian
Domination and gained favour with the last luxury-loving
dynasties and the later Ptolemies. Lucan speaks of Cleopatra's
'white breasts resplendent through the Sidonian fabric.' The
Egyptians were skilled workers of dressed leather, from which
they made corslets, sandals and accoutrements (Pl. 31).

Wigs were worn by both sexes. Often large and ponderous,
they consisted of human hair over which melted beeswax had
been poured. Women wore the wig over their natural hair, but
men appear habitually to have shaved their heads. Men were

invariably clean shaven, using elaborate copper and bronze razors for the purpose, no doubt in conjunction with some kind of perfumed grease or unguent. The beard worn by Pharaoh in frescoes or on mummy cases was a false beard, donned for ceremonial occasions (Pl. 1). The elaborate wig worn in many royal portraits was known as the *nemes* headdress (Pl. 29). In a large number of frescoes a small cone can be seen placed on top of the wig. It was composed of a perfumed oil which slowly melted and ran down over the face and neck, a gratifying sensation in a hot climate.

The principal ornament was the broad bead collar, composed of many rows of different coloured beads strung in intricate patterns. Also worn round the neck were pectorals, commonly of faience but magnificently jewelled in the case of high priests and leading officers of state (Pl. 33-36). Anklets, pendants and rings were worn by both men and women. Earrings were widely in vogue only under the Eighteenth Dynasty, when they reached a great weight and size. The earring was attached to the ear by means of a cylindrical tube, and the size of the tube and the weight of the earring combined in many cases to produce a serious deformation of the ear lobe.

Amulets and scarabs were normal features of dress. The scarab, which had its origin in the cylinder or button seal employed to stamp the locks of houses, tombs and boxes, or to seal jars and documents, came into popular use in the Middle Kingdom. In shape and size it resembled the scarab beetle, of which it was a representation. It was often carved beautifully from such stones as steatite, schist or jasper, but in most cases it was mass produced in pottery and faience. Inscribed with a charm, or with the cartouche of some dead but potent king, or with the picture of a god or a magical pattern, it served to ward off sickness and the evil eye. It was either worn round the neck or else mounted for use as a ring. The *scarabaeus sacer* was sacred to and thought to be a form of the sun god. The female of this species of beetle lays her eggs in a ball of dung, which

33. A JEWELLED COLLAR WITH PECTORAL
From the tomb of the Pharaoh Tutankhamon

34. A JEWEL OF THE EIGHTEENTH DYNASTY REPRESENTING THE GODDESS MAAT HOLDING THE FEATHER OF RIGHT

35. AN ENAMELLED PECTORAL WITH THE CARTOUCHE OF THE PHARAOH SESOSTRIS II

36. THE JEWELLERY OF A TWELFTH DYNASTY PRINCESS
The cartouches are those of Sesostris II and Sesostris I

she rolls about on the sand until it has accumulated enough grains to be as large as the beetle herself. The Egyptians noted this strange proceeding, and with an entirely characteristic identification recollected that the sun god pushes the sun across the sky in a similar fashion. The identification was confirmed when the young of the *scarabaeus* were seen to hatch out of the ball it propelled in front of it. In just such a way had Ra originally created teeming life from within the circle of the sun.

The Egyptians were jewellers of surpassing excellence. Their skill needs no testimonial. The precious and semi-precious stones they used were as follows: agate, amethyst, beryl, calcite, carnelian, chalcedony, coral, felspar, garnet, haematite, jade, jadeite, jasper, lapis lazuli, malachite, olivine, onyx, pearl, peridot, rock crystal, sard, sardonyx and turquoise. The diamond, opal, ruby and sapphire were unknown. Fine jewelry appears in the First Dynasty, and the art reaches its height in the masterpieces of the Twelfth Dynasty, in particular those found at Dahshur and Illahun (Pl. 35, 36).

Egyptian women were adepts in the field of cosmetics. The use of kohl for lengthening eyebrows, lining the outer corners of the eyes and shadowing the lids was practised from the earliest times. The kohl was in the form of a powder into which the finger was dipped. A special implement for applying the powder was invented at the beginning of the Middle Kingdom, but the toilet apparatus was already extensive in the Old Kingdom, as the implements from the tomb of Hetephras demonstrate. Kohl was of two kinds: the green ore of copper (malachite), popular until the close of the New Kingdom, and the grey ore of lead (galena), in use up to Coptic times. A restricted amount of rougeing with red ochre was carried out. Henna was probably used in the fashion current in modern Egypt for dying the hair, the nails, the palms of the hands and the soles of the feet.

Egyptian perfumes enjoyed a great reputation. Distillation and the use of solutions in alcohol were not known, and the perfumes were in reality scented oils. Subtle blending and maturing was effected with the large number of oils available for use as vehicles. Ingredients included myrrh, frankincense, cardamons, cinnamon, galbanum, bitter almonds, sweet rush, wine, honey, balanos oil and olive oil. Perfumes were also used to sweeten the breath.

THE COOK

The Egyptians were restrained eaters, taking a single main meal each day at sunset. Cooking in the houses of the rich was carried on in a separate building, and fare was varied. The staple meat dishes were beef, lamb and goat, supplemented by the flesh of such wild animals as the antelope and the gazelle. Pork was unclean, for the pig was the animal of Seth. Fish also was eschewed, perhaps because of its smell and its resemblance to decomposing flesh. It was freely eaten by the poorer classes. There were many varieties of vegetable. Onions, leeks, beans, peas, lentils, garlic, turnips and carrots, spinach and radishes, pumpkins and water-melons were plentiful. Fruits included figs, dates, grapes, pomegranates and various berries. Wild-fowl were eaten in abundance and large flocks of geese were fattened and forced. Savour was imparted to the dishes by means of salt from the Delta and a number of seeds and spices. Bread was baked in ovens and on stones.

Beer brewing is pictured on the walls of tombs as early as the Fifth Dynasty. Thick loaves of wheat or barley were lightly baked and allowed to ferment in water. Wine jars occur in the First Dynasty and the vine was cultivated in Egypt itself. Old Kingdom wines appear to have been predominantly red, Middle Kingdom wines predominantly white. The Egyptians cultivated an experienced palate, the wine of Buto being particularly relished. Cellars of wine were laid down and carefully inspected at intervals. 'Excellent wine of the king's growth', runs an inscription on the necks of a group of jars.

CHAPTER VII

The Commoner

This chapter is devoted to the social condition of the bulk of the population of ancient Egypt. The common folk may be roughly divided into three great agglomerations: middle class, soldiery and peasantry. In early dynastic times the numbers of the first two classes were small. The number of special occupations, and consequently the persons engaged in them, was restricted. The two main social spheres under the Old Kingdom were the upper class and the lower class, between whom there was fixed a great gulf. The social revolution of the First Intermediate Period, followed by the wider and more complex economic activity of the Middle Kingdom, initiated a change in the balance of the classes. Specialist trades of many kinds were established on a permanent basis, while the foreign campaigns of a succession of self-confident Pharaohs encouraged the growth of a body of professional soldiers. In addition there had taken place a significant increase in the size of independent urban communities no longer reliant upon the presence and patronage of the crown. Owing to the centralized and paternalistic nature of Pharaonic rule, however, the growth of cities was always retarded in Egypt, and cities did not become an important political element in Nilotic life until Greek times. But by the onset of the New Kingdom there had come into existence a large and prosperous class of tradesmen and artisans who, though holding no land and little property beyond their immediate household possessions, may be designated a middle class. The members of this class consisted in the main of the craftsmen whose callings were enumerated in the previous chapter. They were very largely dependent for their livelihood upon the local nobility, for whose tastes in luxury they catered. They would be found dwelling in four or five-roomed houses in the cities, often in special quarters devoted to their own particular trade. It may be supposed that they owed a clearly defined allegiance to were the various guilds. The guilds, while being in no sense trades unions after the modern fashion, would serve to regulate the internal affairs of the trade in question.

The immediate focal point in the life of the tradesman or craftsman, as in the life of the peasant, was of course the family, whose inspiration was the divine family of Osiris, Isis and Horus. The institution of marriage was much respected, and it seems probable that the majority of unions were love matches rather than affairs of purchase or contract. The status of the chief wife was safeguarded by law, for polygamy was practised by anyone who could afford to do so. The really well-to-do commonly kept a number of harîm women as well as secondary wives, the number of a man's concubines being doubtless a badge of wealth and prestige. Man and wife lived on equal terms, the household goods belonging to the chief wife, whose first male child was recognized as a man's heir even if other sons had previously been born to him by minor wives. The necessity for divorce was recognized, though it is not known precisely how it was effected. A solemn statutory declaration in front of witnesses that a man's wife was put away from him seems to have been required. The father was responsible for educating his children and giving them their start in life, while children owed their father implicit obedience. 'A splendid thing is the obedience of an obedient son.' For his part, it was a man's ambition to boast in his funerary inscription that he had been 'beloved of his father, praised by his mother and loved by his brothers and sisters.'

The women of Egypt, though renowned for many excellent wifely qualities, were equally renowned for their habitual and persistent infidelity. Herodotus, gravely considering the incidence of adultery in the ancient world, placed Egyptian women at the top of the poll. He tells the story of a Pharaoh whom the gods struck blind because of his impiety. They promised to restore his sight when he found a woman faithful to her husband. His queens, his concubines, the women of the court and the towns, peasant women, slaves: all were brought before him. And the king remained blind. He was compelled to summon foreign women to Egypt before the cure was brought about. It will be remembered that Potiphar's wife was a Theban woman, and she bears a marked resemblance to the wife who figured in the popular Egyptian *Tale of the Two Brothers.* In this tale the younger of two brothers was desired by his sister-in-law. 'The seed of the god is in you,' she exclaimed as she took hold of him, 'and my heart would know you as one knows a young man! Come, let us lie together for an hour, and I will give you two pretty garments.' The youth fled in alarm from this formidable lady, who promptly complained to her husband that she had been seduced. The husband set out in hot pursuit of his brother, who in a fit of quite unwarranted self-reproach cut off the too-much-admired member and threw it to the crocodiles. No doubt the enthusiasm of a moment, as Frazer remarked of the priests of Attis, thereupon became the regret of a lifetime. Egyptian women were adepts in the art of attracting admiration. Their dress, their perfumes and cosmetics were described in a section of Chapter VI. Garments of 'fine Upper Egyptian linen' were coveted by Egyptian woman as greatly as Roman women coveted the linen of Cos. Frizzed, depilated, with gilded breasts, blue nipples and scented breath, the typical Egyptian beauty bore a close resemblance to Antony's 'serpent of old Nile,' for whom he counted the world well lost. Like most Orientals, the ancient Egyptians were unflinching seekers after excitement. They were industrious swallowers of elixirs and aphrodisiacs, indefatigable collectors of erotic pictures and papyri, resolute frequenters of the celebrated brothels of Thebes and Memphis. The women were as determined sexual adventurers as the men. It was sufficient for a princess to set eyes on a strapping young man-servant for her to send a maid with the royal ukase: 'Come to my pavilion and let us rest there an hour.' Yet the Egyptian wife also inherited the deference which the heavenly family paid to Isis, the first wife. Isis acted as her husband's regent, she sailed the seas to Byblus to recover his body, she travelled the length of Egypt to gather up his mangled remains, she devised a manner of restoring him to life. She brought up her little son in secret, to protect him from the malevolence of his uncle. She was altogether the perfect pattern of wife and mother, and her lustre was shed on all subsequent wives and mothers. Egyptian women would participate, furthermore, in the special honour accorded to their predecessors in predynastic times, when women were regarded as the mysterious source of life, possessors of psychic powers beyond male experience and guardians of the myths and traditions of the race.

The middle class, like the soldiery and peasantry, was fenced about by an acknowledged system of law. No codification of Egyptian law resembling the great Code of Hammurabi has come down to us, however, and it is doubtful whether any such deliberately formulated code was ever attempted. An innate sense of social morality was strong in every citizen, for the habit of discipline had been inculcated in the Nile valley from the earliest times. The ramifications of the legal system (p. 48) indicate clearly that the rule of law was a reality. A mass of documents dealing with civil rights, property, inheritance, censuses and taxation suggest that the ancient Egyptian, perhaps because of his partly Semitic origin, was something of a connoisseur of the art of litigation. Also of a Semitic nature was his single-minded passion for justice. There was an inborn conviction that every man should have his rights which did not need to be written down. There was no equivocation about what constituted transgression. It was abundantly clear what actions were right and what actions were wrong. Right was what Pharaoh loved, wrong was what he hated. Any action that tended to disturb the *status quo*, the precious equilibrium of the state, was abominated. The conviction that things must always remain as they were at the moment was of course somewhat hard on the underdog. Punishments were prompt and severe, although the Egyptian reverence for living things, for the essence of the divine that informed all nature, forbade the use of the death penalty for any but the most repulsive crimes. Fines, nicely calculated beatings, mutilation and the opening of a specified number of wounds on the body were recognized penalties. No doubt the worst punishments were reserved for the poor, for in the ancient as in the modern world to be poor was considered an offence. It may be supposed that the leaders of the community were sufficiently masters of discreet corruption to avoid the heaviest penalties.

A class of criminal which should be singled out for special mention is the tomb robber. Tomb robbery has been an expert branch of crime in the valley of the Nile for five thousand years. The methods are invariable in dynastic as in historic times. The band of thieves burrows its way into the sepulchre from the top or from the side, leaving the official seals on the door untouched. The mummies are then unceremoniously tipped out of their coffins and the bandages ripped off them. The cooler type of thief saves time by making skilful incisions in the cerements at the places where experience tells him the jewels are likely to be. As many portable valuables as can be carried are snatched up and stuffed into linen bags or leather sacks. Tomb robbery was the most execrated of all offences the ancient Egyptian could commit. By his ruthless destruction of the brittle mummy he robbed the deceased person of eternity. In periods of prosperity the necropoles were left unmolested, but when want and famine were abroad temptation proved too strong and superstitious tabus were cast aside. Those who were ragged and hungry were maddened by the knowledge that beneath their feet lay the cadavers of the bejewelled dead. During the Twentieth and Twenty-first Dynasties an epidemic of tomb robbery broke out which the authorities were powerless to stop. The story is contained in the famous Abbott and Leopold II–Amherst papyri. At last the priests were reduced to collecting the royal mummies by night in the Valley of the Kings and interring thirteen of them in the tomb of Amenophis II and thirty-six of them in a secret cache in the cliffs. There they remained until they were discovered in 1881. Many Pharaohs were at various times hustled hugger-mugger from tomb to tomb. The great Ramses III, for example, was reburied three times. Thrashing, cutting off the ears and nose and eventual impalement breech first awaited the convicted tomb robber.

Business in ancient Egypt was carried on by means of barter. Coined money did not appear until the Persians introduced the silver shekel of Darius. In earlier times a complicated scale of comparative values was in existence whereby the value of an animal, a manufactured object or a piece of agricultural produce could be expressed in terms of other articles. A cow, for example, would be exchanged for an agreed but socially acceptable number of bushels of grain or flax. Graduated weights of stone or metal, sometimes marked to show that they were officially certified as accurate, were used in conjunction with the balance, which was of the type pictured in the psychostasia. From Ramesside times onward values were regularly expressed in terms of the gold, silver or copper *deben*, a standard weight of about ninety-one grammes. There were twelve 'rings' to the *deben* , and the Egyptians used ring money similar to that employed by many primitive communities. Bullion in the form of bangles for the neck, arms and ankles served the dual purpose of display and easy transportation. Metal money was also put up in little linen bags in the form of dust, no doubt the sweepings from the metallurgist's workshop. The standard measure for grain was derived in an interesting manner. The Eye of Horus sign (see title-page) was divided into six portions: a half, a quarter, an eighth, a sixteenth, a thirty-second and a sixty-fourth. The Eye was torn out of the god's head during his encounter with Seth, and later it was reassembled by Thoth. Thoth was also the inventor of mathematics, which may explain why the sign was chosen. The sign was also much revered as a protective amulet or as an all-seeing eye painted on the prow of a ship. Presumably the tradesman regarded it as a safeguard against sharp practice. The complete weight of the Eye was the full barrel or *hekat*, roughly equivalent to our modern gallon. In the New Kingdom a standard weight of four gallons or one sack was adopted. Measures of length consisted of the finger, the palm, the cubit (20.6 inches) and the rod of cord (100 cubits). A larger linear measure was the 'river measure,' which consisted of four thousand cubits. It was employed for geographical purposes. The standard measure of area was the square *khet*, a hundred cubits squared, or approximately two-thirds of an acre. Separate jar measures were employed for beer, milk, honey, wine, oil and incense.

The rewards and privileges of the military leaders were touched on in an earlier chapter. It seems likely that a few specialist soldiers existed during the final decades of the Old Kingdom, but experience in warfare only came to the bulk of the population during the First Intermediate Period. During this period and the Middle Kingdom the regular army, as distinct from a levy raised in times of crisis, came into existence. The ancient Egyptians were not on the whole a warlike race. They hated organized warfare and dodged conscription whenever they could. It was no easy matter to rouse enthusiasm for battle in the breasts of the bulk of the population, and it was only the material rewards of conquest that made foreign campaigning acceptable to the people. They possessed no urge towards domination for its own sake: their impulse was always to live and let live. The gift for dragooning these amiable people into service and making presentable soldiers of them was manifested by only a handful of Pharaohs. The Egyptian armies that marched into Asia were invariably supplemented with a large corps of mercenaries. The instinct for fighting was more highly developed in the Upper than the Lower Egyptian, and it was from Upper Egypt that the military leaders and the backbone of the army were drawn.

During the imperial heyday of the New Kingdom the army swelled to a size that made it a recognizable class within the body of the state. Besides awards made for gallantry in the field, soldiers now commonly received an estate in their homeland for distinguished foreign service. In Ptolemaic times it was recorded that this estate consisted of twelve *khet* of land, free of taxation. The grants of land were made in the area of the great military bases, which resembled such Roman *coloniae* in our own country as Lincoln or Colchester. The presence of townships inhabited by reckless men more familiar with barrack life than sophisticated existence proved irksome to the immediate neighbourhood. The citizens of nearby towns often complained of their turbulent, privileged and moneyed protectors. From the Nineteenth Dynasty the soldiery played the dominant rôle in politics. The generals easily prevailed over the pacific multitudes who relied on them to deal with the ever-increasing threat of invasion. In turn Libyans, Nubians and Greeks, who began as small bodies of auxiliaries or picturesque adjuncts to the royal bodyguard, insinuated themselves into power and ultimately seized the throne. The troops whom the Egyptians employed to help them acquire an empire at length became a scourge for the Egyptians themselves. By the time of Herodotus there were nearly half a million cavalry and infantrymen in the Delta alone, all receiving generous rations of bread, beef and wine if they were not actual owners of land.

The lot of the peasantry, the third class of commoner to be considered, was a hard one. In ancient Egypt the rich were very rich and the poor very poor. The condition of the peasant under the absolute monarchy of the Old Kingdom was particularly burdensome, so much so that a savage social cataclysm was provoked. A tiny oligarchy commanded the physical resources of a vast labour force, organized in permanent battalions of fifty or a hundred men. These battalions were composed of small gangs of five men under the orders of a foreman. The gangs may have represented family units. The Old Kingdom peasant was bound to the soil. He was transferred from one owner to another as part of the estate to which he belonged. If he was fortunate he worked on a royal estate, where discipline was commonly less strict than on estates in private hands. For a period of several weeks every year, probably during the slack season of the Inundation, he was placed solely at the service of the king for purposes of forced labour on the royal palace or pyramid. The plight of the peasant was greatly ameliorated by the revolution which preceded the Middle Kingdom. During the course of widespread reorganization and reform the Pharaohs of the Eleventh and Twelfth Dynasties granted liberalistic charters to each agricultural estate, details of which were entered in a kind of Egyptian Domesday Book. Previously the family tie could be cruelly ignored if it interfered with the gang system, but now the peasantry was loosely and humanely rearranged in family groups. The system of the *corvée* or forced labour remained in force, but the events of the First Intermediate Period won for the peasant a release from the shameful anonymity of the slave gang. Men were no longer counted and registered like cattle. Under the new dispensation the skilled occupation of every man was carefully noted on the population returns submitted to the office of the vizier. Not only the growing company of craftsmen but also the peasants were henceforward to be respected as individuals. Under the New Kingdom the progress of the peasant from serfdom to liberty was signalized by the division of arable land into 'Pharaoh's fields,' small equal segments of soil each in the keeping of a single family. These strips of land were hereditary and inalienable, although they still formed part of some larger estate in the hands of king or nomarch. The strips were demarcated by boundary stones, given identifying names and entered in the archives of the royal granary. The peasant paid his own dues and was to a large extent the master of his own affairs. He still farmed his land, however, in accordance with the local practice of the district, growing grain in a grain area or flax in a flax area.

Evidence of agriculture is found in abundance on the earliest ancient Egyptian dwelling sites. The Neolithic farmers whose culture will be described in the next chapter flourished in the Nile valley between about 6000 and 4500 B.C. There seems little doubt that their knowledge of the cultivation of cereals and the breeding of livestock was derived from Hither Asia. Such communities as the villagers of Sialk in Iran and the even earlier peasants of Mount Carmel appear to have utilized sowing and breeding techniques for many centuries before their appearance in the Nile valley. Flint hoes and sickles with serrated teeth of flint secured by gum occur in the earliest Egyptian cultures, while in Lower Egyptian Neolithic stations well-constructed silos lined with straw matting have been excavated. At this remote date the Neolithic settlers were already spinning flax or plant fibre, growing crops and domesticating cattle, pigs, sheep (or goats), dogs and cats. The crops appear to have consisted of wheat and barley. Wild einkorn (*Triticum aegilopoides*), wild emmer (*T. dicoccoides*) and wild barley (*Hordeum spontaneum*) were all found in Syria and Phoenicia at this time, and derivatives of these wild grasses found their way to the valley of the Nile. The principal form of wheat cultivated in ancient Egypt until the Christian era was emmer (*T. dicoccum*). Bread wheat (*T. vulgare*) was apparently unknown.

About 3000 B.C., during the Thinite or Archaic Period, the plough came into use in Egypt at about the same time as it did in Mesopotamia, perhaps as the result of independent invention. It appears to have been a lineal descendant of the primitive digging stick, the flint or copper hoe and the manual plough. Since it lacked the attributes of the plough proper, wheels, coulter and mould-board, it would be more accurate to call the implement by the Scandinavian term of *ard*. The Egyptian plough consisted of a sharpened stick bound to a shaft, a larger and inverted hoe. Its introduction played an important part in the sudden cultural upsurge of Egyptian civilization soon after the dawn of the dynastic era. Hitherto the heavy work of tilling the soil had occupied all available labour for a considerable part of the agricultural year. Now one man with a pair of oxen could accomplish in half the time what it had previously taken a dozen men to carry out. The use of the plough, coupled with an increase in metallurgical science and an expansion of the irrigation system, was responsible for the adjustment of a semi-nomadic people to the historic pattern of Nilotic life. The plough was one method whereby an enormous saving of time and energy could be effected, and the extra time and energy were quickly harnessed by the Thinite rulers to architectural pursuits. Men could at last be spared from the task of food-producing to build stone mastabas, the Step Pyramid and ultimately the Pyramids of Giza. The technical advances of the Thinite period, far from ameliorating the burden of the majority of the population, ultimately led to the imposition of even more wearisome tasks. The sense of comradeship and joint endeavour in taming the forces of nature was replaced in the Old Kingdom by the rigours of Pharaonic compulsion. The attitude of the ruling class at the vital stage of Egyptian development resulted in the stultification of the earlier spirit of adventure. It must be admitted that the civilization of ancient Egypt constitutes from the technological aspect a case of arrested development. After a beginning of unparalleled brilliance and promise there came into operation a system of religious and social tabus that

129

discouraged the inventive capacity. The Egyptians arrived too early at the conclusion that life in the Nile valley was perfect, that they wished to lead the same lives as their ancestors, that they desired to remain in spirit as close as possible to the Golden Age when the gods reigned upon earth. This emotional and intellectual attitude resulted in the eventual paralysis of the inventive faculty. On the other hand, it can equally well be argued that it is not fair to have expected the Egyptians to contribute more to history than the very considerable amount which in fact they did. If Egyptian women were condemned to the immemorial drudgery of grinding their corn on the saddle quern, by hand and upon their knees, so were the women of all the other great nations of the pre-Christian era. The autocratic and conservative methods of government practised by the Pharaohs were the foundation of those grand achievements of ancient Egyptian civilization which we admire today. Humanity being what it is, perhaps the achievements were inseparable from the absolutism.

A particularly arduous agricultural procedure was the raising of water. Before the arrival of the Hyksôs, when half the civilization of the Nile valley had run its course, the task of bringing the water to the fields from the irrigation canals was performed by hand. The Hyksôs made the labour less wearisome by introducing the *shâdûf*, still in use on the Nile today. The *shâdûf* consisted of a long beam supported by two stakes, one end of which was weighted by stones that acted as a counterpoise when the leather bucket at the other end was dipped into and lifted from the stream. The water was then poured into the runnels that led to the growing crops. The operation of sowing was also carried out by hand. For threshing, a large open air threshing floor was prepared, where the ears of grain were trodden out by oxen or asses. The ears were winnowed by throwing them into the air with shovels, when the wind blew away the chaff and the grain fell into linen cloths spread underneath.

The oxen domesticated by the ancient Egyptians were derivatives of the long-horned wild ox or Urus (*Bos primigenius*) (Pl. 42). Sheep were hardly distinguishable at the outset from the proverbial relatives, the goats. Egyptian sheep were descended from the reddish-coated Mouflon (*Ovis musimon*), a native of Hither Asia. The Mouflon was found at Sialk. A ram with peculiar twisted horns was also known at an early period in Egypt, where it lent its appearance to the god Khnum and was worshipped as the Ram of Mendes. It may be the animal called *Ovis longipes palaeoaegypticus*, but it seems more likely to be *Capra prisca*. *Capra prisca* is the model for the celebrated 'Ram caught in a thicket' found in the tomb of Queen Shubad at Ur. It would be instructive to find an identical animal worshipped in both Sumer and Egypt when the First Dynasty of both kingdoms was being founded. The pig does not appear to have been prolific in ancient Egypt, perhaps because it was associated with Seth. Its prototype was the wild boar. Apart from the ox, the ass was the most common beast of burden. It was sometimes used for ploughing and was the medium for the transport of goods. Mule trains from the Red Sea and the desert oases were familiar sights. The camel was never tamed for this purpose in ancient Egypt. The history of the horse in the ancient world is obscure. The tarpan, with perhaps an element of cross breeding with Przewalski's horse, was being ridden on the grassy steppes of South Russia about 3000 B.C., but it was fully a thousand years before it made any significant spread westwards and southwards. It reached Mesopotamia shortly after 2000 B.C., owing to the exertions of the irresistible Indo-European horsemen. It was introduced to Egypt during the interregnum of the Asiatic Hyksôs. The Egyptians rapidly became outstanding charioteers and breeders of horses. It is stated in the Book of Kings that 'Solomon had horses brought out of Egypt,' and that 'a chariot came up and went out of Egypt for six hundred shekels of silver and a horse for a hundred and fifty.' The Egyptians were also great dog fanciers. Handsome *salukis* or *slughis* are frequently portrayed in wall paintings. Originally the domestic dog was possibly a cross between a jackal and a wolf.

Hieroglyphic characters, which are a prime source of information about the fauna of the Nile valley, depict over two dozen different varieties of bird. Wildfowling was a universal pastime. The birds were either taken in the net or stunned by a wooden or ivory throwing-stick shaped like a boomerang. Fish were speared, and the slaughter of hippopotami and crocodiles by means of cudgels and baited hooks constituted an exhilarating pastime. The nobility indulged in constant drives for game. Lions, panthers, giraffes, elephants, gazelles, ibexes, oryxes, bubalises and leopards were all included in the bag. Many of these animals and birds were adopted as the totems of pre-dynastic clans and in dynastic times continued to lend their names to the nomes.

The peasant occupied a small and squalid hut of mud brick or clay-daubed reed matting. Not for him the bedstead with its padded mattress and linen sheets, the woven hangings, the mats, chairs, cushions and inlaid coffers of the well-to-do. If the Cotswold labourer of a century and a half ago received a shilling a day for his services, it is unlikely that the wages in kind of the Egyptian peasant were more substantial. Yet the soil of the Black Land was not the most heartbreaking soil in the world to farm, the bad years were not harder to bear than they were elsewhere, the Egyptian landowner was not notorious as a cruel taskmaster. The peasant was in general a cheerful, indeed a gay person, not commonly stupefied by fatigue and brutalized by apprehensive fear. He had his songs, his pastimes, his children. Above all, he had the sun. The obligation which he owed his master was a reciprocal one, and he was sustained by the knowledge that he was a member of a sound and generally stable social organization. The tomb paintings which have immortalized his activities were not the expression of an arrogant and domineering power bent upon the subjugation of the lower classes. The models and frescoes which the rich man included among his tomb furnishings indicate an understanding and appreciation of the rôle which the peasant played in the conduct of life. In a peculiarly dignified civilization, the peasant too was not denied his proper dignity. At its best the work of an Egyptian estate must have been invested with a kindly, companionable atmosphere in which each man, regardless of his employment, was regarded as the member of a team or family. The history of the Egyptian peasantry in its warm and sunlit retreat is singularly free from the brooding terror which oppressed the poorest classes of the neighbour countries of the ancient Near East.

CHAPTER VIII

History : One

None of the other great nations of antiquity has left behind such a mass of material of all descriptions as Egypt. The ancient Egyptians turned the valley in which they lived into a veritable museum. They bequeathed to the student of their civilization a seemingly inexhaustible supply of documents and artefacts. It would be impertinent to call the builders of Luxor and Karnak a vanished race, yet for all the evidence about them which has been preserved we must confess that we know singularly little. There seems to be no vital principle which we can deduce, no nerve which we can touch, to bring their culture warm and living to the mind's eye. They are veiled from us by a brooding impersonality.

The reason for this is not far to seek. The ancient Egyptians were indefatigable compilers of records, but the records they kept were couched in conventional terms. They evolved certain formulae which they used over and over again. One grave stele is a repetition of another grave stele. A private letter consists of a tissue of blank and formal phrases. A monumental relief celebrates a feat of arms which research shows to have been either inglorious or actually non-existent. The Egyptians had no desire to express originality or individuality: they tried to be as like each other, and as like their ancestors, as possible. They possessed little sense of the dynamic aspect of history as we know it. How could they come to grips with history and personality when their major philosophical preoccupation was to ignore time and live outside it? The stuff of history—cause and effect, rise and fall, ebb and flow—was no subject for speculation among these strange people.

It is therefore not surprising that the Egyptians produced no native historian to evaluate or give a disinterested account of their civilization. The first historian of Egypt was Herodotus the Greek, and after him other classical writers such as Hecataeus, Strabo, Chaeremon, Josephus, Plutarch and Horapollo commented on the Egyptians with a curiosity which the Egyptians never felt about themselves. The only conscious assistance which the Egyptians render us are contained in a few inaccurate KING LISTS: the Palermo Stone (time of Niuserra), a list from Karnak (time of Tuthmosis III), two tablets from Abydos (time of Seti I and Ramses II), a tablet from Sakkara (time of Ramses II), the Turin Papyrus (time of Ramses II), a list by the Alexandrinian Eratosthenes with additions by the pseudo-Apollodorus (third century B.C.) and the list of the scribe Manetho. Where these tablets or papyri are not actively misleading they are in a fragmentary state. The most important of them is the list in Greek compiled by Manetho, a priest in the reign of Ptolemy II Philadelphos (285–247 B.C.). The list has come down to us in commentaries by Africanus and Eusebius on Josephus, in whose polemical treatise against Apion portions of a lost history by Manetho are quoted. It is from Manetho that the arrangement of the Pharaonic succession into thirty dynasties down to the conquest of Alexander is adopted. It must be remembered that these dynasties are all of unequal duration. Some are plainly apocryphal, some exist contemporaneously side by side, and some number only a handful of Pharaohs while others contain a score. Thus the Twenty-eighth Dynasty consists of a single king who reigns for six years, while the Eighteenth Dynasty consists of fourteen who rule for two hundred and sixty. According to Manetho, the Seventh Dynasty comprises seventy kings who altogether reign for seventy days: an utterly incredible piece of fiction. The Twenty-third,

Twenty-fourth and Twenty-fifth Dynasties are now known to have overlapped one another, though Manetho lists them consecutively. These random examples demonstrate the difficulties entailed in disentangling dynastic history even from a fairly promising source. The greater part of our knowledge is not in fact derived from king lists at all, but from the study of literary and religious texts and archaeological remains. Manetho's list has nevertheless provided a useful framework on which to reconstruct the history of the dynasties. It has served for so long as a set of universal terms of reference in Egyptological literature that any attempt to substitute a revised scheme would be pointless. Familiarity with the list accustoms the student to its shortcomings.

The problems of ancient EGYPTIAN CHRONOLOGY are extremely complex. The Egyptians numbered their years regnally, not continually from a certain fixed point determined by the dawn of an era. Where we might write: 'In 1951 A.D., in the reign of King George VI,' an Egyptian would write: 'In the twenty-fifth year of the reign of the Pharaoh Menkheperra Tuthmosis.' Thus the beginning of every reign constituted a new dating point. The Egyptians were not given to thinking in terms of dynasties, neither were Pharaohs accustomed to call themselves Amenophis, Ramses or Tuthmosis I, II, III or IV. The Pharaoh we name Tuthmosis I is called in his monuments and official documents Akheperkara Tuthmosis, Tuthmosis II is Akheperenra Tuthmosis, Tuthmosis III is Menkheperra Tuthmosis, and so on. Pharaohs went by names, not numbers. Since the length in years of the vast majority of individual reigns is unknown to us, we cannot reckon back towards the date of the first Pharaohs by the simple expedient of adding together all the reigns of their successors. The only method open to us is to rely on astronomical calculations based on similar calculations made by the Egyptians themselves. Unlike most nations in antiquity, the Egyptians used the solar and not the lunar calendar. The moon played an unusually minor rôle in their mythology. The Egyptian year was divided into twelve months of thirty days, to which were added five epagomenal or extra days, making three hundred and sixty-five days in all. The first day of the year began on the first day of the Inundation, the nineteenth of July (Julian). Thereafter the twelve months, each containing three weeks and ten days, were grouped in three seasons of four months' duration: Inundation, Germination and the Warm Season.

The Egyptian year of three hundred and sixty-five days was not quite in accord with the true solar year, which lasted an additional quarter of a day. Each year the fixed ceremonies of the temple and the palace were increasingly if almost imperceptibly retarded. Only the official year was affected, for the agricultural year followed a natural and inevitable cycle. Inundation, sowing and harvest do not depend on any man-made calendar. Early one morning, before dawn on the first day of the Inundation, one of the first astronomers of the academy at Memphis or Heliopolis was watching the sky. He noticed that the bright star Sothis (Sirius, the Dog Star) appeared on the eastern horizon on this particular day at the same moment as the sun. He and his colleagues were profoundly impressed with this heliacal rising of Sothis, and they decided to make it a subordinate point of departure for the Egyptian year. But the rising of Sothis was equally affected by the quarter day solar error, which lost the Egyptian calendar a whole day every four years. It was calculated or observed by successive generations of astronomers, all of whom kept meticulous records, that the three events—rising of sun, rising of Sothis, start of Inundation—occurred in conjunction only once every one thousand four hundred and sixty years. This immense period, invaluable in astronomical and calendrical computation, constituted a 'Sothic cycle.' Modern research establishes that a Sothic cycle would have commenced between 1325 and 1322 B.C., during the Nineteenth Dynasty. This fact is confirmed by ancient scribal records. Therefore the previous cycle would have begun in the Pyramid Age, between 2785 and 2782 B.C. There are certain passages in the Pyramid Texts which seem to convey, albeit obscurely, references not only to the Pyramid Age cycle but to an even earlier cycle which would have commenced between 4245 and 4242 B.C. If this reading of the Pyramid Texts is correct, we may surmise that the Egyptian astronomer gazed at the morning sky at Memphis during the predynastic era, when the Egyptian calendar was devised. There are also excellent reasons for thinking, however, that the calendar was not in fact introduced until the reign of Zoser in the Third Dynasty, perhaps by Imhotep. There are also scribal notations which enable us to fix with certainty the dates of three reigns, those of Sesostris III of the Twelfth Dynasty and Amenophis I and Tuthmosis III of the Eighteenth Dynasty. By combining such astronomical data with dates given in king lists and especially the cross-dating obtained from the histories of neighbouring countries, a tentative date of about 3300 B.C. or 3200 B.C. can be given for the beginning of the dynastic epoch. It so happens that this date also corresponds with the approximate date of the first rudimentary hieroglyphic inscriptions on stone vases, clay seal impressions and wooden and ivory tablets. Thus if we accept Tylor's classic definition of civilization as 'the literate culture of cities' we find that the commencement of dynastic civilization conveniently coincides with the commencement of writing.

The history of the predynastic occupation of the Nile valley was entirely unknown to ancient historians. Information about Egyptian culture anterior to the First Dynasty has been elicited by modern archaeology, for the most part during the course of the last half century. With the most remote division of the predynastic period, the PALAEOLITHIC or OLD STONE AGE, we shall not long concern ourselves. The successive cultures of the Egyptian Palaeolithic belong to a time when the geography of the Nile valley and the whole of North Africa

was so different from that of the present day as to be un-
recognizable. The climate was equatorial, the steaming and
swampy river flowed down the whole breadth of its valley, the
desert may have been covered with luxuriant forest. The
development of the stone industries along the sedimentary
terraces of the Nile resembled the Western European sequence.
Large Chellean and Acheulean hand-axes were succeeded by a
smaller Levalloisean-type industry, known as the Aterian. A
microlithic or small blade industry called the Sebilian occupies
the position of the Upper Palaeolithic horizon in Europe. We
may perhaps hazard a guess that the makers of these stone
industries were wandering bands of huntsmen, but they left
behind such scanty evidence of their mode of life that we
cannot make any profitable comment about them. It can safely
be said that they made no positive contribution to the later
grandeur of ancient Egypt.

The history of ancient Egypt properly began to unfold when a
cooling climate initiated the desiccation of the fertile Sahara
at the end of the Upper Palaeolithic epoch. This drastic change
of climate was interconnected with a contemporary climate
change in Europe which stimulated the rapid recession of the
glaciers. By the onset of the NEOLITHIC or NEW STONE AGE, to
which a very rough date of 6000 B.C. may be given, the valley
of the Nile was assuming the configuration it possessed in
dynastic times. The Sahara, except for its oases, now consisted
of withered scrub unsuitable for the survival of the large
mammals which roamed North Africa in Palaeolithic times.
The only animals to survive the climate crash in any quantity
were the rhinoceros and the hippopotamus, and it may have
been in quest of dwindling herds of these animals that bands
of huntsmen began to pay regular visits to the banks of the
Nile. The huntsmen, who soon began to settle in the valley
and make it the base of their operations, were probably of
mixed Semitic, Bantu and Berber stock, tribesmen from Hither
Asia commingling with tribesmen from the African Interior.

The subsequent racial amalgam consisted of non-Negro and near-Negro types. After some time, perhaps owing to influence from the culturally advanced settlements of Mesopotamia, villages were founded, leading strains of domestic animals built into herds and the rich black Nilotic soil sown with vegetables and primitive forms of grain. It is probable that the first settlers were for many generations semi-nomadic, alternating their agricultural activities with far-flung hunting expeditions.

There were two main concentrations of these Neolithic cultivators and pastoralists. In Middle Egypt and on the borders of the Delta existed a culture of settled habits known as the MERIMDEAN culture, closely allied to the culture of the FAYÛM. In Upper Egypt there dwelt the members of the quasi-nomadic TASIAN culture. The names of predynastic cultures are derived from sites where they were first unearthed or where they appear to be most representative. The Merimdean and Tasian cultures both possessed beautifully executed flint industries, comprising slate palettes, polished axes, many varieties of arrowheads and bone harpoons, needles and fish hooks. Merimdean pottery consisted of a series of coarse un-decorated baked clay pots and a range of fine red and black ware. The characteristic Tasian pot is a pointed 'tulip vase' with white encrusted geometrical patterns on its black surface. In Merimdean villages the crops which had been cut with wooden sickles with serrated flint teeth were stored in mat-lined silos. In both areas the dead were buried seated or lying in a curious doubled-up posture. Vases containing the remains of food and drink and hunting weapons were enclosed with the dead man. On occasion a handful of grain appears to have been sprinkled over the corpse as it lay in the grave. This custom, no doubt intended to quicken the dead flesh or to be symbolic of its resurrection, anticipates later representations of crops growing from the buried body of Osiris.

It is remarkable that two distinct cultural groups should

already exist in the Nile valley at this remote epoch. The villagers of the Merimdean group, occupying oval huts clustered inside a palisade, showed a greater subtlety in their manner of manufacturing tools and pottery than the Tasians. The invasion of Upper Egypt by the Followers of Horus from the Delta is thus early foreshadowed. The dual nature of Egyptian history, divided between the sophisticated lowlanders and their brothers from the uplands, is apparent at the outset of Nilotic history. It seems likely that the Delta dwellers established themselves in Egypt at a slightly earlier date than the Upper Egyptians and brought their agriculture and science more rapidly to perfection. Some scholars nevertheless refuse to accept this hypothesis of the early supremacy of the Delta. They prefer to believe that the predominant influence was exerted by Upper Egypt, whose inhabitants may have reached Egypt from the direction of the Red Sea. The larger extent and better state of preservation of the predynastic cultures of Upper Egypt is advanced as an argument in favour of this view. It may be noted that the ancient Egyptians themselves appear to have been convinced that their place of origin was African rather than Asian. They made continued reference to the land of Punt as their homeland. In dynastic times ambitious trading expeditions were despatched to Punt, which has been identified as modern Somaliland.

The development of the Merimdean culture during the major part of the ENEOLITHIC or COPPER AGE is unfortunately little known, perhaps because the damper conditions of the atmosphere of Lower Egypt are more inimical to the survival of dwellings and artefacts than the dry heat of Upper Egypt. The term Eneolithic signifies the addition of a small number of copper tools and copper objects to the Neolithic inventory. The Eneolithic phase may be said to open about or after 4500 B.C. In Lower Egypt the phase is represented by the MAADIAN culture, and it may have been representatives of this culture who were the Followers of Horus who marched against

Upper Egypt. A likely date for this invasion is about 4245 B.C., the period when the Egyptian calendar may have been invented by astronomers who can be shown to have made their observations in the latitude of Memphis and Heliopolis. The civilization of Lower Egypt was almost certainly more advanced at this date than the civilization of Upper Egypt, and such characteristics of Lower Egyptian culture as fine stone vases and the rectangular house are found in Upper Egyptian contexts. The ascendancy of the Delta dwellers was nevertheless short-lived, for in Upper Egypt the Neolithic Tasian culture was superseded by the powerful BADARIAN culture which grew steadily in strength until it entirely reversed the earlier balance of power.

The Badarian villagers appear to have inherited the sites of the Tasians about 4000 B.C. with no break in continuity. Over a dozen Badarian settlements have been excavated, yielding a great wealth of objects. The standard hut was of oval shape and light wood construction. Skin garments were now supplemented with linen, and ornaments consisted of carved ivory combs, pieces of ostrich egg shell, quartz and felspar beads and necklaces composed of little copper tubes. Copper was at first used sparingly and cold hammered, but under the Badarians the practice of casting came into use. Blue-green faience and enamels composed of pounded rock crystal were introduced. The leading ceramic was a skilfully fired burnished red pot with black edges. Burial followed the fashion of the previous period, clay or ivory figurines of naked women being sometimes placed in the grave. It is indisputable that Asian ideas were reaching Upper Egypt at this time, some no doubt from Lower Egypt, but others from the direction of the Red Sea. The boats which the Badarians used were of the type common in the Persian Gulf, and it was by this route that Upper Egypt was chiefly fertilized by notions from Asia. Two facies of the Badarian culture deserve mention, the AMRATIAN and the GERZEAN. The Amratians were contemporaries of the earliest

Badarians, and their activities are particularly remarkable in the stage known as NAGAADA I. The Gerzeans may have represented a late influx of individual character into Badarian society. It is possible that they brought with them from the environs of Syria important agricultural innovations. The Gerzeans were chiefly in evidence in NAGAADA II. Both Amratians and Gerzeans produced exquisite flint implements, which rank as among the most beautiful ever made. Their pressure-flaked comma, swallow-tail and scimitar knife blades are so delicate that they could only have been employed for ceremonial purposes.

What can legend and later record tell us about the political relationship between Upper and Lower Egypt in predynastic times? In Pharaonic times it was always recognized that Egypt was divided from the dawn of its history into two states with rigidly demarcated frontiers. There were two treasurers, two viziers, two residences and two crowns in Pharaonic times. Certain legitimate conclusions may be drawn from the twin nature of the state about the character of predynastic government. In the kingdom of Upper Egypt, differentiated geographically and perhaps ethnographically from its rival, there ruled at Hierakonpolis a king who wore a white crown. The name of the capital, which signifies Falcon Town, was perhaps a legacy from the dominion of the Followers of Horus in 4245 B.C. The realm of the white crown was placed beneath the protection of the vulture goddess Nekhebet, whose shrine was situated on the opposite side of the river to Hierakonpolis at el-Kab. The emblem of the kingdom was the sedge. In the Delta there ruled in the city of Pe a king who wore a red crown. His realm was protected by the cobra goddess Buto, whose home was at nearby Dep. The emblem in this case was the bee. Upper Egypt was divided into twenty-two and Lower Egypt into twenty nomes, separate administrative areas each with its own capital, governor and fetish. The fetish or standard, dedicated to a specific god or goddess, is suggestive of the clan totem.

Upper Egypt was under the patronage of the god Seth, but during the dual monarchy of Hierakonpolis and Pe his overlordship was renounced in favour of Horus. Horus was the god of Lower Egypt, and it was in 4245 B.C. that he achieved the subjugation of Seth, after the epic battle recounted in religious literature. It is not easy to determine whether the father of Horus, Osiris, belonged initially to Upper or Lower Egypt. Probably he was commonly worshipped in both kingdoms. Soon after 4245 B.C. the grip of Lower Egypt was relaxed, and the two kingdoms existed side by side as independent entities for a thousand years. It was during this millennium that each evolved its indestructible autonomy.

The struggle between the red and white adversaries was renewed about 3300 B.C. A decorated macehead from Hierakonpolis records the resounding victory of 'KING SCORPION' over the armies of the Delta. The principle which underlies the writing of hieroglyphs is the rebus, and probably the conqueror's name as it occurs on the macehead was pronounced in the same manner as the word for scorpion, in the way a man called Penn might sign a letter by drawing a picture of a pen. It seems likely that the Scorpion's conquest did not extend beyond Memphis, the Delta remaining a bastion of lowland resistance. The effective unification of the Two Lands was carried out by the Scorpion's successor, NARMER, whom later Egyptians called Menes. A great schist palette and a macehead depicting the triumphant conclusion of his campaign against the Delta were unearthed at Hierakonpolis (Pl. 26, 27). On the reverse side of the palette the king, wearing the white crown, smashes the skull of a member of the Harpoon Nome. On the obverse, wearing the captured red crown, he marches forward preceded by the standard-bearers of the conquering nomes.

Narmer was the first king of dynastic Egypt. His successors during the First and Second Dynasties ruled from the unidentified town of This, which was in the locality of Abydos. These two dynasties comprise the THINITE PERIOD or ARCHAIC

PERIOD, dated between 3300 and 2778 B.C. The king lists and Manetho are unreliable guides to this period, which has been reconstructed to some extent from archaeological sources. These sources are themselves exiguous, which is peculiarly exasperating in view of the fact that in the five centuries from the battles of the Scorpion and Narmer to the beginning of the Third Dynasty an amazing cultural advance was made. In this relatively short space of time the Egyptians developed the complete theory and practice of hieroglyphic writing. They brought architecture to the high pitch to which the Step Pyramid of Zoser, first Pharaoh of the Third Dynasty, is ample testimony. They evolved their civil and religious institutions in all their essential complexity, and the central power of the state was consolidated. These achievements suggest that the kings of This were building on firm foundations laid by the predynastic kings of Hierakonpolis and Pe. The second king of the *First Dynasty*, Aha, appears to have been buried at Sakkara, which would suggest that the situation of Memphis as the most satisfactory administrative centre was already recognized. Aha's mastaba is a remarkable building, and another First Dynasty mastaba at Sakkara which deserves note is the large tomb of Hemaka, chief minister of the Pharaoh Wedimu. The six successors of Aha, however, were all buried in their homeland, in the ROYAL TOMBS of the holy city of Abydos. The tombs contained no bodies, and may in fact be cenotaphs. The grave goods of the Royal Tombs consist of beautifully wrought copper vessels, stone vases and ornaments of gold, lapis lazuli and turquoise. It is evident from their burials that these early kings were able to maintain specialist craftsmen and to command the manufactures of foreign craftsmen by trade. Already the young state was sufficiently confident to undertake organized expeditions to Libya, Nubia and Sinai for the dual purpose of obtaining raw materials and taking punitive measures against local tribes. The names of these first Pharaohs are carved in the quarries and their achievements recorded on tablets of ivory. Among the religious ceremonies instituted in this dynasty were the coronation, the Two Lands festival and the Heb-Sed feast, all celebrated regularly in later periods. The ceremonies were designed not only for religious purposes, but also to concentrate worship and power on the person of the king. The absolute character of the monarchy clearly emerged at this remote period.

Under the seven kings of the *Second Dynasty* these tendencies were carried farther. The Second Dynasty kings were buried at Memphis, which confirms the shifting trend of the administration. The religious prestige of Memphis and Heliopolis no doubt helped to attract them towards the Delta, for the Thinites were already patrons of Ptah and were soon to fall beneath the spell of the sun cult. The decision of the monarchy to employ religion as a major instrument of policy was reflected in the regularity of religious observance. Nevertheless no parallel simplification of the pantheon accompanied the simplification of the machinery of government. The ancient gods and demons of the nomes remained unaffected and retained their primitive appeal. The Pharaoh Peribsen, perhaps indignant at the unshakable ascendancy of the intellectual ideas of Lower Egypt, attempted to reassert the supremacy of Seth, the patron of his Upper Egyptian forefathers. He boldly substituted the name of Seth for the name of Horus in the royal titulary, but his gesture of nonconformism quickly proved abortive. Peribsen joins the later Pharaohs, Shepseskaf and Akhenaton, in the roll of kings who tried unsuccessfully to challenge the power of the priesthood.

The legal and fiscal organizations which operated in the nome capitals throughout Egyptian history appear to have been defined during the Thinite Period. Already a paramount duty of the nomarch, revealed in his official titles, was the maintenance of the canals and dykes in his territory. A macehead of King Scorpion shows the king lifting the first spadeful of soil for a new canal, and care of the waterways was always to be one of

Pharaoh's most urgent tasks. From Thinite times dates the accurate measurement and meticulous recording of the yearly height of the Inundation. It can be claimed that under the dispensation of the kings of the first two dynasties the land of Egypt progressed from the sophisticated barbarism of the Neolithic and Eneolithic periods to the proud status of civilization. This progress was to a large extent a matter of necessity. The catastrophic desiccation of North Africa threw together a great mass of human beings into a narrow fertile valley. To maintain the large population and to exploit the full potentialities of the new skill of agriculture demanded the maximum amount of co-operation between neighbours. Every clan in the crowded valley had to learn how to live harmoniously with the clans which jostled it on either side. Mutual action in the erection of irrigation works for the common benefit engendered a sense of discipline and cohesion. But it was not the challenge of nature alone which impelled the ancient Egyptians towards their ultimate triumphs. Their inborn genius also played its part, a genius perhaps produced and fostered by the apparently unpromising admixture of racial strains of different attitude and experience

The OLD KINGDOM opens about 2778 B.C. with the *Third Dynasty* (2778–2723 B.C.), although the crystallizing processes at work under the Thinites continued until the Fourth Dynasty. The first Pharaoh of the Third Dynasty, ZOSER, was himself a Thinite, for he was the son of Khasekhemui, last king of the previous dynasty. Zoser was the first great terrestrial Pharaoh to the later Egyptians, and his vizier IMHOTEP (p. 50) was considered as mighty a man as his master. The Step Pyramid, grand memorial to their joint endeavour, was described in Chapter V. Zoser's large mastaba at Beit Khallaf near Abydos was probably built before his pyramid, but at some time in his reign the king decided to make his permanent residence at Memphis. Subsequent Old Kingdom Pharaohs invariably ruled from Lower Egypt, which gives rise

147

to the term *Memphite Empire* as an occasional alternative for Old Kingdom. Zoser continued the expeditions and razzias of the Thinite kings into foreign territory, quarrying granite at Aswan, limestone at Tura and copper at Sinai. The end of the Third Dynasty, like the end of all the dynasties with three or four exceptions, is obscure. We are also ignorant in the majority of cases of the precise relationship between each Pharaoh and his successor.

The *FOURTH DYNASTY* (2723–2563 B.C.) represents the peak of Egyptian accomplishment under the Old Kingdom. The founder of the dynasty, SNOFRU, was evidently a man of great character and energy. His two recorded campaigns in Nubia and Libya led to the capture of seven thousand and eleven thousand tribesmen respectively, and his name and titles are recorded on the rocks at Sinai. He built two pyramids at Dahshur, and the Palermo Stone credits him with the construction of many temples and fortresses. He seems to have imported wood for his buildings from Phoenicia, where an Egyptian colony was established at Byblus early in the Old Kingdom. It is unfortunate that the records are less informative about the successors of this formidable dynast: CHEOPS, CHEPHREN and MYCERINUS. By one of the characteristic mischances of history, the entries on the Palermo Stone relating to the reigns of these three kings are mutilated. Their fame lingered in the memory of the Egyptians, for many apocryphal and outrageous anecdotes were related about them to the avid and credulous Greek historians, who like all Greeks possessed a taste for scandalous gossip. It is evident from their monuments that the three Pharaohs were men of overwhelming authority: the pyramids of Giza could have been raised only under an exceptionally wealthy and well-organized government. The successor of Mycerinus was probably the little-known Dedefra, who built his pyramid at Abu Roash. The last king of the dynasty, Shepseskaf, appears to have rebelled against the growing authority of the sun priests of Heliopolis, for he refused

37. PAINTED WOODEN STATUES OF MAIDSERVANTS
From the tomb of Meketra at Thebes
Eleventh Dynasty

38. A SHIP UNDER SAIL

39. SPINNERS AND WEAVERS AT WORK ON AN ESTATE
Models from the tomb of Meketra
Eleventh Dynasty

to take the title 'Son of Ra,' borne by the successors of Cheops, and instead of a pyramid he erected an odd sarcophagus-shaped mastaba at Sakkara. He succumbed after a reign of four years, whereupon the Heliopolitan priesthood were quick to seize power.

The kings of the *Fifth Dynasty* (2563–2423 B.C.) made a point of adding the title 'Ra' to their names, as Khafra (Chephren), Menkaura (Mycerinus) and Dedefra had done. The papyrus Westcar relates that the first three kings of the dynasty, Userkaf, Sahura and Neferirka, were triplets begotten by Ra on the wife of one of his priests. This legend indicates that the priests of Ra-Atum may have elected their nominees or even their own high priests to the throne. All six kings of the dynasty were slavish devotees of the sun god, to whom they built rich temples of novel design in which are found the inscriptions known as the Pyramid Texts. They do not seem to have exercised a strict sacerdotal dictatorship over their people, for from this time can be traced the rise of Osirianism, the popular religion. The monarchs of the preceding dynasty were gods: they alone after death were privileged to journey across the heavens with their retainers in the divine barque. The religious squabbles of Shepseskaf with the priests damaged the majesty and authority of this conception in the eyes of the populace, and Shepseskaf cast additional discredit on the royal office by marrying his daughter to a court official, thus corrupting the sacred blood of the royal line. Under the Fifth Dynasty a distinctly more democratic habit of thought is discernible, for which the weakening of central control was responsible. Priests seldom make efficient kings. The nomarchs began to assert themselves so effectively against the monarchy that a vizier for Upper Egypt was appointed in the second half of the dynasty. The vizier was probably an Upper Egyptian nomarch whose specific duty it was to keep his fellow nomarchs in order. The monarchy contributed to its own downfall by making generous grants of land and money to the nobility and priesthood, a dangerous practice which was to assume serious proportions towards the close of the Sixth Dynasty. The kings of this religious dynasty were nevertheless given to mundane activities, which included foreign campaigns on an increasing scale. Sahura in particular was responsible for major operations against the Asiatics in the form of sieges and pitched battles.

These military proclivities were even more pronounced under the Pharaohs of the *Sixth Dynasty* (2423–2300 B.C.). Expansion southwards now became a fixed idea. One after another the kings of Egypt fought their way into Nubia, and their prolonged effort in this direction may have contributed to the fatal exhaustion at the end of the dynasty. Lengthy concentration of troops in Upper Egypt for the purpose of sustained assault in Nubia would render Lower Egypt, her defences neglected, a tempting prey to the tribesmen of the eastern desert who eventually overran the Delta. It appears that only the inhabitants of the traditionally warlike uplands received adequate military training at this time: the untrained lowlanders would therefore be burdened with an additional handicap when confronted with the fierce Bedouins. The nomarchs of Upper Egypt, who supplied the king's armies and acted as his generals, steadily increased their prerogatives until they became petty potentates in their own right. The nomarch of Elephantine became especially powerful. He regulated affairs in Nubia and was permitted an unprecedented measure of personal initiative. With the king spending much of his time in far-away Memphis, the balance of power weighed more and more heavily in favour of the barons of Upper Egypt. While they preoccupied themselves with their own diminutive kingdoms and their thrusts into Nubia, Lower Egypt fell into the clutches of the enemy.

The Sixth Dynasty nevertheless numbers two kings of outstanding ability, Pepi I and Pepi II. PEPI I ruled for over half a century. His troops not only made the customary forays to mines and quarries but penetrated as far as Palestine. The general on this last occasion was Weni, whose autobiography was quoted in Chapter IV. Weni was sent five times against the various Bedouin tribes, finally launching a surprise attack on their Palestinian base after a journey by sea. Pepi was an energetic builder, and remains of his temples have come to light at Bubastis, Tanis, Dendera, Koptos and Abydos. He was sufficiently self-assured to marry the two daughters of a magnate of Abydos, probably in defiance of a ban by the Heliopolitan priests. By the elder sister he had a son called Merenra and by the younger the future Pepi II. Merenra was a gifted young man whose five-year reign opened auspiciously. He sent the experienced statesman Merira to Edfu as nomarch, with instructions to prepare a detailed plan for the annexation of Nubia. The nomarch of Elephantine, Iri, and his son Herkhouf were sent on three long voyages of discovery to the land of Yam in Southern Nubia. The two explorers opened up hitherto unknown trade routes and persuaded the native chieftains whom they encountered during their travels to make peaceful submission to Merira. The ideal of the youthful Pharaoh was to colonize Nubia by pacific methods, not to crush and terrorize it. This enlightened project was not to be realized, for on his death the regents of his six-year-old halfbrother Pepi embarked on a policy of repression which resulted in a series of Nubian revolts. Herkhouf made yet a fourth journey, however, bringing back from the African Interior one of the Danga dwarfs who were a constant source of amusement at the courts of the Pharaohs. The reign of PEPI II was the longest in Egyptian history. He died a centenarian. The first half of his reign was brilliantly prosperous and uneventful, but during the decades of the king's senility the shadows began to fall upon the bright glories of the Old Kingdom. The populace took advantage of Pharaoh's impotence and the self-absorbed manoeuvring of the nomarchs to press for social reforms which were too readily granted them. Perhaps the atmosphere of the court had grown supine, luxurious and liberalistic, in contrast to the vigorous and ascetic spirit which pervaded it in the heyday of the Memphite Empire. The decrepit king gave way to the greedy clamour of the priesthood and the nomarchs for additional lands and privileges. The priests in particular were avid in their demands for tax-free gifts of land from the crown estates, which the pious old Pharaoh was not reluctant to grant them. It is possible also that the economic structure of the Old Kingdom had been undermined by excessive architectural activity from the Fourth Dynasty onwards. Only the group of nomarchs in the extreme uplands near the Nubian border and in the environs of Thebes seem to have shown self-restraint in their dealings with one another and to have stood steadfast in the face of growing popular agitation. They were thus able to hold firm when the invader flooded into Lower Egypt at the precise moment when the populace broke into open rebellion. The Delta and Middle Egypt were plunged into fearful chaos. Their nobles were dispossessed, a reign of terror commenced, palaces and temples were destroyed. For nearly three hundred years, from the closing years of Pepi II to the foundation of the Middle Kingdom, anarchy ruled in Egypt.

This confused and imperfectly understood epoch is known as the FIRST INTERMEDIATE PERIOD (2300–2065 B.C.). The period is so called because it stands intermediate between the Old and Middle Kingdoms. The events of these centuries are difficult to reconstruct. A remarkable account of them is given in a long text called the *Admonitions of a Sage*. Since it gives a vivid picture of the state of the country at all similar periods of social upheaval, the text is worth quoting at some length. 'The rabble is elated,' laments the Sage, 'and from every city goes up the cry: "Come! let us throw out the aristocrats!"' The land is full of rioters. When the ploughman goes to work he takes a shield with him. The Inundation is disregarded. Agriculture is at a standstill. The cattle roam wild. Everywhere the crops rot. Men lack clothing, spices, oil. Everything is filthy: there is no such thing as clean linen in these days! The dead are thrown into the river. People abandon the cities and live in tents. Buildings are fired, though the palace still stands. But Pharaoh is kidnapped by the mob. The poor have become rich. The man who went barefoot now owns a fortune. The woman who used to study her complexion in the pool now possesses a bronze mirror. Slaves wear ornaments of gold, lapis lazuli, silver, malachite and carnelian. Luxury is rampant, but the ladies of the nobility exclaim: "If only we had something to eat!" They are ashamed of being seen in rags. They are embarrassed when someone greets them. They are forced to prostitute their daughters. They are reduced to sleeping with men who were once too badly off to take a woman. Today there is no trading with Byblus. No one can get pine wood for coffins, funerary materials or the oils for embalming which were once brought from as far afield as Crete. There is a gold shortage, and raw materials for proper burial are exhausted. Nowadays it seems very important that the oasis dwellers should bring in caravans of their once despised produce!'

Manetho's *Seventh Dynasty*, numbering seventy kings in seventy days, was almost certainly fictional. Perhaps Manetho inserted such a topsy-turvy entry in his list for the purpose of conveying in a picturesque manner the utter confusion of the political scene. The Memphite succession was assumed down to about 2242 B.C. by the feeble *Eighth Dynasty*, which maintained nominal rule over Lower Egypt in desperate circumstances. In Upper Egypt the eight nomes nearest the Nubian border banded together under the nomarch of Koptos, though it was necessary to coerce the nomarchs of Hierakonpolis, Edfu and Elephantine into the confederation. This division of the country lasted for a half century, when a more definite grouping began to emerge. The nomarch of Herakleopolis, a determined person called Kheti I, wrested the throne of Lower Egypt from the tottering Eighth Dynasty and founded the *Ninth (Herakleopolitan) Dynasty* (2242–2150 B.C.). He also led an army against the Upper Egyptians grouped around the ensign of Koptos and inflicted a sharp defeat on them. It was nearly a century before the Upper Egyptians found a real champion among their number, but eventually he appeared in the person of Intef I, founder of the *Eleventh (Theban) Dynasty*. At about the same time the Herakleopolitans, who had been ruling effectively in Lower Egypt, were credited with the establishment of a second dynasty, the *Tenth (Herakleopolitan) Dynasty* (2150–2060 B.C.), which in reality was a mere extension of the Ninth Dynasty upon the accession of Kheti II. War between the Thebans and the Herakleopolitans was now joined in earnest. Intef and the two namesakes who followed him adopted the hollow title of King of Upper and Lower Egypt and attempted to march their troops down the valley. At first the Herakleopolitans had no difficulty in containing their enemies. More, they invaded Theban territory and captured Abydos.

Eventually, however, after a century of bitter skirmishing, the fifth leader of the Theban party, MENTUHETEP II (2065–2060 B.C.), proved to be a general of outstanding skill. He not only recaptured Abydos: he forced his way downstream until he had made himself master of the whole of Egypt. His conquest was not effected without much bloodshed. The Herakleopolitans, perhaps weakened by their altruistic campaigns under Kheti II to rid the Delta of the invader, contested the Theban advance strenuously. The nomes of Asyut and Hermopolis in particular put up a resolute resistance. But at last Mentuhetep bestrode the Two Lands as a much-needed supreme chief, bringing to an end the sorry interlude of civil war.

The *ELEVENTH DYNASTY*, from the year 2065 B.C., undertook the resumption of coherent rule in Egypt for the first time since the end of the Old Kingdom. From the date of Mentuhetep's victory is reckoned the second classic epoch of Egyptian civilization, the MIDDLE KINGDOM (2065–1580 B.C.). The work of pacification was carried on by MENTUHETEP III (2060–2010 B.C.). An uneasy truce was proclaimed with the tribesmen of the eastern and western deserts and control over Nubia was gradually reasserted. The power of the nomarchs was not easily broken after so long a period of individual action in the sphere of politics, but internal policy demanded the deprivation of a large part of their former freedom. Accordingly the hereditary succession of the nomarchs was abolished, the office becoming once more a crown appointment. The nomarchs of Beni Hasan alone escaped the ban, perhaps because of a bargain they struck in throwing in their lot with the Thebans at a critical juncture in the civil war. Mentuhetep III revived the system of centralized administration which made his country great under the Fourth Dynasty and was soon to make it equally great under the Twelfth. It was of course the only possible system of rational government for a land with the physical conformation of the valley of the Nile. From the very beginning the Pharaohs of the Middle Kingdom were preoccupied with the reformation of the legal system. They were great law givers, obsessed with the ideal of Justice. All men were to be considered equal in the eyes of the law. The democratic impulses of the Old Kingdom, which had been so disastrously stifled, were prudently acknowledged and ennobled by the great kings of the Middle Kingdom.

The new policies restored the country to a thriving condition. Sensible and authoritative direction put fresh heart into the people. The king paid special attention to the regulation and improvement of the water supply and the reconstruction of irrigation works shattered or neglected during the years of anarchy. It was under the two illustrious Mentuheteps that the cult of Amon-Ra began to emerge, encouraged by the monarchy as a counterbalance to the fervid enthusiasm for Osiris which was sweeping through the country. Amon-Ra was the god of Thebes and after the triumph of the Theban party he became the national, or rather nationalist, deity. His association with the Theban royal family and his military reputation ensured him continued prosperity under the New Kingdom. Nevertheless the most striking religious feature of the dynasty was the immense prestige now enjoyed by Osiris.

It was at the end of the Fifth Dynasty that the faithful began
to make the Osirian pilgrimage to Abydos and not to Heliopolis, which gives point to the long tussle for Abydos between
the forces of Thebes and Herakleopolis. The two sides were
fighting for possession of the shrine of Osiris, which far out-
weighed the strategic importance of Abydos as a town. The
proletarian uprisings which brought the Old Kingdom crashing
down firmly established the popular god in public esteem.
The Theban princes paid homage to him, while adopting Amon-
Ra as their own aristocratic god. The mysteries of Osiris at
Abydos now assumed great importance. From this time onwards every dead man, whether Pharaoh or commoner, was
entitled to be judged before Osiris and declared 'justified.'
Under the Eleventh Dynasty the political and religious
resurgence was accompanied by a new cultural impetus. There
was a daring re-interpretation of artistic tradition, manifested
in novel architectural conceptions and a rough and invigorating
approach to sculpture. The centuries of disruption rendered
Egypt indirect service in that they ultimately induced a mood
of enterprise and decision.

The destinies of the ephemeral Mentuheteps who conclude
the Eleventh Dynasty are obscure. It is possible that the throne
was wrested from the last Mentuhetep by the vizier Amenemhat or one of Amenemhat's family. The vizier is known to
have led ten thousand men on a campaign in the eastern
desert under Mentuhetep IV, and it was an Amenemhat who
became first Pharaoh of the resplendent *TWELFTH DYNASTY*
(2000–1785 B.C.). The capacity for administration shown by
AMENEMHAT I (2000–1970 B.C.) accords well with the suggestion that he was connected with the vizierate. He moved the
capital once more to Memphis, though the influence of Thebes
and its god was in no way diminished. He then turned his
attention to internal affairs. He began by constructing a
defence line called the Wall of the Prince across the entire
eastern frontier of the Delta. The line was intended to prevent

any repetition of the Bedouin incursions which devastated
Lower Egypt three hundred years before. He next occupied
himself with the thorny problem of apportioning water rights,
also a source of dispute among a people to whom supplies of
water meant not only prosperity but life itself. He redefined
the frontiers of the nomes with exact precision, shrewdly
encouraging the nomarchs to abandon their military pretensions in favour of the peaceful routine of administration.
Under his wise direction the Two Lands attained a high level
of ordered affluence. He also resumed the grasp of Nubian
affairs which was to some extent relaxed in the last years of the
previous dynasty and began the sporadic forays against the
Libyans which were to be continued throughout the reigns of his
successors. His thirty years of sagacious activity were ill rewarded:
he fell victim to that occupational hazard of the Egyptian
Pharaoh, a harîm conspiracy. There was some justice, however,
in the fact that he was thus paid out for his own probable
usurpation.

His son, SESOSTRIS I (1970–1936 B.C.), was campaigning in
Libya when the news of his father's assassination reached him.
He rushed back post-haste to Memphis to prevent the conspiracy from spreading. From what we know of this martial
young man, we may be sure that he dealt with the plotters
with resolute severity. With great foresight he afterwards
elevated his eldest son to the rank of co-Pharaoh, thus pro-
viding a loyal and watchful regent whenever he was absent
from Egypt with his armies. This procedure became almost
standard practice with subsequent Pharaohs, to whom plots
concerning the succession were a constant source of anxiety.
Sesostris was not content, like his father, to occupy himself
exclusively with internal politics, but set off on a series of
expeditions which were more ambitious than those of any
previous Pharaoh. He penetrated into Nubia as far as the
Third Cataract, securing during his march a region rich in
gold. Trade became a prominent feature of Egyptian life

during the reign of Sesostris I, owing largely to the king's interest in external affairs. Contracts with Crete, Byblus and the Syrian seaboard, the land of Punt and Hither Asia were extended and regularized. Altogether the reign of Sesostris I was among the most distinguished in Egyptian history.

During the next half century the stability of the dynasty was maintained by the Pharaohs Amenemhat II and Sesostris II, of whom little is known. Sesostris II began the important work of irrigating the Fayûm, moving his capital from Memphis to Illahun to facilitate the work of supervision. SESOSTRIS III (1887–1850 B.C.) was remembered by the Egyptians as one of their outstanding sovereigns, and his fame was known to the Greeks. He emulated the feats of Sesostris I in Nubia and the Sudan, while his thrust into central Palestine was a sustained operation on a scale very different from the raid of Weni in the time of Pepi I. Sesostris III was the precursor of the imperial Pharaohs of the New Kingdom. At home he found it necessary to suppress the office of nomarch almost entirely, leaving it with barely nominal authority. It took a potent and ruthless man to eliminate the provincial aristocracy. A measure of his might is revealed in the triumphant conclusion of the cultivation and colonization of the desert Fayûm, now turned into a fruitful oasis. His successor, AMENEMHAT III (1850–1800 B.C.), improved on the titanic work of reclamation that had caused the desert to blossom like the rose. He built in the Fayûm the massive palace of Hawara, the largest inhabitable building ever constructed in ancient Egypt. Herodotus reported that it contained three thousand rooms. By the time Herodotus visited Egypt the palace was in ruins, but its remains were still impressive enough to account for the manner in which it gave rise to the legend of the Labyrinth.

After the death of Amenemhat III the historical story is once more interrupted. The Twelfth Dynasty peters out in an unaccountable fashion under a mediocre king and an insignificant queen. Why a dynasty as securely based as the Twelfth should suddenly be extinguished is a mystery. We know only that the entire fabric of the state, woven by kings of pre-eminent statesmanship, disintegrated entirely within a single generation. Perhaps expensive architectural and agricultural schemes strained the economy for a second time and brought a great kingdom crashing down. The SECOND INTERMEDIATE PERIOD (1785–1580 B.C.) was as puzzling a phenomenon as the First Intermediate Period. Until about 1730 B.C., when a people from Asia called the Hyksôs invaded Egypt, we are virtually without information. The *Thirteenth Dynasty* and the *Fourteenth Dynasty* number between them some thirty Pharaohs so inextricably jumbled together that it is not possible to assign the majority of them either to the earlier or the later dynasty. The relics by which they are known to posterity are meagre and insubstantial: a scarab, a broken relief, a statue, a funerary stele, a shattered column. Few of them, if any, appear to have ruled over both Upper and Lower Egypt. Most of the men who figure in the king lists were either short-lived opportunists or petty nomarchs of the Delta and the Thebaid, ruling contemporaneously with each other and in the latest cases with their Hyksôs conquerors. Although the apparently adamantine structure of Twelfth Dynasty rule had been burst asunder, it does not appear that the Second Intermediate Period or the Hyksôs domination were years of such intense stress and misery as the First Intermediate Period. The Egyptians forbore to make war on each other and managed to avoid famine by keeping their agricultural and irrigation works intact. The grim lesson of the First Intermediate Period was heeded. It may be that the Thirteenth and Fourteenth Dynasties represent a period of apathy after the concentrated zeal of the Middle Kingdom rather than an epoch of violent upheaval. Nubia broke away, extra-territorial ambitions were renounced. The population of the Nile valley carried on its normal existence in a spirit of profound apathy. After a half century had passed it fell placidly, if shamefacedly, beneath the yoke of the Asiatic.

CHAPTER IX

History : Two

God was displeased with us,' wrote Manetho, 'and there came up unexpectedly from the East men of ignoble race who had the audacity to invade our land.' The invaders were the HYKSÔS, who ruled a large part of Egypt from about 1730 to 1580 B.C. Manetho translated the word Hyksôs as 'Shepherd Kings,' but the more correct version is 'Foreign Kings.' The movement of the Hyksôs into the Nile valley was part of a sweeping folk migration taking place all over Hither Asia at this time. The Hittites were establishing themselves firmly in Anatolia, the Kassites were founding a dynasty in Babylon, the Hurrians were spreading across Mesopotamia in a belt reaching from Kirkuk to the old Amorite trading cities of Aleppo and Carchemish. Among the Hurrians the most important element were the Mitannians, their newly arrived leaders and overlords. The Mitannians, who founded a kingdom of their own which was to play an interesting rôle in Egyptian affairs, were Aryans of some denomination, and it was to an influx of Indo-European aristocrats that the entire sequence of folk movements was directly attributable. It appears probable that the Hyksôs were related to the loose racial conglomerate of the Hurrians. The Hurrians were certainly leading exponents of the new art of chariotry which the Hyksôs used with great effect against the Egyptians. The forms of their names indicate that they were Semites, and there would be no question of their Semitic origin if they were in fact not Hurrians but warlike Syro-Palestinian nomads who, finding the way northward and eastward blocked by a confederation of Hittites and Hurrians, broke out towards the south-west. It may be noted that the Ramessides of the Nineteenth Dynasty, who hailed from the ancient capital of the Hyksôs at Tanis and were patrons of the Hyksôs god Seth, were of marked Semitic appearance.

At first the Hyksôs occupation of Egypt was confined to the Delta, but with the arrival of a new Asiatic wave under a chieftain called Salatis (the Sultan) a campaign was mounted against Upper Egypt. The Hyksôs easily prevailed against the Egyptian troops, demoralized by the brisk tactics of chariot warfare. Upper Egypt was nevertheless never systematically administered by the intruders, who were doubtless content to levy annual tribute. The six Hyksôs kings known to us from a few insignificant inscriptions adopted the cartouche and the title Son of Ra, but it is unlikely that they lived in much better style than that of nomad chiefs of the more colourful variety. Manetho saw fit notwithstanding to dignify them with the award of two dynasties, the *Fifteenth Dynasty* and the *Sixteenth Dynasty*. Like the Kassites in Babylon, the invaders never seem to have accustomed themselves to urban existence. Their capital before they moved to Memphis was a fortress on the shore of the Delta called Avaris, a massive-walled military encampment garrisoned by heavily armed troops: a fitting point of departure by barbarian terrorists in search of plunder. That their terrorism was effective is suggested by the fact that Manetho compares them to the Assyrians, whose name was a byword for cruelty in the ancient world. Later Egyptians held the Hyksôs in peculiar abhorrence, but it is curious to find that not long after their departure the Egyptians were enjoying the most cordial relations with the probable countries of their origin, Hurri and Mitanni. There is also no trace of the sack of Thebes with which the Hyksôs king Khian was credited. Perhaps the damage inflicted by the Hyksôs affected national prestige more than material possessions. To be conquered by Assyrians and Persians was pardonable: to be conquered by a horde of nomads was a lasting humiliation.

The detested Hyksôs succeeded, in fact, in making two very important contributions to Egyptian civilization. The first was the practical matter of the introduction of the horse and chariot. The horse and chariot had not been evolved or adopted in Egypt because there had existed no pressing need for them. The Nile provided an admirable highway and the Egyptians devoted their ingenuity in the matter of transport to devising many different types of boat. The Hyksôs wars quickened the pulse of Egyptian life, and in a new expansive mood the Egyptians were not slow to comprehend the possibilities of the chariot. With it their kings were soon to win an empire. The Egyptians never rode the horse itself but always used the chariot, although the Nubian warriors of the Twenty-fifth Dynasty were accustomed to ride on horseback.

The second Hyksôs contribution was an intellectual one. Egypt had never before in dynastic times been entered by invaders from so far afield, and the Hyksôs incursion made the insular Egyptian suddenly aware of wider horizons. Hitherto his colonial ambitions had been confined either to the Nile valley or to its Nubian extension. With the exception of heavily protected forays to mines and quarries, he had never wandered any great distance from his native river. Now he began to take a growing interest in the increasing complexity of Asian affairs. If the Asiatics could invade Egypt, why should not the culturally advanced Egyptians carve out for themselves an empire in Asia ? Furthermore it was becoming evident that the destinies of the Two Lands were inextricably bound up with events in Asia. The Wall of the Prince which Amenemhat had thrown across the Eastern Delta had proved as inadequate in the face of determined assault as such passive defence lines always are. It was clear that the best defence against external attack rested in treaties and alliances with the potential aggressors in Hither Asia. Once the Egyptian began to indulge in this novel kind of political thinking it was not many decades before he came to the conclusion that the frontier of Egypt lay on the River Euphrates.

About 1680 B.C., when the invader had been installed for over half a century in the Delta and Lower Egypt, the nomarchs of Thebes became sufficiently prominent to be considered a separate dynasty, the *Seventeenth Dynasty*. Again it was a nomarch called Intef, as in the First Intermediate Period, who was instrumental in embodying the Upper Egyptians in what was to become a liberating force. The office of nomarch at this time had not been restored to the hereditary principle of which Sesostris III had deprived it, but was elective. The ninth of these elective Theban nomarchs, Sekenenra, struck the first blow in the struggle for freedom almost a full century after the founding of the Seventeenth Dynasty. The papyrus Sallier I tells how the Hyksôs king Apopi sent a message to Sekenenra ordering him to abolish the hippopotamus pool near Thebes because the noise of the beasts could be plainly heard in Avaris and was keeping Apopi awake at night. This cryptic utterance, couched in Oriental circumlocutions, was no doubt designed to inform Sekenenra in a tone of veiled contempt that his plotting with his Theban cronies was well known to the Hyksôs chief. In the upshot, the lord of Thebes accepted the challenge and resorted to active defiance, of which we possess dramatic testimony. When the mummy of Sekenenra came to light in the Valley of the Kings, the head was seen to bear a number of really fearful wounds and gashes. It seems reasonable to suppose that these injuries were inflicted in battle. Sekenenra's son, Kames, achieved some measure of revenge, for he carried on the war so energetically that he wrung Lower Egypt from Apopi's grasp, perhaps to the extent of reaching Memphis. Both Kames and his father were hampered in their courageous undertaking by the cautious, perhaps craven attitude of their subordinate nomarchs. The great concerted effort to oust the invader was not made until the reign of Ahmosis, the successor of Kames.

Ahmosis was a Pharaoh of commanding stature whose accession marks the beginning of the *EIGHTEENTH DYNASTY* (1580–1320 B.C.), the most memorable dynasty in Egyptian history. From the inception of the Eighteenth Dynasty is dated the NEW KINGDOM (1580–1085 B.C.). Egypt embarked in this period on the great imperial adventure in Hither Asia that made her the most important power in the world. From the position of a remote but respected realm, she became the leader and arbiter of the nations. Fantastic riches poured into her treasure houses. She commanded boundless resources of men and materials. Yet the old austere and native qualities were lost irretrievably. After four heady centuries she succumbed to the exhaustion which followed a sustained imperialist effort. Luxury and cosmopolitanism sapped the tough fibre which was the strength of the Old and Middle Kingdoms. The narrow durability, the stubborn rigour were gone. But for all that, in the infinite count of years that composed her history, this was her glittering, flamboyant moment of fulfilment.

The first task to which AHMOSIS (1580–1558 B.C.) set himself was to regain Nubia from the native rulers who held sway during the Second Intermediate Period. With indefatigable energy he brought Nubia once more under Egyptian control in three campaigns, during the course of which he may have reached the Second Cataract. When this task was accomplished he ventured into Palestine, where he laid the foundation-stone of the subsequent empire by annexing the wealthy and strategically important ports of Phoenicia. The capital remained at Thebes under Ahmosis and his successors for two cogent reasons. The first was· that the lords of the city had demonstrated their indisputable claim to moral and military leadership. Secondly, the priesthood of Amon-Ra, the local god of Thebes who had led Egyptian armies to victory on two

164

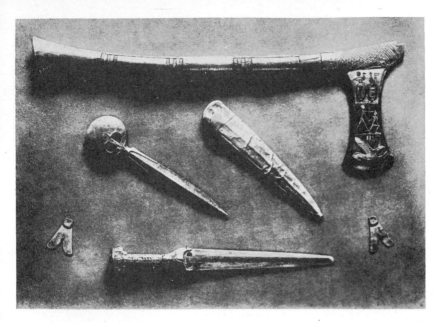

40. THE CEREMONIAL WEAPONS OF THE PHARAOH AHMOSIS
Eighteenth Dynasty
A battle axe, two daggers and two flies

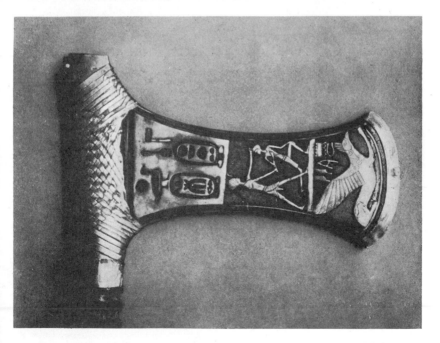

41. THE BATTLE AXE OF THE PHARAOH AHMOSIS
A detail of the axe shown above

42. A NOBLEMAN AND HIS SECRETARIAL STAFF
INSPECTING CATTLE
A model from the tomb of Meketra

43. THE CARPENTERS' WORKSHOP
ON AN ESTATE
A model from the tomb of Meketra

44. AN EIGHTEENTH DYNASTY VILLA
A modern reconstruction

occasions, was emerging as the most potent political factor in the state. Ahmosis followed royal practice in marrying his sister Nefertari, who bore him the Pharaoh AMENOPHIS I (1557–1530 B.C.). Nefertari was apparently a woman much loved by her family and by the people, and her cult remained in vogue for many centuries. She was the first of a series of royal women who played an important part in the history of the dynasty. Her son Amenophis carried on the Nubian policy of his father, but we are ignorant of his endeavours in Asia. It is likely that his campaigns there were extensive, for his successor TUTHMOSIS I (1530–1520 B.C.) stated at the outset of his reign that the boundary of Egypt was the river Euphrates. Tuthmosis was the son of Amenophis by a concubine, but he rapidly reinforced his claim to the throne by marrying his half-sister Ahmosis, daughter of his father by his legitimate queen. In Nubia he penetrated as far as the Third Cataract and his activities in Asia followed the same pattern as his predecessors: he took his armies across well-charted routes with the aim of striking fear into the tribesmen and exacting tribute. There was no attempt at establishing a chain of fortresses or lines of communication, and no attempt to organize systematic colonial administration.

Like his father and grandfather, Tuthmosis II (1520–1505 B.C.), of whose reign we know very little except that he was called upon to quell revolts in Nubia and Syria, left the question of succession in a lamentably indecisive condition. Once more the royal offspring consisted of two legitimate daughters and the illegitimate son of a concubine. On this occasion the issue was complicated by the fact that the boy was only six years old on his father's death. The dynastic wrangles which followed are the subject of prolonged debate among scholars and the account given here adheres to the simplest and most feasible version. According to this account the little boy was proclaimed Tuthmosis III, but because of his minority his aunt HATSHEPSUT (1505–1484 B.C.) was appointed regent. Hatshepsut, who was Tuthmosis II's half-sister and his wife, married the child to her own daughter by Tuthmosis II. During the course of the regency her appetite for power became so inordinate that she boldly mounted the throne and declared herself Pharaoh. She laid emphasis on her legitimate descent, insisted that her father Tuthmosis I had always destined her for the crown, and maintained that she was begotten by Amon-Ra in person. She caused reliefs to be cut portraying the god coupling with her mother in which she herself was depicted in male garments and with a breastless body. She adopted the full masculine titulary, omitting only the traditional attribute of 'Mighty Bull': a claim which even a Hatshepsut was unable to sustain. She surrounded herself with a junta of brilliant individuals, which included the vizier and high priest of Amon-Ra, Hapuseneb, and the architect of genius, Senmut. Despite her formidable nature, Hatshepsut was a woman of taste and discrimination. As a ruler she was able and unbellicose. It was hardly possible in any case for a woman to lead armies in person into the field, and in the sphere of foreign relations she contented herself with peaceful commercial enterprises. The most famous of these was the expedition to Punt which is recorded in her temple at Deir el-Bahri. Her indifference to the loss of the Asian Empire and the civil temper of her cabinet enraged the military leaders, chafing with inactivity and hungering to repeat the exploits of the early Pharaohs of the dynasty. In time they formed a cabal of their own round the person of the adolescent TUTHMOSIS III (1505/1484–1450 B.C.). The military ardour and physical prowess with bow and chariot of the young man made him the darling of the army. The fiery prince was irked by the authority of his aunt, but he was nearly thirty before he was released from bondage either by her death or by a military coup d'état. His fury at his long constraint, his hurt pride that it had been inflicted upon him by a woman and a usurper, induced him to carry his vengeance to immoderate lengths. He hacked

166

her cartouche from her monuments and either substituted his own or those of his father and grandfather, whose cartouches had earlier suffered eradication at the hands of Hatshepsut.

No sooner had Tuthmosis III assumed sole power than he set off immediately on the first of his incessant campaigns. He is one of the great soldiers of history, and he has been aptly named the Napoleon of Egypt. His mummy proves him to have been a man as small in stature as the Emperor of the French, with whom he possessed in common more than the ordinary endowment of will and energy. He executed no less than seventeen distinct campaigns, interspersed with regular tours of inspection of the mighty empire. The record of his feats of arms were carved on the walls of Karnak, which received the lion's share of the booty which the king brought back to the Nile valley. The first campaign was one of the most momentous, for it concluded with the battle of Megiddo, an unusually bitter and protracted affray for the ancient world, in which the Pharaoh vanquished the first of many coalitions formed to resist him. Thereafter he annexed the rich harvest lands of Syria, whence with the academic instinct of Napoleon he sent back wild animals and botanical specimens to Egypt. The sons of Syrian reigning families were despatched to Thebes, not only as hostages for the future good behaviour of their fathers but also to be indoctrinated in Egyptian manners. He secured Palestinian ports as points of departure for his armies, thus manifesting his grasp of the importance of sea power. The climax of his career came in the thirty-third year of his reign, when he was thirty-nine years old. In this year he won two pitched battles at Carchemish and Aleppo, floated his army across the Euphrates on rafts and advanced across Mitannian soil to defeat the Mitannians, his principal foes, in their own homeland. He then recrossed the river and set up a stele beside the stele of his grandfather Tuthmosis I to mark the Euphrates as the eastern limit of his empire. For nine years more he was occupied with stamping out minor revolts, but in 1464 B.C. he wrecked the last Mitannian coalition by taking the citadels of Tunip and Kadesh. Until his death fourteen years later he received regular tribute from the conquered provinces, while Babylon, Assyria, Hatti, Mitanni, Crete and the Mediterranean islands all vied with each other in sending him sumptuous presents. He also found time to conduct a campaign in Nubia, pushing with characteristic *élan* as far as Napata, near the Fourth Cataract. His constant desire was to emulate the deeds of the great Sesostris III of the Twelfth Dynasty, to whom he built a temple at Semna, beyond the Second Cataract. In this aim he succeeded, for he is without question the most remarkable of all Egypt's Pharaohs. The wealth which flooded into Egypt from the empire was responsible for such a high standard of living that he was freed from the necessity of keeping close watch on domestic affairs, although his almost continuous absence from Thebes permitted the priesthood of that pampered city to tighten its grip on the reins of government. Tuthmosis built the colonnade at Karnak, where he set up a pair of the splendid granite obelisks which he was fond of erecting throughout the land. One of them, from Heliopolis, is the 'Cleopatra's Needle' of the Thames Embankment, while its twin stands in Central Park, New York. After his death, as was fitting, he joined his great forebears in the Valley of the Kings, outside their native city.

To avoid the disputes over the succession which had previously racked the dynasty, Tuthmosis took the precaution of elevating his son AMENOPHIS II (1450–1425 B.C.) to the throne as joint ruler the year before his death. Amenophis was a tall, broad young man, totally unlike his father in physique. It was said that nobody could bend his bow. Otherwise he much resembled his father, as the Syrian princes who took the opportunity to rebel on the death of the great Tuthmosis found to their cost. Amenophis crushed the revolt and captured

45. THE PHARAOH TUTHMOSIS III
Eighteenth Dynasty

46. THE PHARAOH TUTHMOSIS III MAKING AN OFFERING TO
AMON-RA, KING OF THE GODS
A painted relief

seven of the ringleaders, whom he brought to Thebes. There he sacrificed them alive in front of the statue of Amon-Ra, hanging six of the bodies on the walls of the city and sending the seventh to be similarly exposed in distant Napata as a warning to the Nubians. In this piece of blatant savagery he showed himself not only unworthy of Tuthmosis III, but of the prevailing spirit of ancient Egypt. Such an act is almost without parallel in dynastic annals. TUTHMOSIS IV (1425– 1405 B.C.), who may have been the eldest son of Amenophis II, made a tour of the Asian Empire and a tour of Nubia. He cemented an alliance with the now quiescent Mitannians, who were facing a new enemy in the form of the Hittites, by marrying the princess Mutemuya. Mutemuya, daughter of king Artatama, was the mother of Amenophis III.

AMENOPHIS III (1405–1370 B.C.) has been called the Caesar Augustus of ancient Egypt. His reign represents the high summer of Nilotic civilization. During the first ten years of his reign Amenophis fought a Nubian campaign and made a reputation as an intrepid huntsman. In this decade he issued a special scarab to celebrate the killing of a hundred and ten lions. After these preliminary exertions, however, he lapsed into the lethargic and voluptuous existence of an Oriental despot. He married a commoner called Tiy on whom he bestowed the title of 'Great Royal Wife.' Tiy was a woman of long-suffering character and also of compelling physical appeal, for she maintained her influence over her husband despite the monotonous importation into his harîm of the choicest princesses the Near East could provide. One of his greatest pleasures was to sail with Tiy in his boat *Splendour of the Aton* on the artificial lake in the grounds of his palace. Tiy may herself have been of Asiatic blood, like the royal wives Gilukhipa and Tadukhipa, daughters of the Mitannian kings Shuttarna and Tushratta, or the daughter of Tarkhundaraba of Arzawa in Cilicia. By the end of the reign of the son of Mutemuya, the blood which flowed in the veins of the

169

Egyptian royal family was almost entirely alien. There also emerged at court a taste for Asiatic fashions in dress and manners, together with an ominous taste for Asiatic religion. The spell of the great Vedic and Aryan gods of the Mitannians, such as Indra, Varuna and Mithra, began to exert itself among the Egyptian aristocracy. We noted that the name of Amenophis' pleasure-barge was *Splendour of the Aton*, and it seems certain that the cult of the Aton, which is related to Mitannian sun worship, began to come to the forefront in the reign of Amenophis. Atonism, monotheistic in conception, was championed at this time by the priests of Heliopolis, jealous of the favoured treatment accorded for so many years to Theban Amon-Ra. As excuse for this whoring after a strange god, they could plead the similarity between the worship of the sun god in both Egypt and Hither Asia. But in this as in other matters, Amenophis preferred that Asia should come to him rather than that he should go to Asia. He could not be persuaded to undertake the unsparing tours of the empire instituted by Tuthmosis III and scrupulously maintained for a further half-century by his two successors. The colonial government of Amenophis was lax in the extreme, and the royal indolence was particularly inexcusable in view of the fact that the Hittites had found a great fighting king in the person of Shubbiluliuma. The surveillance of such a sprawling empire, compounded of so many races and nations, demanded a vigilant monarch. While Amenophis basked in the mellow sunshine of dominion, away to the north the storm clouds were gathering. Shubbiluliuma was busy encouraging an alliance of Syro-Palestinian princes which was to act decisively during the reign of Amenophis' feeble son. Meanwhile Pharaoh degenerated into a senile voluptuary, taking his ease in the fabulous palace at Thebes which was built for him by his friend and favourite Amenhetep. Amenhetep also constructed his master's funerary chapel, of which only the two Colossi of Memnon survive, and the magnificent temple of Luxor. It cannot be denied that as a whole the reign of Amenophis III was distinguished by a truly Augustan breadth and majesty.

The celebrated and dramatic story of the following reign brings a human and pathetic touch into the historical story. In the fourth year of his rule AMENOPHIS IV (1370–1352 B.C.) changed his name from Amenophis to AKHENATON. Amenophis signifies 'Amon is satisfied,' while Akhenaton means 'Glory of the Aton.' The king sailed downstream from Thebes to found in the inhospitable wastes of Middle Egypt a new capital city called Akhetaton, 'Horizon of the Aton,' near the modern village of el-Amarna. At Akhetaton he erected temples to the Aton, which he worshipped in opposition to Amon-Ra. Whereas the Aton had been regarded by his father and perhaps his grandfather as only one god among many, the casual addition of an exotic deity to an already well-stocked pantheon, Akhenaton recognized in the Aton the sole god of Egypt. The Aton represented the creative principle of the sun, source of life and universal demiurge, and to adore the Aton was to know simple gaiety and intellectual freedom. Despite the carefree abandon which was supposed to characterize the worship of his new god, Akhenaton proceeded against Amon-Ra, the fountainhead of his dynasty, with all the fury of a joyless bigot. The name of Amon-Ra was chiselled out of every monument on which it figured, even where it occurred in the former royal name of Akhenaton himself. The king became high priest and prophet of the new deity, to whom he dedicated a series of moving hymns. Beside a purely religious motive, Akhenaton was actuated in his religious warfare by a political consideration: he wished to break the iron hegemony of the priesthood of Thebes. It appears that his wife Nefertiti identified herself with this ambition. She supported her husband's ill-conceived defiance of Amon-Ra through thick and thin, her fanatical devotion to the cause of the Aton surpassing Akhenaton's own. It is possible that Nefertiti was actuated in the matter by the fact that she may have been a

Mitannian princess. It has been suggested that she was Tadukhipa, the young woman sent to marry Amenophis III. Amenophis may have died before he celebrated the nuptials, whereupon she was wedded by his son. Tiy, the queen mother, took a moderate and conservative view of the Atonist controversy. Distressed by the acrimony of the schism, she made attempts to reconcile her son with the Theban priests and acted as mediator when at last he was forced to capitulate. The surrender was brought about, we may suppose, mainly by economic pressure. The king had isolated himself in the barren desert, his expenses outrunning his income, while the bland priests controlled the chief sources of revenue and in particular the gold supply. It is also likely that public opinion was on their side from the first, since the sedate Egyptians would not look upon the clumsy rooting-up of their entire religious system with a kindly eye. In the end the will-power and the staying power of the king proved inferior to that of the priesthood. He could in any case hardly have hoped to prevail against a high priest whose implacable opposition was reinforced by the knowledge that he was supported by two thousand years of traditional belief. This opposition was not softened by the conviction that the royal heresy struck at the very foundations on which the civilization of the Two Lands rested. Akhenaton, his frail body worn out by his fierce idealisms and the heat of the contest, sent his son-in-law to Thebes to discuss the terms of capitulation. Nefertiti completed his personal tragedy by sundering herself from him and taking his other young son-in-law to live with her in a palace on the outskirts of Akhetaton provocatively named 'Fortress of the Aton.' There is ample testimony to the deep love that existed between these two headstrong people in a score of intimate frescoes and reliefs in their ill-fated capital. While the domestic dreams of the would-be progressive crumbled about him, Hittite-inspired Asians were throwing off Egyptian shackles. The prince of Kadesh captured the Syrian plain, the prince of Amurru

captured Phoenicia, the Palestinians captured Megiddo and
Jerusalem. The increasing plight of the Egyptian empire is
recounted in the wonderful *Amarna Letters*. These letters, which
were found during modern excavations at Akhetaton, comprise
official letters received and copies of letters sent between the
Egyptian government and the princes of Asia, including those
of Mitanni, Babylon and Ashur. The letters are written on small
clay tablets in the diplomatic language of the time, Akkadian
cuneiform. They cover a substantial period of the foreign
policy during the reigns of Amenophis III and Akhenaton, and
reflect no credit on the grasp of affairs of either of these kings.
Loss of the Asian empire and its tribute was a serious blow to
Egypt, which had come to rely heavily upon the wealth that
came from abroad. A state of near famine ensued in the Nile
valley, to which the internecine squabbles between the leaders
of the country contributed. It is likely that even in his lifetime Akhenaton was execrated as he was in later years as 'the
great criminal of Akhetaton.' However, the heretic was spared
the worst humiliation of his defeat by his premature death.

Smenkhara, the young man whom Akhenaton had sent to
the priests at Thebes, perhaps as a pledge of his change of
heart, did not long survive his father-in-law. The ten-year-old
boy called Tutankhaton whom Nefertiti was keeping at her
side at Akhetaton thereupon succeeded to the throne. The
origins of both Smenkhara and Tutankhaton are obscure. It
seems that Akhenaton and Nefertiti, in common with so
many royal couples of the dynasty, were unable to supply a
male heir, although they produced an abundance of girls. For
two of their six daughters, Meritaton and Ankhesenpaaton,
they chose the boys Smenkhara and Tutankhaton as husbands.
It is possible that Smenkhara was a son of Tiy, but there is no
clue to the family history of Tutankhaton. Nefertiti managed
to keep the lad with her for a further three years, but at the end
of that time the priests of Thebes were not to be gainsaid, and
he was brought to Thebes. There his name was changed from

Tutankhaton to TUTANKHAMON, 'Living Image of Amon,' an ironic comment on his father's change of name nearly twenty years before. The name of the offensive Aton was also removed from the name of Tutankhamon's girl wife, Ankhesenpaaton, who henceforward was known as Ankhesenamon, 'She lives in Amon.' Nefertiti, alone in her empty palace, seems to have made a curious appeal to the Hittite king Shubbiluliuma to send her one of his sons as a husband. The reason for this appeal is not known. Perhaps Nefertiti was actuated by treacherous and revengeful thoughts of confusing the already delicate matter of the succession. Or it may simply have been that the unfortunate lady was lonely and craved a handsome young companion of her own Asiatic kind. After some hesitation the Hittite king, then in camp at Carchemish, complied with the request, but the young prince was ambushed and murdered on his way to Egypt. The author of this deed was probably the distinguished general Horemhab, presiding genius of the Theban party and leader of the Amonian counter-revolution. Horemhab had restored a measure of Egyptian prestige in Asia by several vigorous campaigns during the reign of Tutankhamon. When the boy king died, the general placed a second puppet on the throne in the person of Ay, an aged priest or courtier. Ay also succumbed after a very short interval, and Horemhab forsook the rôle of grey eminence and proclaimed himself Pharaoh.

The tomb of the luckless little Tutankhamon remained un-disturbed for three thousand years, until it came to light in the Valley of the Kings in 1922. Thieves had made an abortive attempt in antiquity to rob the tomb, but the last set of seals of the necropolis officials of the New Kingdom remained intact upon the outer doorway. The antechamber was piled high with a haphazard mass of objects. In appearance it resembled a fantastic warehouse in which were heaped the personalia of the dead king. There were jewelled and gilded chairs, stools, couches, chariots, weapons and model boats. There was the famous chair, with a representation of the king with his wife Ankhesenamon (Pl. 12). Inlaid chests and coffers contained such objects as clothing and mummified birds. A second sealed door, guarded by two life-size statues of the king, led from the antechamber to the actual burial chamber. Here were even greater marvels. Inside the golden shrines, the outermost measuring seventeen feet by eleven, lay a fourth shrine draped by a linen pall. Inside the fourth shrine lay the stone sarcophagus. The sarcophagus itself contained three coffins, the third of which consisted of twenty stone of solid gold encrusted with lapis lazuli, turquoise, carnelian and other precious stones (Frontispiece). The king was depicted bearing the insignia of his great office, enwrapped within the golden wings of the guardian goddesses. On the mummy of the king lay an exquisite mask (Pl. 29). When the mask was removed the excavators could see how faithfully the ancient artificers had wrought their portraits of their master. In another room were the king's canopic chest, a box containing cult objects guarded by Anubis and coffers which held such things as a beautiful ivory fan with its feathers in a state of perfect preservation. Altogether the tomb of Tutankhamon represents the greatest discovery from the ancient world ever made. It is unlikely that a comparable find will present itself. The objects it held are testimony to the unrivalled art of the Eighteenth Dynasty. One is left with the reflection that if such magnificence attended the obsequies of an eighteen year-old boy, disregarded by the nobility, despised by the priesthood, interred hastily in a borrowed tomb and in a broken sarcophagus, what must have been the funerary splendours of a more illustrious resident of the Valley of the Kings?

HOREMHAB (1330?–1320 B.C.) was a descendant of the nomarchs of Alabastronpolis. He seems to have been a man of harsh and uncompromising character. He sanctioned a rigorous reaction against the Aton and its adherents, usurping for himself the monuments of Akhenaton and Tutankhamon.

He dated the beginning of his reign from the death of Amen-ophis III, as though to erase forever from men's minds the memory of the disastrous Atonist experiment. With the efficiency of a general staff officer he put in hand the thorough repair of the civil administration. There is good reason to consider this somewhat grim but efficient personage as the first king of the *NINETEENTH DYNASTY* (1320–1200 B.C.) rather than the last king of the Eighteenth. He chose as his successor an elderly fellow-general named Ramses, who be-longed to a Tanite family that was almost certainly of Hyksôs descent. His main titles tell us that he had served as Chief of the Archers, Vizier and High Priest of Seth. During his short reign of two years he continued the reinvigorating policies of Horemhab and sent his son at the head of an army into Nubia.

This son was the forceful SETI I (1318–1298 B.C.), who before his accession held the same posts as his father. Seti dealt firmly with native tribesmen in Palestine who had seized many of the fortresses along the main trade routes. He then went on to fight the most brilliant campaign in Egyptian military history. Encouraged by the Hittites, the Amorites and Aramaeans were marching by separate routes to join the army of the prince of Hamath. Seti made an inspired decision. Dividing his own forces into three corps, the army of Amon, the army of Ra and the army of Seth, he despatched them severally against the enemy. His bold tactics proved a complete success. Seti found himself in control of a large part of Palestine and the trading cities of Phoenicia. He fought a victorious engagement against the Hittite armies of King Muwattalish, but was afterwards unable to use his advantage to dispel Hittite supremacy in Syria. He was a great builder. His chief memorial was the splendid Osirian temple at Abydos, with its sensitive reliefs. From this temple came the king list known as the Tablet of Abydos, containing the names of seventy-six Pharaohs from the accession of Menes. Seti I also contributed to the gigantic hypostyle hall at Karnak, begun by Ramses I, and

47. A WIFE OR DAUGHTER OF THE PHARAOH RAMSES II
A painted limestone bust from the Ramasseum

48. THE PHARAOH RAMSES II
Nineteenth Dynasty

hewed out for himself a great tomb in the Valley of the Kings. His superb alabaster sarcophagus is in Sir John Soane's Museum in Lincoln's Inn Fields.

RAMSES II (1298–1232 B.C.), Seti's son, has always bulked large in accounts of ancient Egypt. Early Egyptologists bestowed on him the title of 'the Great,' for he bequeathed to posterity a series of monuments executed on a staggering scale. Among them were his rock temples in the Sudan, the Ramasseum at Thebes, the completed hypostyle hall at Karnak, extensive additions to Luxor and the reconstruction of the city of Tanis, his family seat. He was a lavish usurper of the buildings of his forerunners and an untiring fabricator of obelisks and colossal statues. His prenomen and nomen, Wesermaatra-Ramses, were corrupted by Greek writers into Ozymandias. 'Look on my works, ye mighty, and despair!' The self-glorification of his monuments and the pomposity of his inscriptions have caused modern Egyptologists to view him with rather a jaundiced eye. The evidence of his achievements is nevertheless plain for all to see, and he supplemented his claim to greatness by procreating over fifty daughters and a hundred sons. Four years after he came to the throne the young Pharaoh, greedy for renown, led a strong force into Palestine. The Hittite-Egyptian stalemate, which persisted for a decade after the efforts of Seti I, was coming to an end. Muwattalish had bought or bludgeoned into existence a coalition of more than twenty states, and Ramses marched forward confidently to meet them, his armies disposed in four corps. The king himself headed the column with the army of Amon, followed at a distance of some miles by the army of Ra, while the armies of Ptah and Seth formed the rearguard. Pharaoh took the army of Amon across the Orontes and encamped before Kadesh. The main body of the Hittites, observing the scattered disposition of the Egyptian forces, then executed a crafty manoeuvre: they stole round by night between the besieging troops and the river. When the army of Ra forded the river the next morning it was treated to a murderous reception. It broke and ran for Kadesh. Ramses found himself facing superior forces with a mere army and a half, and the fugitives from the army of Ra can have added little to the morale of the army of Amon. Meanwhile the armies of Ptah and Seth were a hopeless distance away on the wrong side of the Orontes. Ramses buckled to and managed to make an excellent fight of it, handling his troops with coolness and courage. In the end the battle was drawn, neither side gaining a decisive advantage, although perhaps the Egyptians had slightly the better of it. For the moment the political initiative remained with the Hittites, who lost no time in fomenting rebellion in Egyptian-occupied territory. But Ramses was equally prompt in his reply. He reduced the strongholds of rebellion in Canaan and marched north into Naharina, scene of many of the triumphs of the Eighteenth Dynasty. The Hittites rushed troops to the defence of the town of Tunip, which Ramses quickly took. By his energy and determination the young king had in some degree recreated the empire of Tuthmosis III. An uneasy peace followed his defeat of the Hittites and their allies in the field, during which both sides viewed with increasing uneasiness the encroachments of the Assyrians. When the forces of Ashur under their first great warrior king, Shalmaneser I, swallowed up Mitanni and reached the Euphrates, Ramses and the new king of Hatti, Hattushilish III, decided that the time had come to patch up old enmities and unite against the common foe. In 1277 B.C. the Hittite king sent a silver tablet to Ramses at Tanis on which was engraved in cuneiform the draft of a proposed treaty of alliance. The terms of the treaty were afterwards transcribed on the walls of Karnak and the Ramasseum. The contracting parties swore eternal peace, promised each other mutual assistance in the event of foreign aggression and made provision for the extradition of political prisoners. These prisoners were given up, however, on the understanding that they were to be humanely treated. Syria was carefully divided into spheres of influence. Fourteen years after the signing of the treaty Hattushilish visited his ally in person, bringing with him to Egypt one of his daughters to be Ramses' bride. The occasion was celebrated with great public festivities. The remarkable *entente* between the two great powers brought peace to Asia for over half a century. It was not until both royal signatories were old men that a series of disturbances commenced with which they were impotent to deal. Hordes of immigrants and swashbuckling soldiers of fortune were flowing across the plains of Hither Asia from the Balkans and the Black Sea. Ramses watched events from the Nile valley with a weary eye, completing his sixty-year building programme and dreaming of Kadesh, a battle that became a more famous victory with every year that passed.

It was MINEPTAH (1232-? B.C.) who inherited the problems that perplexed his father. In Asia the son of Shalmaneser I, Tukulti-Ninurta I, had sacked Babylon. At the end of the long reign of the last powerful king of Hatti, Todhalijas IV, Hattushilish III's son, the Hittites were to experience one of their incessant internal crises, which on this occasion was to prove fatal to their survival as a nation. Mineptah seems to have put down a revolt in Palestine early in his reign, and he is known to have sent a consignment of wheat to the foundering Hittites. But it was from the west that Egypt was now called upon to face her most dangerous antagonist. The Libyans, with whom Seti I had fought a sharp encounter, were now reinforced by a contingent of the Sea People, whom we shall meet in the sequel. The Libyans marched on Memphis, only to be cut down by Mineptah's army. Ramses II was a centenarian when he died and Mineptah, his thirteenth son, cannot have been a young man when he became Pharaoh. He nobly shouldered his responsibilities, although the nation's fortunes were now in perceptible decline. Hitherto it was Egypt which had marched against Asia: now it was Asia which marched on Egypt. The Nineteenth Dynasty came to a dismal end with five

179

usurpations. Ironically enough, it was more perplexing for Ramses to leave a hundred sons than it was for Amenophis I or Tuthmosis I to leave no son at all. The usurpers Mineptah–Siptah and Seti II, who each reigned for six years, were probably both descendants of Ramses' royal brood. The final usurper was an impious naturalized Syrian called Yarsu, an ignominious state of affairs which could only have been brought about by prolonged disorganization of the political machine. Eventually, after a lapse of two more decades of confusion, a powerful individual called Setnakht seized power about 1200 B.C. and founded the *Twentieth Dynasty*. In a short reign of two years he achieved a notable revival of strong centralized government.

The second king of the *TWENTIETH DYNASTY* (1200–1085 B.C.) was Setnakht's son RAMSES III (1198–1166 B.C.). The claim of Ramses III to be called 'the Great' is at least as valid as Ramses II's. He continued the work of rescuing the country from the plight in which his father found it, paying particular attention to a revision of the class system. The status and rights of every member of the community were clearly redefined, a much needed reform in view of the social havoc wrought by indiscriminate immigration, weak administration and regal usurpation. Under Ramses III's guidance Egypt seemed to return for thirty years to the palmy days of the Eighteenth Dynasty. The worship of the gods was restored to its former dignity, trade flourished, mining expeditions were sent out and the empire paid regular tribute. The king beautified Thebes and made additions to Karnak, and at Medinet Habu he built a great palace-temple worthy of an imperial Pharaoh. But Ramses was required to wage unrelenting war on his country's ever-threatening antagonists. The Libyans, undaunted by the thrashing administered to them by Mineptah, tried a second time to march on Memphis. Ramses got wind of their intention and fell upon them before their plans matured, making prisoner all whom he failed to massacre. In the eighth year of his reign the Sea Peoples, who were the instigators of the Libyan troubles, were considerably reinforced, and they now felt strong enough to make a direct frontal attack on Egypt. The Sea Peoples had been for three centuries the scourge of Hither Asia. Pouring in from the Russian steppes and south-eastern Europe, they comprised either wild tribesmen or ferocious sea raiders. Everywhere they acted in concert. They lent the Mycenaeans their aid in destroying Crete, they joined with the Phrygians in undermining the Hittites, they overran Cyprus, Carchemish and Cilicia. In the grand assault on Egypt six groups of the Sea People banded together their forces. The most formidable were the spike-helmeted Shardana, probably from Lydia, who ironically enough had taken part as mercenaries on the Egyptian side in the battle of Kadesh. They were almost certainly the Sardinians of later date. A second group were the Shakalsha, from Sagalassus in Phrygia, who eventually sailed westwards to colonize Sicily. Thirdly came the Danuna, the Danaans, shortly to play their part in the Trojan Wars. A fourth element were the Washasha, perhaps the Oassians of Asia Minor. The last two tribes in the Egyptian account were the Pulesati and the Zakkala. The Pulesati appear to have been refugees from Crete who became the Philistines of the Palestinian mainland, while the Zakkala too were Mediterranean sea wanderers of some denomination. Among other members of the confederation of Sea People who made an appearance in Egyptian history at this or other moments were the Luka, or Lycians, and the Tursha, from Tarsus in Cilicia. Ramses was confronted with a simultaneous sea and land attack by these formidable professional buccaneers. A pirate fleet sailed on the Delta while an army of Sea People set out overland from Southern Palestine. A tremendous sea battle, dramatically depicted on reliefs at Medinet Habu, was fought near the mouth of the Delta. The Egyptian bowmen annihilated the pirate crews with their accurate fire, then rammed, boarded and sank the enemy craft. 'I capsized their ships and their riches fell into the water,' boasted Ramses. The Egyptians then turned at leisure to chase the Pulesati and their fellow bandits back into the desert. Undaunted, the Sea Peoples again coalesced with the Libyans to attack Memphis four years later. Again they were repulsed with fearful loss. The aged Libyan leader came personally to Pharaoh to beg the life of his son, who had been taken prisoner. Ramses' answer was to imprison the old man and put his son to death. Other captives were apportioned as slaves to fortresses and temples or branded and set to work as oarsmen in the Egyptian galleys. Many became shepherds of the flocks of Amon-Ra. For twenty years after these splendid victories Egypt enjoyed untroubled prosperity, but the last years of the king were clouded by a conspiracy aimed at his life. A first conspiracy was an unimportant affair concocted by a disgruntled provincial vizier at Athribis, but the second was a well thought out major attempt emanating from the king's own household. One of the king's minor wives determined to seize the throne for her son, who joined her in the plot against his father's life. Two high dignitaries at court were also persuaded to become accomplices. A sorcerer was called in to make wax models of the king and his chief officers on which malign spells were written. In the upshot the deadly harîm conspiracy was unmasked. Pharaoh became 'like a panther' with rage. The ringleaders were put on trial, and during the proceedings it came to light that three of the judges and two police officials were in league with the accused persons. They were thereupon arrested and put in the dock. One of the judges was found to be innocent, but the other two were sentenced to have their ears and noses cut off. Ramses permitted the chief conspirators, including his son, the boon of 'dying of themselves,' that is, of taking their own lives. The fate of the treacherous wife is not recorded. Altogether forty men and six women were executed, including the Steward of the Harîm, the Majordomo, the Captain of the Bowmen and the Fan Bearer.

In the course of the following eighty years eight other Ramses ruled in Egypt. They were men of little character whose ineptitude brought the New Kingdom to an inglorious close. The order in which they reigned is disputed, but the Pharaohs labelled Ramses IX and Ramses XI ruled for nineteen and twenty-seven years respectively. The greater portion of the wealth accumulated during Ramses III's campaigns in Asia was poured into the treasure-rooms of Amon-Ra, and on the king's death the god's devotees were supreme in the state. While the members of the Ramesside family bickered among themselves for possession of the crown of their mighty namesakes, the priesthood of Amon-Ra unobtrusively organized itself into an impregnable hierarchy. The monarchy, relying for authority on religious approval, was assisting in its own downfall. It is significant that on the large relief at Karnak in which the high priest of Amon-Ra acknowledges the receipt of gifts from Ramses IX the figure of the priest is carved on the same heroic scale as that of his sovereign. The Theban priests, nevertheless, were unfortunately immersed exclusively in political machinations. Firm central government ceased to exist. The population began to go hungry. The sad condition of the country led to a terrible outbreak of tomb robbery during the reign of Ramses IX. In vain the priesthood strove to stop the desecration of the hallowed necropoles. It became necessary to re-inter the royal mummies with unseemly haste and despatch. Finally the Ramessides became the puppets or virtual palace-prisoners of their own ecclesiastics. The urban mobs were showing every sign of restlessness. Imperial Thebes was in decline.

CHAPTER X

History: Three

From the beginning of the Twenty-first Dynasty may be dated the LATE PERIOD (1085–332 B.C.) of ancient Egyptian history. Some authorities refer to it less politely as the Decadence. The Late Period, which continued until the extinction of the last native dynasty by the conquest of Alexander the Great, was nevertheless by no means an epoch of hopeless declension. Within its span of seven hundred and fifty years were numbered several brilliant reigns.

With the ineffectual close of the Ramesside era the Two Lands once more found themselves divided. The nominal head of the state was the titular founder of the *Twenty-first Dynasty* (1085–950 B.C.), an elderly vizier of Lower Egypt called Smendes. The claim of Smendes to the succession may have derived from the royal origin of his wife, Tentamon. He ruled from his native city of Tanis, in the Delta. The real power in the land was located at Thebes, where the high priest of Amon and vizier of Upper Egypt, Herihor, was installed. Herihor, also an elderly man, appears to have been a soldier who was presented with the office of high priest by the last of the bankrupt Ramessides. On his death he was succeeded by his son Piankhi, who after a short interval was followed by his own son, Pinodjem I. Pinodjem married the daughter of Smendes' successor, Psousennes I, and for a short period he was ruler of a united country after the death of his father-in-law. It fell to Pinodjem to rewrap the bodies of the Pharaohs whose tombs in the Valley of the Kings had been violated. He gave orders for them to be interred in a secret place behind the

184

Temple of Hatshepsut, where they lay undisturbed for three thousand years.

Pinodjem I appears to have carried on his somewhat unsteady rule from Tanis, after relinquishing the Theban pontificate to his sons. One of the high priests, Menkheperra, put down a revolt of the citizens with great severity. Many of the leaders were executed or sent as exiles to the desert oases. The troubled unity of the Two Lands was sundered with the death of Pinodjem I, when the Theban priest-kings once more reverted to virtual independence under the nominal suzerainty of Tanis. Menkheperra was succeeded by Pinodjem II, who transferred the mummies of the great kings of the Nineteenth Dynasty from their own gorgeous sepulchres to the tomb of an obscure queen. Even this precaution was unable to secure undisturbed repose for their remains. The arch-thieves of the Twentieth Dynasty had spawned a host of worthy disciples. In Lower Egypt the Twenty-first Dynasty came to an end with two monarchs called Amenophthis and Siamon, the latter the only Tanite king to leave behind him many monuments. At Thebes the line of priest-kings terminated after the reign of Pinodjem II with a ruler called Psousennes II. Throughout the entire dynasty the real ruler of the kingdom was neither priest-king nor Tanite, but the god Amon-Ra. The priesthood did not scruple to play upon the superstition of the god's worshippers for purely mercenary reasons. Political decisions were taken by Amon-Ra as a matter of course. The written petition was laid before him and the deity either signified or withheld his approval. Under the New Kingdom the will of the god had been consulted only in cases of special importance. Horemhab, for example, had done so in order to impart conviction to the way in which he rigged his election to the throne. Under the dispensation of the high priests, however, the oracle boomed forth its mandates from morning till night. The head of the sacred image wagged incessantly, manipulated like a ventriloquist's doll by a concealed cleric.

After an undistinguished century during which the stand-ing of Egypt throughout the ancient world dwindled to nothing, imperial rule was assumed about 950 B.C. by an energetic soldier called SHASHANK I (950–929 B.C.), founder of the *TWENTY-SECOND* and *TWENTY-THIRD (LIBYAN) DYNASTIES* (950–730 B.C.). Shashank was a Libyan prince by part descent, and his Libyan successors were to rule Egypt for over two centuries. His forebears were the captives or mercenaries engaged by Ramses III to hold the Libyans and Sea People at bay. Ultimately large numbers of the enemy were employed to keep their own fellow-countrymen from Egyptian soil. The formidable Sea People eventually intermarried with their Libyan allies and acquired the status of a dominant caste, from which sprang the ancestors of Shashank. At first his family were commanders of the military colony at Herakleopolis, but when the divided rule of the Twenty-first Dynasty reduced Middle Egypt to a kind of political no-man's-land the Libyan generals took control of their own destinies. In the closing years of the Tanite kings they extended their influence as far downstream as Bubastis, which they later made their capital. When the time came for him to mount the throne, Shashank was careful to secure the semblance of legitimate succession for his heirs by marrying his son Osorkon to the daughter of Psousennes II.

The history of the Bubastites is highly confused. The native population continued as always to pursue its traditional manner of life under a frank military dictatorship. The Libyan princes, with the backing of their legionaries, maintained themselves in power despite perpetual disputes among them-selves. They constantly regrouped into different factions, and the cadet branches of their families were a continual source of trouble. Shashank I lost no time in proclaiming his son chief priest of Amon-Ra, thereby implanting a Bubastite viceroy in the territory of the disgruntled priesthood. These viceroys later tended to carve out an individual realm for themselves or even actively to rebel against the authority of the Delta. The office of chief priest was therefore abolished in an attempt to remedy the situation, and a chief priestess appointed instead. The chief priestesses, known as the Divine Worshippers of Amon-Ra, ruled at Thebes from the middle of the Twenty-third to the end of the Thirtieth Dynasty, but it cannot be said that the new essay in political stability was an unqualified success. It was found that in unsettled periods the rule of a woman needed to be supported by the local military leader, whose tool she thereupon became. The device served a useful purpose, however, in that it enabled the immense wealth of Shashank I to be transmitted from one of his heirs to another with the minimum of discord, in accordance with the custom of a matriarchal society. Shashank had amassed this wealth during his short and spectacular Palestinian campaign of 935 B.C. He took skilful advantage of the split which occurred in Palestinian government after the death of Solomon. Ten of the twelve tribes formed themselves into the Kingdom of Israel under the leadership of Jeroboam, with the secret connivance of Egypt. The tribes of Judah and Benjamin became a separate little kingdom under Roboam, Solomon's son. Under the pretext of assisting Jeroboam, Shashank, the Shishak of the Book of Kings, fell upon the Kingdom of Judah and sacked Judah and Jerusalem. From the Temple and the Treasury at Jerusalem he carried off the almost legendary wealth accumulated by David and Solomon. The booty was sufficiently extensive to provide the Libyan kings of Egypt with great personal fortunes during the entire period of their ascendancy.

For nearly a century and a half the Two Lands were administered by a single Libyan royal house, but during the fifty-year reign of SHASHANK III (823–772 B.C.) the Upper Egyptians broke away from the Delta under the influence of a second branch of the Bubastite Libyans. The Bubastites continued to be known as the Twenty-second Dynasty, while the overlapping Theban dynasty constituted the Twenty-third. Both

187

contained rulers with the characteristic Libyan surnames of Shashank, Osorkon and Takelot. The rift between the kingdoms was the beginning of a more serious disintegration of the fabric of government. Opportunist nomarchs or army officers were prompt in making their authority absolute in their own district, with the result that the local governors of Hermopolis and Herakleopolis eventually claimed royal honours in addition to the legitimate rulers. It was perhaps as well for the security of the Nile valley in this period of political distraction that the campaign of Shashank I had raised Egyptian prestige in Asia to a high pitch. Cordial relations once more existed with the trading cities of Phoenicia, which under the Twenty-first Dynasty had insulted Egyptian ambassadors with impunity. The small states of Hither Asia, which were to turn again and again to Egypt for help in their hour of need, were nevertheless to discover that they had sadly overestimated the reputation of Egyptian arms. During the entire Late Period the allies of Egypt found her, in the contemptuous words of Sennacherib, a broken reed.

Towards the year 730 B.C. the lord of Saïs in the Delta, a prince named Tefnakht, undertook the task of subduing his neighbouring dynasts. After annexing the Western Delta he captured Tanis and Bubastis, strongholds of the Eastern Delta, and then turned towards Upper Egypt. The self-constituted kingdoms of Memphis and Hermopolis succumbed to him, and he then set about the siege of Herakleopolis. At this point an extraordinary and dramatic event occurred. The king of Nubia, PIANKHI, decided to invade Egypt, perhaps to prevent the able prince of Saïs from penetrating beyond Middle Egypt and consolidating a power which could challenge the growing strength of his country. Piankhi was considered by later Egyptians to be the founder of the *TWENTY-FIFTH (ETHIOPIAN) DYNASTY* (730–656 B.C.). It no doubt appears strange that the former colony of Nubia could exert its will over Egypt in this manner, but history furnishes many instances of colonies which outgrow the parent country. The conquest by the Mycenaeans of their Cretan homeland is an obvious example. The creation of the viceroyalty of Nubia at the majestic apogee of the Eighteenth Dynasty was described in Chapter IV. The 'royal son of Kush' introduced into savage Nubia a replica of the manners and mode of government of the royal court at Thebes. The viceroy comported himself as a miniature Pharaoh, and in consequence the Negro became acquainted with the ways of civilization. In particular the strong ties which grew up between their capital at Napata and the holy city of Thebes made a deep impression on their minds. They developed into dignified and devout worshippers of Amon-Ra. The priest-kings of the Twenty-first Dynasty, who contrived to maintain a firm hold on Nubia for the sake of its gold supplies, were not slow to imprint respect for the great nationalist god still more indelibly upon the imaginations of the simple blacks. Soon afterwards the priest-kings themselves were expelled in large numbers from Thebes by Shashank and his Libyans, and it is probable that a portion of the clergy of Amon-Ra took refuge in Napata, where they would be sure of a loyal welcome. Napata became the Avignon of the cult of Amon-Ra, and during two centuries of Libyan rule in Egypt, when Nubia and Egypt were irrevocably sundered, the Nubians evolved a richly barbaric version of Nilotic culture. When Piankhi set out on the conquest of Egypt from the huge Temple of Amon-Ra at Napata, he may have regarded himself as a crusader, the spiritual heir of the Theban monarchy, destined to restore to a forgetful nation the traditions his own people had carefully nurtured. The temple at Napata, on the slopes of the mountain of Geb el-Barkal, was completely Egyptian in style, with meticulously accurate reliefs and hieroglyphic inscriptions. Egyptian was the official language of the country, and the Nubians had even affected the use of the pyramid (p. 75).

Piankhi had ruled at Napata for over twenty years before his incursion into Egypt. The Nubians appear to have been content

189

with their previous state of prosperous isolation, and the invasion was perhaps due to the personal initiative of their king. The expedition set sail in well-found ships, encountering the forces of Tefnakht in the region of Thebes. From the ensuing battle Piankhi emerged victorious, and it was altogether characteristic of the pious Negro to delay the campaign by lingering at Thebes to celebrate the New Year festival. We can picture the exaltation of the black soldier when he was conducted into the original sanctuary of the god of his country. On resuming the fight, he first besieged Hermopolis, where the townsfolk managed to put up a sturdy resistance. But the resistance of the Hermopolitans was nothing in comparison with the gallant struggle of the Memphites to prevent him entering the Delta. For a time Piankhi was baffled, before he noticed that the garrison, anticipating an attack by land, had neglected their riverward defences. The Nubians promptly made a waterborne attack in their neat craft and overwhelmed their opponents. Tefnakht rallied his last battalions and made a stand in the Delta, but the result of the campaign was a foregone conclusion. Both commanders had proved themselves during the course of hostilities to be skilful tacticians, although the initial advantage lay always with the resolute, aggressive and inspired negroes. The local nomarchs came to Piankhi's camp at Athribis to make formal surrender, and were shortly afterwards followed thither by the reluctant Tefnakht. The prince of Saïs was honourably and courteously treated by his conqueror. Then, doubtless to the astonishment of the entire country, the Nubians suddenly decided to make their way back to Nubia. Why they should elect to do so is obscure. Perhaps they came to Egypt equipped only for a short campaign, perhaps as negroes they felt ill at ease among the fair-skinned Egyptians, perhaps they were overawed by the splendours of a land which for generations had been a legend to them. Or perhaps they were merely homesick for their own country. Piankhi was in any case a shrewd enough general to realize that the unexpected completeness of his victory did not necessarily imply the smooth administration of the conquered territories. Whatever the reason for their decision, the Nubians departed as rapidly as they came. A surprised and thankful Osorkon, last king of the Libyan Twenty-third Dynasty, was left to reoccupy Thebes. The irrepressible Tefnakht at once reimposed his sway on Memphis and the Delta.

During the decade which followed the departure of the Nubians, Tefnakht once again exerted himself with remarkable success. He became undisputed lord of the Delta. He was succeeded by his son Bocchoris, and together father and son comprise the brief Twenty-fourth Dynasty (730-715 B.C.). In Upper Egypt the Nubians exercised control through nominees who received orders from Napata. Bocchoris was remembered with affection by the Egyptians as a wise law giver and a valiant if unfortunate defender of his native land. He certainly inherited his father's political ability, for unlike his Libyan predecessors and his Nubian successors he was able to appreciate the growing menace of Ashur. He sent judicious presents to Sargon II, at the same time surreptitiously inciting revolt against the Assyrians in their Palestinian dependencies.

Bocchoris was beginning to feel his way into Middle Egypt when Piankhi's son SHABAKA (716-701 B.C.) determined that the time was ripe to bring the Nubians again into Egypt. This time the Twenty-fifth Dynasty was to entrench itself firmly on Egyptian soil. According to Manetho, Shabaka captured Bocchoris and burned him alive, which suggests that the son did not inherit his father's chivalry. He established his capital at Thebes, and with the solemn piety of all the kings of his dynasty set about the renovation of religious buildings up and down the entire country. After a reign of fifteen years, during which he practised a half-hearted policy of appeasement towards Sargon II, he died and was succeeded by his son Shabataka. The power behind the throne during the ten-year reign of this unassuming monarch was the young prince

Taharka, an able and ambitious son of the great Piankhi. Taharka led an army into Palestine to attempt to bolster up one of the endless coalitions against Ashur, now ruled by Sennacherib. The pitiless armies of Ashur were busily laying siege to Jerusalem, and Taharka, with more courage than sense, determined to march to the relief of the embattled Ezechias of Judah. Fortunately for the black generalissimo and his Palestinian ally the forces of Sennacherib were at this juncture decimated by the mysterious pestilence described in the Second Book of Kings. The Assyrian remnant made off homeward, leaving Egypt and Palestine to enjoy a short respite. In 690 B.C. Sennacherib was assassinated by his sons, and according to Manetho it was in this same year that TAHARKA (690–664 B.C.) murdered Shabataka and ascended the throne. He appears to have been madly possessed by a fantasy of restoring to Egypt her lost empire. He moved his court to Tanis in the Eastern Delta, where he could more conveniently direct Palestinian resistance to the new king of Ashur, Esarhaddon. To control Theban affairs he appointed a governor called Mentuemhat, a functionary whose membership of the priesthood of Amon-Ra was purely honorary. The priests of Amon-Ra were at this time prohibited from interference in civil matters. Taharka was politically more sapient than his Nubian forebears, and he decided to set up a military dictatorship of a more thorough-going character than the Libyans had done. Possibly a second governor was installed in distant Napata. The kingdom of Egypt now stretched from the Mediterranean to the junction of the White and Blue Niles.

The axis of the ancient world was shifting. The blissful isolation of Egypt was a thing of the past. This new and uncomfortable orientation had become manifest during the struggle between Ramses III and the Sea People. It was suggested in the first chapter that the ideal centre of government was Memphis, a city within easy reach of each of the Two Lands. The emergence of a closely knit Eastern Mediterranean world required the capital to be sited at some vantage point on the Mediterranean littoral, which inevitably resulted in the dislocation of administration. Events in Asia were now moving with an increased momentum. The dreaded Assyrians were again on the march in Palestine, where they were sacking town after town and sowing salt, as their custom was, upon the smoking ruins. In 671 B.C. Esarhaddon finally tired of the continual provocation sponsored by Taharka and planned a direct assault on Egypt itself. He thrust across the desert with his incomparable troops in a series of forced marches and swooped at once on Memphis. Taharka, whose information service and sense of strategy were somewhat inadequate for a soldier who aspired to world conquest, had massed his forces in the Delta, anticipating that Esarhaddon's blow would fall on Tanis. By taking Memphis the army of the Assyrians bestrode Taharka's lines of communication. The resistance in the Delta collapsed and Pharaoh's family and harîm fell into the hands of the invader. Taharka himself fled to Nubia, leaving to Mentuemhat the distasteful obligation of surrendering Upper Egypt to Esarhaddon. The king of Ashur could not afford to spend many weeks in the valley of the Nile, and he soon returned to war-troubled Asia, leaving behind a small garrison. The local princes of the Delta became Assyrian governors, many of them adopting Assyrian names both for their cities and themselves. The lord of Saïs, Bocchoris' son Neko, was among the number who performed this ignoble act. On the departure of Esarhaddon, Taharka emerged once more and retook Memphis, with the help of several of the governors appointed by the Assyrians. Enraged at this news, the king of Ashur marched immediately on Egypt, only to fall sick and die *en route*.

But Assyrian vengeance was merely postponed. In 666 B.C. Ashurbanipal pounced on the Two Lands, and on this occasion Thebes was occupied for good measure. The treacherous princes of the Delta were deported to Nineveh, where no doubt a grim fate awaited them. The servile Neko paid what appears to have been a state visit to the capital of Ashur, for he was sent back to his native Saïs laden with gifts. The diplomatic Mentuemhat succeeded a second time in saving Thebes from the sword, but it was to be systematically pillaged two years later when Ashurbanipal made a second punitive expedition to Egypt to drive back an attempt at liberation. The forces of Nubia and Egypt were on this occasion led by Tanutamon, who reigned at Napata since the death of Taharka in 664 B.C. The third Assyrian invasion dealt the Nubian dynasty its death-blow. Henceforward the Negro abandoned all pretensions beyond their own frontiers. They retained their autonomy until the dawn of our own era, but after leaving Egypt they quickly reverted to a savage mode of life. The capital was removed deeper into the African interior, from Napata to Meroë, between the Fifth and Sixth Cataracts. A purely African language was adopted and a script known as the Meroïtic script was introduced.

The Ethiopian Dynasty yielded power to the last great independent dynasty, the *TWENTY-SIXTH (SAITE) DYNASTY* (663–525 B.C.). For a brief century and a half the Egyptians were to enjoy a mellow St. Martin's summer of prosperity. The capital of the new dynasty was located at Saïs, the Delta city which was patronized by the Assyrians. PSAMMETICHUS I (663–609 B.C.), a distant relative of the resolute Tefnakht of the Twenty-fourth Dynasty, was the son of the abject Neko, the prince who collaborated with the invader. Psammetichus accompanied his father on his visit to Nineveh, when Neko was fêted by Ashurbanipal, and on his return the boy was appointed prince of Athribis. After the Egyptian *débâcle* under Tanutamon, Psammetichus wiped out the shame of his country, his province and his family by rousing his countrymen and driving the Assyrians pell-mell into Palestine. He chased them far from the Egyptian frontier, and there is a record of the long siege which he made of the Assyrian strongpoint at Ashdod.

Once more the states of Asia were losing any semblance of political stability, even under the aegis of some single tyrant. A bare half century after the triumph of Psammetichus the Medes were to sweep across from Ecbatana to help the resurgent neo-Babylonians sack Nineveh, whereat a mighty howl of joy was uplifted all over the ancient world. The victory of Psammetichus was achieved largely with the help of foreign mercenaries, the bulk of whom were Greek. The greater proportion of the mercenaries was composed of troops sent to the assistance of Psammetichus by Gyges, king of Lydia. After the war these Ionian, Carian and Rhodian troops were settled on great military reserves outside the urban areas, where they encountered much local hostility. Their proved ability as fighters also led to their disposal at vulnerable strategic points. At Daphnae in the Eastern Delta, for example, they formed the bulwark of Egypt against the Asiatics, while in far-off Elephantine they were charged with the task of guarding the gates of the valley from a belated attempt at reconquest by the Nubians. Libyan and Nubian detachments still formed part of the Egyptian army, but the king now relied increasingly on his Greek contingents. The navy fell under the influence of the Corinthians, who were masters of the arts of ship-building and navigation. After the mercenaries came the traders. At first, like the soldiers, the Greek merchants were compelled to form small colonies in the Delta. They soon showed so marked a mercantile flair that such emporia as Naucratis rapidly became the richest cities in Egypt. At the end of the Saïte Dynasty the rules regulating the movements of immigrants were relaxed and bodies of Samians and Milesians spread to Middle and Upper Egypt.

Psammetichus, a man of sagacity and will, was faced with a delicate problem of government in Upper Egypt. It was imperative that he should remain at Saïs in order to survey the busy world of the Mediterranean, but the elderly Mentuemhat was still in control at Thebes, where he demonstrated a

ANCIENT EGYPT

commendable loyalty towards the lost cause of his former masters, the Nubians. A further complication was that the spiritual ruler of Upper Egypt, the Divine Worshipper of Amon-Ra, was a daughter of Piankhi. Psammetichus therefore installed his own daughter Nitocris as ward of the Ethiopian princess. Since the line of the chief priestesses had acquired substantial property in the territory between Thebes and Elephantine, he took care to appoint a reliable governor of the nomes in the vicinity of the Nubian border. This governor was stationed at Edfu, while another governor was placed at Herakleopolis to administer the country between the Thebaïd and the Delta. In the Delta itself he followed the same wise policy of conciliation as in Upper Egypt, for Herodotus records that by origin he was merely one of a Dodecarchy or confederation of twelve powerful princes, the remainder of whom he successfully appeased on his accession to the throne. The economic recovery of the Two Lands during the course of his reign was also due in large measure to the extraordinary recrudescence of the national spirit apparent at the beginning of the Saïte epoch. The expulsion of the Assyrians, like the expulsion of the Hyksôs, was accomplished by a monarch of vigorous personality in command of a nation united in its desire to expunge the memory of foreign occupation. In the case of the Saïtes this desire was increased by the previous subservience of the country to a long succession of Libyan and Nubian rulers.

The spiritual revival, the new awareness of the great destiny of Egypt, was revealed in every phase of national life. There was a universal determination to cleave to traditional ways, to repeat the glories of the past. In politics this determination to redefine a pattern of behaviour which was innately and specifically Egyptian took the form of an intense dislike of the foreigner, particularly when he dwelt on Egyptian soil. No doubt Psammetichus encountered many difficulties in his championship of the Greeks, who were guilty of the additional

196

crime of deserving well of their hosts. The Greeks were held in such repugnance by the natives that we are told that no Egyptian would kiss a Greek or use a Greek's knife. In religion the new tendency manifested itself in the abjuration of all exotic gods and the adoration of the most venerable deities. In a period which gave itself up to intense intellectual and artistic activity the cult of Ptah became particularly prominent. The ancient cult of Neith, patroness of Saïs, was also intensified. In place of the recensions of the Book of the Dead on rolls of papyrus, wealthy citizens now sanctified their tombs with spells from the Old Kingdom Pyramid Texts inscribed upon the walls. Some Saïte tombs were exact replicas of Old Kingdom mastabas. Every religious, artistic and architectural device of the Old Kingdom was passionately imitated. Egypt was attempting to recover her lost youth. The pristine forms of hieroglyphic characters were laboriously copied, while literary productions of the early periods were closely studied and their style emulated. Old Kingdom statuary was reproduced with such skill that without an accompanying inscription a Saïte statue is frequently impossible to distinguish from a statue of the Fourth, Fifth or Sixth Dynasty. In general, however, Saïte statuary is paradoxically too perfect: the astounding technical skill of the sculptor becomes virtuosity indulged in for its own sake. Saïte artists, exulting in their powers, executed works of a florid character that bespeak a civilization which has become like a ripe fruit, ready to fall. Side by side with idealized statues are statues carved with an almost macabre realism. Flattering portraits alternate with clinical studies of ugliness and old age. Yet in its own over-sophisticated manner Saïte art is superb. Two peculiarities of Saïte statuary may be mentioned: firstly, the predilection for hard and sombre materials, and secondly the occasional use of the so-called 'archaic smile.' The archaic smile was a peculiarity of Greek sculpture which may have found its way to Egypt from increased intercourse with Cyprus. The soft-fibred sculptors of the Saïte revival misunderstood the intention of the archaic smile. In early Greek religious statuary it was meant to be a symbol of inhuman and remote benevolence, of kinship with the high gods. The Saïtes reduced it to the fatuous simper on the face of a scribe. Its employment on statues which in all other respects are formally of Old Kingdom appearance is a subtle indication of Saïte ignorance of the true temper of the centuries of early greatness. To the sculptor of the Old Kingdom, with the conception of his work outlined in Chapter VI, the archaic smile would have been akin to blasphemy. It has been said, in conclusion, that the history of art is the history of revivals, but it would not be too much to say that the intellectual nostalgia of the artists of the Saïte epoch, with its pathological overtones, is only paralleled in art history by the antiquarian mania of Renaissance Italy.

The sound domestic policy of Psammetichus restored Egypt to a state of affluence which encouraged his son NEKO (609–594 B.C.) to pursue the old imperial dream in Asia. The Saïtes were striving to identify themselves not only with the inward spirit of their ancestors but also with their outward panoply. Neko no sooner came to the throne than he led his troops eastwards. His ostensible aim was to assist the shattered armies of the Assyrians, under their last emperor Ashuruballit II, against the neo-Babylonians under Nabopolassar and the Medes under Cyaxares. At Megiddo the Egyptians fell upon Josias, the king of Judah, who had allied himself with Babylon, killing him and routing his forces. After installing the compliant Joiakim in his place, Neko subdued Syria and resumed his march towards the Euphrates. For one dazzling moment the flame of conquest was rekindled: the empire of Neko was the empire of Tuthmosis III. The Saïtes had resumed the mantle of their forefathers, albeit with the assistance of a legion of Greeks. But the imperial torch was quickly quenched. In 605 B.C. the young Babylonian heir-apparent, Nebuchadnezzar, met the Egyptians at Carchemish and totally crushed them.

Neko's broken forces fled for Egypt, leaving the Asian empire to crumble. Nebuchadnezzar would no doubt have followed up his victory by invading Egypt itself, but the sudden death of his father obliged him to return to Babylon. Neko's hopes of re-entering Asia were extinguished by the Babylonian annexation of Palestine. At the end of his reign he pinned his faith to a sea invasion, to which end he began to build an impressive fleet. He appears to have been more adventurous in his conception of sea power than previous Pharaohs, perhaps because he inherited and developed his father's policy of extensive overseas trade. It was Neko who began the construction of an overland link between the Red Sea and the Mediterranean, precursor of the Suez Canal. He also despatched a squadron of hardy Phoenicians on an examination of trade routes around the coast of Africa. The mariners appear to have accomplished the periplus or circumnavigation of the entire African continent, an enterprise which took them three years.

The six-year reign of Psammetichus II (594–588 B.C.) is ill-documented. An ill-assorted brigade of Greeks, Phoenicians, Egyptians and perhaps Jews made the kind of armed foray into Nubia that belongs in spirit to an earlier age. The army, commanded by the future Pharaoh Amasis, at this time a professional soldier, penetrated as far as the Second Cataract. Some of the Greek mercenaries carved their names on one of the colossi of Ramses II at Abu Simbel, now deep in hostile territory. Psammetichus also seems to have made a state visit to Phoenicia. The relations of the next Pharaoh with Phoenicia were less amiable, for Apries (588–568 B.C.) lost no time in besieging Sidon and blockading Tyre. His Phoenician war was a failure, however, and he was forced to abandon any larger scheme for combating the influence of the Babylonians in Asia. It was during the reign of Apries that the Jews were led off to the Captivity. Jewish refugees flocked to Egypt, where Pharaoh, no doubt prompted by the mercantile instinct of the Saïtes, settled them in colonies extending as far upstream as Elephantine. The end of the reign of Apries was unfortunate. About 570 B.C. the Greek colonists at Cyrene came to blows with their Libyan neighbours. The Libyans appealed to Apries, who dared not use his Greek troops in a dispute where Greeks were involved. His expeditionary force of Egyptians was soundly beaten, and during the subsequent outcry at this affront to tender national susceptibilities the general charged with ending the disturbances led a rebellion against his sovereign. After two years of uncertainty the crisis was resolved in favour of the general, AMASIS (568–525 B.C.), the popular favourite. Amasis was a bluff, crafty, Falstaffian personage, much addicted to wine and women. He ruled with marked ability for over forty years, surviving an early defeat by Nebuchadnezzar on the borders of the Delta and contriving, according to Herodotus, to occupy Cyprus. He soothed the indignation felt by his countrymen against the Greeks with such adroitness that he was ultimately able to allay Greek anxiety by marrying a Cyrenian princess. His reign was exceedingly prosperous, although this genial fellow hardly recommended himself to posterity by instituting the income tax. In the field of foreign affairs the problems he bequeathed to his successor proved insuperable. He watched the advance of the Medes and Persians with disquietude, and he joined with Nabonidus of Babylon and Croesus of Lydia to oppose them. Sparta and Samos were also leagued with many other nations in opposition to the new power. But Cyrus, the young Persian who beat his overlord Astyages the Mede and yoked his power with his own, was a military leader of genius. He defeated Nabonidus and Croesus, leaving Egypt to await the Persian onslaught bereft of allies.

The Egyptians were attacked by Persia in 525 B.C., when the unfortunate Psammetichus III had been Pharaoh for less than a year. CAMBYSES (525–522 B.C.) annihilated the Egyptian army after a hotly contested engagement at Pelusium. The Persian victory was due in no small measure to the commander of the Egyptian fleet, who not only delivered up his ships to

Cambyses but also betrayed the defence preparations of Psammetichus. The disaffected Cyrenians also came to offer their services to the conqueror. Psammetichus stuck it out until the surrender of Memphis, when he committed suicide. Despite the horrific tales related to Herodotus, Cambyses evidently behaved with restraint. He is the founder of the *TWENTY-SEVENTH (PERSIAN) DYNASTY* (525–405 B.C.). Like many a conqueror before him and after him, he adopted the full titulary, observed the rites of Egyptian religion and respected native customs. He inspected Upper Egypt, tried without success to reach Napata, and then left the Nile valley. The great DARIUS I (522–485 B.C.) came to Egypt in 518 B.C. to quell disturbances with which the Persian satrap had dealt ineptly. He too imitated the native Pharaohs, ordering a great temple to be built to Amon-Ra in the great oasis of el-Kharga with stone from the ancient quarries of the Wadi Hammamat. He completed Neko's canal between the Mediterranean and the Red Sea. The Persians took pains to secure the proper administration of Egypt because it was the richest of all the provinces of their empire. The provinces or satrapies of the Persian empire were organized with great skill and good sense, and Persian methods contributed much to the government of the later empires of the ancient world.

Egypt, which had experienced outside interference so many times before, was not at all overawed by the armed might of Persia. The brutish XERXES (485–464 B.C.) arrived in person to put down a revolt stimulated by the defeat of Darius at Marathon four years previously. The revolt seems to have occurred in 486 B.C., and the success of the Greeks in repelling Xerxes at Salamis in 480 B.C. encouraged the Egyptians to further resistance. There was a major revolt against ARTAXERXES (464–424 B.C.), whose army was defeated at a great battle at Papremis in the Delta. The leader of the Greek mercenaries and the Persian satrap were both killed in the ferocious encounter, in which the Egyptians were assisted by a fleet of

Athenian warships which had hurriedly set sail from Cyprus. Within two years the Persians turned the tables. The satrap of Syria was despatched with a large army and the Phoenician fleet, and in the subsequent battle Inaros, the Libyan patriot chief who appears to have been a son of Psammetichus III, was wounded, captured and sent to Susa, where Artaxerxes put him to death. His lieutenant, Amyrtis, prince of Saïs, carried on guerilla warfare in the Delta until 449 B.C., when the new satrap, Sasarmas, offered honourable terms of surrender. The war of liberation was not resumed for another forty years, when Amyrtis (404-398 B.C.), one and only representative of the *Twenty-eighth Dynasty*, took advantage of Persian distractions in Asia to drive out the foreign garrisons. Little is known of Amyrtis, a son or grandson of the earlier Amyrtis, but his gallant campaign is sufficient to assure him an honoured place in Egyptian annals.

The four Pharaohs of the short-lived *Twenty-ninth Dynasty* (398-378 B.C.), which originated from Mendes, were Nepherites I, Achoris, Psammouthis and Nepherites II. With the exception of Achoris, who ruled for twelve years, they were all ephemeral monarchs, hindered at every turn by the subterfuges of rival dynasts. In the Late Period strong kings with universally acknowledged authority were rare, and for a Pharaoh in the real sense of the word it would be necessary to glance backward to the New Kingdom. But it must not be thought that the constant drumming and trampling up and down the valley, or to and from Asia, represented a complete dislocation of the traditional mode of existence. Superficially the Egyptian scribe, priest, artisan and peasant lived the same life as his forefathers. The time-honoured patterns of behaviour remained intact. Kings and kesars traipsed here and there with frenetic energy: the dwellers in the Black Land continued to recite their litanies to Osiris and Amon-Ra, to manufacture scarabs and *ushabtis*, to build pylons and hypostyle halls. The habits of mind and body ingrained during the progress of three millennia were not easily abandoned. The presumptuous conqueror could bring little that was novel or attractive to a land so old, so noble and so rich in experience. During the Late Period, nevertheless, the vital spark was slowly fading, until during the Ptolemaic epoch the indwelling spirit was totally extinct and all that remained was a lifeless, meaningless code of conduct.

The story of the dynasties is now almost at an end. Nepherites II was dethroned after four months by the founder of the *Thirtieth Dynasty* (378–341 B.C.), a prince of Sebennytos called Nectanebo I (378–361 B.C.). Nectanebo regarded himself as the inheritor of the Saïte virtues, and he delighted to honour the goddess Neith. He attempted to loosen the ties which had bound the Twenty-ninth Dynasty to the Greeks, for he allowed the mercenaries who assisted Achoris to return home. This gesture nearly proved fatal to him. The satrap of Syria marched on Egypt and was on the point of taking Memphis when a fresh outbreak of the war with Greece compelled him to hurry homewards. Nectanebo was the last of the great native builders and traces of his handiwork are found scattered throughout Egypt from Philae to Bubastis. His son Teos (361–359 B.C.) revived the Greek alliance and yearned, rather late in the day, to reconquer the East. The young man spared no one in pursuit of this aim, levying huge imposts on every section of the community to raise funds for the enterprise. A year after his accession he landed on Syrian soil with an army composed of eighty thousand Egyptians, ten thousand Athenian mercenaries and a thousand Spartan hoplites. At first he swept everything before him, but at a critical moment his young brother Nectanebo deserted him in the field and decamped with a large part of his forces. Teos suffered the eventual humiliation of surrendering to the Persians. Nectanebo returned to Egypt and proclaimed himself Nectanebo II. After suppressing a Mendesian rebellion he ruled quietly until about 350 B.C., when he was called upon to repulse the first wave of a fresh Persian offensive. He contrived to hold the Persians at bay until 341 B.C., when the personal presence of the Persian monarch in the field, coupled with the defection of numbers of his own Greek mercenaries, combined to bring about his downfall. Thus, after three thousand years of settled government, the last Egyptian king of Egypt passed from the stage of history.

The *SECOND PERSIAN DOMINATION* (341–332 B.C.) was far less humane than the First Domination, or Twenty-seventh Dynasty. The new King of Kings, Artaxerxes III Okhos (341– 338 B.C.), was possessed of an almost maniacal desire to bring Egypt once more under Persian rule. After the abortive initial attempt of 350 B.C., he finally organized an army of three hundred thousand men which hurtled irresistibly into the Delta. The last native Pharaoh went down fighting before him. Once in Egypt, Artaxerxes behaved like a greedy ruffian, and during his reign and that of his son and successor Oarses (338–335 B.C.) the Egyptians were submitted to a persistent policy of looting and terrorization. Eventually Artaxerxes and Oarses were poisoned by a eunuch called Bogoas. Bogoas offered the throne to Darius III Codoman (335–332 B.C.) and was suitably rewarded by being made to swallow a poison of his own concocting. The Egyptian satraps of Darius III were no less rapacious than their predecessors. When Alexander chased Darius through burning Persepolis after destroying the hege-mony of the Persians at Issus in 332 B.C., the Egyptians voluntarily invited the young hero to take the Nile valley under his protection.

With the coming of ALEXANDER THE GREAT the old Hebrew prophecy was fulfilled: 'There shall be no more a prince out of the land of Egypt.' The Egyptians considered Alexander to be an 'Ionian dog,' but at least he had brought to an end the dominion of the Persians. The new king made the gesture of worshipping Zeus-Ammon, and it was the Egyptian god who revealed to him the fact that he was divine. The kings of none of the other great nations of antiquity claimed this honour for themselves, and to Alexander's followers it must have seemed the height of folly and presumption. After founding the city of Alexandria, the conqueror marched away to die at Babylon of the ungodlike illness of typhoid fever. After his death the province of Egypt was administered by one of his generals, Ptolemy Lagos, who in 305 B.C. became the founder of the Greek dynasty. Among later Ptolemies the following may be singled out. Ptolemy II Philadelphos (285–247 B.C.), builder of the Pharos at Alexandria, one of the wonders of the ancient world, and patron of the famous library there. Ptolemy III Euergetes (247–222 B.C.), a soldier of ability in whose reign occurred a terrible famine. Ptolemy V Epiphanes (209–182 B.C.), who made extensive gifts to the temples. In 51 B.C. Ptolemy XIV ascended the throne with his wife and sister Cleopatra. The pair were under the protection of the Roman Senate, which nominated Pompey for the post of guardian. Soon afterwards Ptolemy quarrelled with Cleopatra and banished her. After the battle of Pharsalia the defeated Pompey escaped to Egypt, where his erstwhile ward caused him to be murdered. In 48 B.C. Ptolemy had reason to regret the assassination of so able a general, for Caesar brought an army to Egypt and crushed Ptolemy's forces. He himself was drowned. Caesar restored Cleopatra to the throne and appointed Ptolemy XV as her co-regent. In 45 B.C. Cleopatra ordered Ptolemy to be killed and elected her son by Caesar, Ptolemy XVI, co-regent in his place. Fifteen years later, when Antony lost the battle of Actium to his fellow triumvir Octavian, Egypt was declared a Roman province.

The Ptolemies, who do not properly belong to our story, made a wholehearted attempt to copy the manners of the true Pharaohs. They proclaimed themselves gods and even went so far as to practise incestuous marriage. The Egyptians never ceased throughout to look upon them as interlopers. The Ptolemies tried hard to conform to Egyptian standards: much

205

harder than their Greek subjects, who flocked to Egypt after the disappearance of the indigenous dynasties and the collapse of the Greek city-states. The Ptolemies instituted the worship of the divine triad Serapis, Harpocrates and Isis. The Greek immigrants paid their devotions to Zeus, Apollo, Demeter or Aphrodite. The Ptolemies continued to extend pious patronage to the temples. Their Greek followers had a derisive proverb: 'Like an Egyptian temple, magnificent to look at, and inside a priest singing a hymn to a cat or a crocodile.'

The newcomers openly despised the natives. They made it abundantly clear that they regarded Egypt as a land to despoil. Egyptians were rigorously excluded from the management of their own affairs. The profitable office of nomarch was every-where assumed by the Greeks. All the chief administrative posts were in foreign hands within a few years of the arrival of Alexander. The Greeks brought their own culture with them and refused to absorb or even respect the ancient traditions of the valley of the Nile. They showed themselves indifferent to the indignities suffered by the dispossessed nobility. They mocked the plight of the Egyptian masses, reduced in the midst of plenty to a condition of dire poverty. There were strikes, riots and appeals to Rome. The Greeks, brought together only by the desire for profit, lived in their own com-munities. The three main centres were Ptolemais in Upper Egypt and Naucratis and Alexandria in the Delta. At Alex-andria, described by Strabo as a 'universal reservoir,' were to be found Greeks, Italians, Libyans, Arabs, Ethiopians, Jews, Cilicians, Phrygians, Phoenicians, Lydians, Persians, Scythians, Bactrians and even Indians. With the influx of this alien and polyglot population, the present account of the civilization of ancient Egypt comes inevitably to a conclusion.

Tout lasse, tout casse, tout passe.

BIBLIOGRAPHY

SMITH, W. STEVENSON. The History of Sculpture and Painting in the Old Kingdom. (1946)

CRAFTS

LUCAS, A. Ancient Egyptian Materials and Industries. (1948)

SOCIAL LIFE

BLACKMAN, W. S. The Fellâhîn of Upper Egypt. (1927)
MONTET, P. Scènes de la Vie privée dans les Tombeaux de l'Ancien Empire. (1925)
PEET, T. E. The Great Tomb-Robberies of the Twentieth Dynasty, 2 vols. (1930)
PETRIE, W. M. F. Social Life in Ancient Egypt. (1924)
PIRENNE, J. Histoire des Institutions et du Droit privé de l'Ancienne Égypte, 3 vols. (1935)

Index

(The pronunciation is indicated in brackets after certain proper names)

INDEX